James H. Langstaff, M.D.
Box 46
Fairbury, Illinois 61739

ck Newcaſtl Tyne

The concise book of the
HORSE

The concise book of the
HORSE

Edited by
Candida Geddes

ARCO PUBLISHING COMPANY, INC.

New York

Published 1976 by Arco Publishing Company, Inc.
219 Park Avenue South, New York, N.Y. 10003

Copyright © 1973, 1975 by Ward Lock Limited

All rights reserved

Printed in Great Britain
Published in Great Britain by Ward Lock Limited, London

Library of Congress Cataloging in Publication Data

Main entry under title:

The Concise book of the horse.

   Includes index.
   1. Horses.   I.   Geddes, Candida.
SF285.C577   636.1   76–1874
ISBN 0–668–03965–5

Contents

Contributors

The editor and publishers would like to extend their grateful thanks to the following contributors to *The Complete Book of the Horse* whose work has been re-used or adapted in order to make the present book possible:

Hugh Condry

Anthony Crossley

Anthony Dent

Neil Dougall

Elwyn Hartley Edwards

Jean Froissard

Frank Haydon

Ann Hyland

Elizabeth Johnson

Lord Langford

Patricia Lindsay

Pamela Macgregor-Morris

Daphne Machin-Goodall

G. W. Serth

Alan Smith

Diana Tuke

Marylian Watney

J. N. P. Watson

Dorian Williams

Jennifer Williams

Acknowledgements

The editor and publishers gladly acknowledge the owners and copyright holders of photographs reproduced in the book. We hope that any inadvertently omitted from this list will accept a general acknowledgement.

Australian News & Information Bureau 60, 61, 148, 149, 150, 151, 153, 163 (lower); Barnabys Picture Library 45, 49, 66; A. S. Barnes 139, 140; Buckingham PR 53; Central Press Photos 125; Kenneth Collier 47 (upper); Findlay Davidson 136; Deford Studio 42; Fiona Forbes 26; Fores Ltd 15; Fox Photos 128; Francis-Thompson Studios 157; Freudy Photos 146; Jean Froissard 46 (upper); Clive Hiles 121 (lower); Keystone Press Agency 58, 114; Leslie Lane 12, 15, 16, 23, 24, 29, 31, 36, 46 (lower), 50, 106, 112, 131 (upper), 133, 144, 159, 160, 162; Mrs Mackay-Smith 48; Frank H. Meads 138; Monty 19, 25, 27, 143; Director of the National Studs of France 17; John Nestle 56 (lower); Novosti 55 (upper), 56 (upper), 152; Photonews 55 (lower); Photostore 44; Pictor Ltd 33, 52; Picture-point 51, 102, 119, 120; Popperfoto 90, 126; PA Reuter 47 (lower); Mike Roberts 101; Peter Roberts 34, 35, 40; A. Ruddle 20; A. Russell 59; G. W. Serth 97; Sport & General 19, 21, 25, 30; *Stable Management* 65, 67; Peter Sweetman 121 (upper), 130, 131 (lower), 132; United Press, Paris 163 (upper); Marylian Watney 39; Foto Werner 134.

Part 1
Horses of the World

1 Origins of the horse

The modern horse, known as *equus caballus*, has descended in gradual stages from a creature which existed some sixty million years ago called the Eohippus. Within the last hundred years it has been proved that the development of *equus caballus* took place in what is now North America. The land masses of the world were differently disposed at that time, and *equus caballus* was able to move freely, travelling over land from North America across Asia and into Africa and Europe, before the land bridges were submerged beneath the rising sea level caused by melting ice in the post-Ice Age period. There are several theories about the origins of the domestic horse. One widely accepted scheme suggests that four primeval types of horse existed, all of which were domesticated, though at different times and in different parts of the world. For the sake of convenience two of these are known as ponies and two as horses, though one of the 'horses' is believed to have been quite as small originally as the smaller of the pony types.

The first of these four types, which let us call Pony I, was to be found in north-west Europe and was more or less identical to the 'Celtic Pony'; it would have resembled closely the modern English native pony, the Exmoor. As near as we can determine its height would have averaged 12·2 hands; a 'waterproof' animal, brown or bay in colour.

Pony II, native to northern Eurasia, was heavier in build and in bone than the first type, with a coarser head, and was better at trotting than at galloping. It would frequently (if not invariably) have had an eel-stripe running down its back, and was a dun colour which might be so pale as to be almost a cream, like some Przewalski foals, or might almost verge on chestnut. This pony was 'frost-proof', and has a typical modern descendant in Przewalski's horse with its stiff mane hairs, though the abundant and wavy tail it carried is not a characteristic feature of the Przewalski strain.

The third strain, Horse III, inhabited the central Asian areas, extending westward in pockets north of the Alps as far as Spain. One can still see examples of it in the kind of nightmare that is sometimes thrown up in Thoroughbred families: a long, narrowish head with a straight or 'Roman' profile, long straight neck, sloping croup, long ears with a tendency to lop, slab-sided, rather shallow hooves which are broader than those of other races, and a sparse, lank mane and tail. The nearest living equivalent of this type is the marsh-dwelling, clay-coloured horse discovered by d'Andrade as an unfashionable domestic breed in the Douro valley where the river marks the frontier with Spain. Evidently this was the ancestor, or *an* ancestor, of the Andalusian. It was much the largest of these early types, averaging some 15 hands – and is the 'drought-proof' horse.

Horse IV, the last of these, was native to western Asia. It was small – only about 12 hands – and fine-boned, with a straight or concave facial profile, silky, abundant mane and tail – in other words, with most of the attributes now regarded as indications of 'quality'. It had a flat-topped croup at the same height as its withers, with a high-set tail. The nearest modern representative of this 'heat-proof' horse is the recently-identified Caspian pony.

The potential increase in size of each of these early types is known to have varied. The Shetland pony, for example, is a dwarf variant of type I which, if of unmixed blood and living in the relatively mild, wet environment of western England or Ireland would not grow any larger. Type II was capable of the greatest variation in size: under favourable feeding conditions of open forest or natural water-meadows it would achieve massive proportions. Types III and IV would both grow bigger in a favourable environment, as would a cross-bred from any two of the four types. Such crosses are

STAGES IN THE EVOLUTION
OF THE HORSE

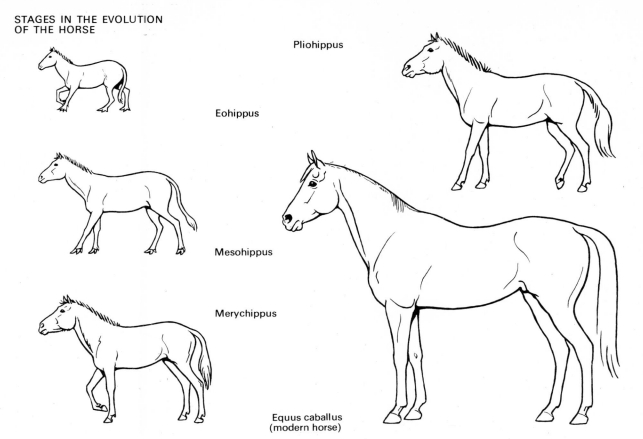

Pliohippus

Eohippus

Mesohippus

Merychippus

Equus caballus
(modern horse)

thought to have existed in a wild state and to have become much more numerous in even the early stages of domestication. Thus the heavy draught breeds of today are crosses of types II and III; light horses are crosses of types III and IV; while most of the ponies native to north-west Europe have the blood of types I and II in varying proportions.

The different environments, climates and conditions in which these early horse-types lived produced in them different characteristics. The first domesticators of the horse inherited the results of nature's fierce test of survival.

The earliest generations of horse-breeders, in their first home on the Asiatic steppe, had no choice in the matter of sires; they had to take what foals the local variety of wild horse would get off their mares. At this stage it was quite beyond the capabilities of early pastoralists to cope with adult stallions, and their domesticated mares were covered by their being tethered, when they came into season, where it was hoped the wild stallion would come out of the steppe

and cover them. The pastoralists' economy was based on mares' milk and the meat of the year's colts; only the filly foals were allowed to grow on. The breeding would have attempted to produce the milkiest mare and the most meaty colt; two qualities inherent, luckily for the owners, in pony type II which was the type of horse most common in north-central Asia.

When it came to breeding horses for work in a later age, the desired type was a packhorse. The use of animals for pack arises sooner or later among all nomadic pastoralists who have been living quite well on meat and milk but are getting tired of carrying their own bedding, tents and cooking pots. The analogy of primitive camel-breeders, donkey-herds, even of ancient cattlemen and yak-breeders, bears this out.

Only after this stage does any significant divergence in the desired type of horse arise. Now the option is between a saddle horse and a harness horse. In the ancient world, one might almost say in the pre-Biblical world, those who bred for riding lived on the Mongolian or north-eastern side of the primeval horse-rearing region, while the breeders of harness horses inhabited the south-western or Iranian side. The distribution of primitive types, either in their wild state or recently domesticated, did not fit in with the requirements of the two groups and their preferences led to the beginnings of horse trading on an international scale, and also to wars of conquest with almost the sole object of acquiring by force working horses and breeding stock.

The invention of body-armour suitable for horsemen and the adoption of the lance both occurred in Persia in remote antiquity, and started a chain reaction in striving for the Great Horse which lasted many centuries, culminating in the international, almost uniform west European charger of the late Middle Ages, from which many heavy breeds still seen today derive. But for many centuries Persia had a head start because horse type III, the tallest of the primitive breeds, was native to that region. The discovery that crossing type III with type II, very common in Europe north of the Alps,

would produce a hybrid bigger than either parent, was a fortunate one. Most of the mediaeval records of horse-breeding that survive in Europe west of a line drawn roughly between Venice and Stettin are concerned with the product of this cross, because it was ridden in war and on ceremonial occasions by kings and nobles who, even if they could not actually write themselves, employed people who could.

With perhaps the single exception of the Andalusian, few breeds of horse extant today can be traced back with convincing continuity to the era of classical antiquity, but many can be shown to have their roots in well-known mediaeval breeds. This is because of the great technical gulf that separates, say, the world of Julius Caesar from that of William the Conqueror. The ancient world was a stirrupless world, a fact which greatly influenced the choice of types of horse for riding. By Roman standards the mediaeval world was a roadless world, and this in turn had a profound effect on mediaeval ideas of what could be expected of a harness horse. When European road surfaces later

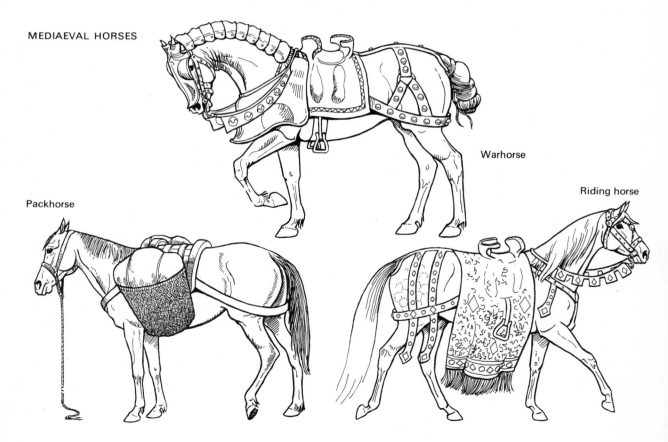

MEDIAEVAL HORSES

Warhorse

Riding horse

Packhorse

achieved the standard, on some stretches of expensive turnpike, that had been common-place throughout Roman Europe, the whole nature of harness and methods of harnessing had undergone such a radical change, making different demands on equine anatomy, that comparisons between the harness horse of antiquity and that of eighteenth-century England, for example, are simply not valid. It is perhaps enough just to point out that the Graeco-Roman horse could not 'throw its weight into the collar' because there was no collar!

Modern harness horses are derived from what were originally riding types. Hackney horses, and most carriage types most effective at a trot, have a foundation in breeds such as the Norfolk Roadster, which had a reputation in the pre-macadam era as a fast *ridden* trotting horse. Throughout Britain and the whole of the continent of Europe a profound modification overtook light horse breeds when parish roads became good enough for the farmer to go to church and market in a gig. As long as he had to travel in the saddle, with his wife riding pillion behind him, he both demanded and bred for himself an 'easy going' sort of horse that would amble or pace. Once the gig was a practical means of transport, however, whether in Norfolk or in Normandy, he went in for a 'hard trotting' horse. Only in peripheral areas such as Iceland, Portugal and Spain is the utility light horse of local pony blood still a pacer, ambler or 'racker'.

During the eighteenth century the packhorse, which had carried most of the goods traffic of Europe since the days of antiquity, also became obsolete except in certain obstinate mountain regions such as the Pyrenees, and was converted into a harness horse of about 'vanner' size. This is true of, for instance, the Fjord pony, the now extinct Devon packhorse, of Fell and Dales ponies and the Arriegeois of south-eastern France, among many others.

The picture in eastern Europe, and over a large part of Scandinavia, is a rather different one. There the harness horse had its chance to excel, not on road surfaces (which were no better than elsewhere) but on frozen snow over several months of the year. It was as much before the sleigh as before the trap that the light horse breeds of Hungary, Poland, Sweden, etc., put up their most impressive records. Even the celebrated Dutch Harddraver performed at its fastest not on the roads but on frozen canals.

2 From Arab to Thoroughbred

It is virtually impossible accurately to date the emergence of the Arab horse as a breed. All that can be said with certainty is that the Arab is the oldest of the world's recognised breeds and that he has had the greatest influence on the world's horse population.

The creation of the Thoroughbred is undoubtedly the greatest achievement of the Arabian horse, but it must also be recognised that all of the established warm-blood breeds of the world either originally contained Arab blood or have, at some time in their history, been improved by the introduction of that blood. Additionally, not a few of the heavy, cold-blood breeds of north-west Europe were at some time influenced by the Arab.

The unique position held by the Arab can be attributed to three principal factors: first, to its antiquity as a breed of fixed type and character; second, to the development and improvement effected by the desert Bedouin over a period of centuries, and especially to the Islamic religion, which virtually incorporated the keeping of horses as an article of faith; and finally, as a result of these two factors, the supremacy of the Arab is due to the inherent qualities of stamina, hereditary soundness, conformation, courage and speed with which the Arab characteristically stamps his stock. Furthermore, Arab blood has the capacity to mix with virtually any other and effect an improvement in the resulting progeny.

Today the Arab horse is bred all over the world, and he retains all the characteristics so highly valued by his original masters. All horses in competitive sport derive from the Arab to some extent and as a pure-bred he is still supreme in the long-distance endurance rides, though in his pure form he plays hardly any part in show-jumping or three-day events. Arab blood, outside strictly Thoroughbred

Lady Anne Lytton's famous Polish-bred stallion, Grojec. He has the classical Arabian head, and displays all the essential characteristics of the top-quality Arab.

breeding, continues to play a vital part in the development and up-grading of other breeds.

The danger facing the future of the Arab horse today, when his breeding has long since passed out of the hands of the occupants of his original desert habitat, is that the breed will become too popular for its own good. Already Arab 'studs' proliferate throughout Europe, America and Australia and exist in some numbers in Scandinavia. Careless overbreeding could result in the production of inferior specimens lacking the true Arabian characteristics. This would be a disaster, not only for the breed but for the whole world of horses, which still depends to a very considerable extent on the maintenance of these properties in the Arab.

In the light of what in certain areas may be termed promiscuous breeding it may be of interest to consider the perfect Arabian horse that breeders ought to be trying to produce. The head should be very short and of great refinement, and the face pronouncedly concave or 'dished'. A straight face is not, under any circumstances, acceptable. The muzzle is tapered and very small—so small, indeed, that it should fit into a half-cupped hand. The nostrils are exceptionally large in comparison and of great elasticity, being flared in excitement. The texture of the muzzle skin is especially soft in the high-class Arabian; any coarse feeling that it gives to the fingers denotes lack of breeding. The eyes are set lower than in other horses and are widely spaced as well as being very large. R. S. Summerhays, an authority of standing, says that 'in appearance they must be dark and deep in colour, very soulful in the mare, in the stallion capable in an instant of showing great alertness, with enormous challenging dignity'. In many respects this typifies the Arabian: no horse is as masculine as the Arab stallion; none as feminine as the Arab mare. The ears are shapely, small, well defined, set apart and always carried alertly, exhibiting 'a most exquisite curve' (Lady Wentworth). Ears in the mare are usually longer than in the male. A further feature of the head, differing from that of other breeds, is the generous rounding of the jaws. It should be possible to insert a closed fist between the spread of the jaw-bones.

The neck should be long enough but not excessively so. In the Arab it is the *mitbah*, the angle at which the neck and head meet, which is important. There must always be a distinctive arched curve formed by the angle, peculiar to the Arab, at which neck and head join. The more accentuated this feature, the greater the degree to which the head may move freely in all directions. The texture of the mane is another distinguishing feature: fine, silky and soft.

The body must next be considered. The shoulder, a particularly important feature in the riding horse, must be sloped and long, with well-defined withers. An excessive slope, though possibly desirable in the Thoroughbred, is untypical of the Arab and the withers, although pronounced, are not so high. The back is short, slightly concave, very strong across the loin and carried on a level croup. Ribs are rounded and the girth deep. The chest, of which Lady Wentworth once wrote that 'it cannot be too broad' in fact certainly *can* be too broad, just as it can be too narrow. Too broad, with legs consequently set far apart, it is a 'harness' chest, whereas it should be normal in appearance and of usual riding type.

The quarters are generously proportioned with the croup level, long and wide. The Arabian differs from other horses in the number of its ribs and lumbar bones, and this is responsible for the particular and unmistakable formation of its back and quarters. The root of the tail sets into the croup and its uppermost line and is carried arched and high in movement. Extreme length from point of hip to point of buttock is expected in the Arab, though it is not always found except in the highest class. The gaskins should be strong and prominent, and the hair of the tail should be similar to that of the mane.

Arab limbs are strong and hard and with clean, well-defined tendons. Knees are flat and low to the ground and the cannon bones short in consequence. Since the bone of the Arab is of greater density than that of other breeds the measurement below the knee need not be as great. Pasterns must be neither too upright nor too sloping and the joints should be flat and well formed. The hind leg is a weakness in the majority of Arabian show class entries. In the ideal Arab it is straight and not in any way sickle-shaped, bent or cow-hocked. Hocks must follow the line, turning neither in nor out, and they too must be set low to the ground. The

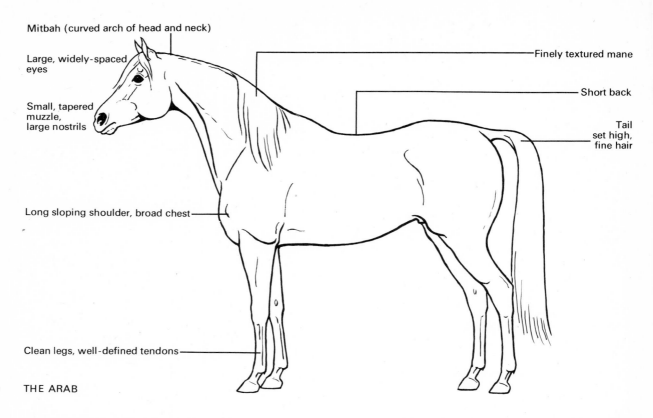

Mitbah (curved arch of head and neck)

Large, widely-spaced eyes

Small, tapered muzzle, large nostrils

Long sloping shoulder, broad chest

Clean legs, well-defined tendons

Finely textured mane

Short back

Tail set high, fine hair

THE ARAB

feet of the Arab must be near-perfect; this is a fundamental characteristic of the breed, and any weakness or malformation is a serious fault.

Like so many other things Arabian the action is unique. It is characterised by a floating appearance, the horse moving as on springs and with the greatest of freedom in all his paces. The tail is always held high and bannered. The trot pace is not, as executed by the Arab, anything at all like the exaggerated, daisy-cutting toe-pointing of the show animal. Rather it is full, free and generous but with, nonetheless, little or no knee action.

Perhaps the most vivid description of the Arab is that written by Homer Davenport in his authoritative book, *My Quest of the Arabian Horse*, published in New York well over half a century ago. He concluded a detailed descrip-tion of the breed by declaring: 'The build of the Arab is perfect. It is essentially that of utility. The space for the seat of the rider at once fixes his true position and his weight is carried on that part of the frame most adapted for it. If he be carefully examined it will be found that all the muscles and limbs of progres-sion are better placed and longer in him than in any other horse. Nature, when she made the Arab, made no mistake.'

THE ENGLISH THOROUGHBRED

It was due to the importations of these Oriental horses into England that the next great development, that of the emergence of a super-horse, the English Thoroughbred, was achieved.

The exact origin of the world's premier breed of horses is a matter of some controversy, and there are authorities who disagree with the late Lady Wentworth's positive and sweeping assertion that the Thoroughbred is entirely and exclusively the product of Arabian blood.

Racing and racehorses were in fact an integral part of the English sporting scene for centuries even before the formative period of the Thoroughbred during the hundred or so years following the Stuart Restoration in 1660. It would therefore be reasonable to assume that native elements already existed which, when crossed with the Arab, contributed to the combination of qualities characteristic of today's Thoroughbred.

This theory is based upon the belief that there was a well-established breed of native 'running horses' in Britain before the large importations of Oriental blood (known variously as Barb, Turk or Arabian) that took place in the latter part of the seventeenth century and continued well into the eighteenth. On the other hand, it is known that efforts were made to improve the native horses by the importation of Oriental sires and mares well back into English history, and so it can be argued that the running horses might well have carried proportions of Oriental blood. At this distance in time, however, no certain proof is available.

What is fact, however, is that James I had Arabians, among them the Markham Arabian, in his stud of racehorses, these being brought to England by Sir Thomas Esmond.

Sir John Fenwick, Master of Horse to Charles II, is said to have furthered the influx of Oriental blood by bringing back, at the command of his master, the Royal Mares, as well as some stallions from the Levant. That, at any rate, is the General Stud Book explanation of the Royal Mares found in so many early Thoroughbred pedigrees. It is more probable, however, that these mares were supplied from various sources by James D'Arcy, Master of the Royal Stud, who had a contract with King Charles to supply 'twelve extraordinary good colts' each year for the royal stud at Sedbury, in Yorkshire, for an annual payment of £800.

During the period 1721–59 some 200 Oriental horses are listed in Volume II of the General Stud Book. Of these 176 were stallions, of whom three exerted a particular influence on the subsequent development of Thoroughbred stock, all modern Thoroughbreds being descended from them in the male line. These were the Darley and Godolphin Arabians and the Byerley Turk.

The Darley was the founder of the Eclipse line, the horse that inspired Dennis O'Kelly, his owner, to make the now-famous remark, 'Eclipse first, the rest nowhere', and how right he was, for this son of Marske was never beaten up to the time he retired from the racecourse in 1760. From Eclipse, and so from the Darley Arabian, descend today's important male lines of Blandford, Phalaris, Gainsborough, Son-in-Law, Boss, Teddy and St Simon. The Darley was also responsible for another famous son, Flying Childers, the first great racehorse out of an Oriental mare, Betty Leedes, and so exclusively of Eastern descent. The Darley also heads the direct sire lines of Sun Chariot and Big Game.

The Godolphin Arabian came to Britain in 1728 and lived to the ripe old age of twenty-nine, dying in 1753, in Cambridgeshire, at the Gogmagog estate of his owner Lord Godolphin. The Godolphin founded the Matchem line; Matchem, foaled in 1748, being by the Godolphin's son, Cade. Matchem, although not as successful on the racecourse as his half-brother, Gimcrack, who is perpetuated by the Gimcrack Stakes for two-year-olds held at York in August, far exceeded the latter as a stallion and was the leading sire in the north of England, his fee starting at five guineas and rising to the then astronomical sum of fifty guineas as his fame spread. The Byerley Turk was the first of the three to come to England. Byerley's Turk sired Jigg, to found the Herod line from whence came the Tetrarch, among other great horses of our own century.

The Godolphin Arabian. (*Fores Ltd*)

The Darley Arabian. (*Fores Ltd*)

Quality Fair, an outstanding modern Thoroughbred stallion.

There were, of course, other Oriental stallions whose influence still remains, although not in the male top line. The Leedes Arabian, for instance, appears in more pedigrees than any other horse and every grey Thoroughbred traces back to Alcock's Arabian.

In order to establish and improve a breed it is imperative to keep reliable records of pedigrees and matings, as well as records of performance in the case of racehorses. Early records of the Thoroughbred are naturally enough not entirely comprehensive, but by 1791, when the first of Weatherby's General Stud Books appeared, a definite pattern had been established. Today's GSB, still published by the same family, includes all pure-bred mares and their progeny together with pedigrees of both mares and sires. Only animals entered in the GSB are eligible to compete on licensed courses in Britain. Loosely, therefore, the English Thoroughbred can be defined as a horse of proved pedigree eligible for entry in the GSB.

The word Thoroughbred, as applied to the racehorse, was not used until 1821 when it appeared in the second volume of Weatherby's GSB, and it was not until much later that Arabian outcrosses ceased and the English Thoroughbred was established as a breed in its own right. Indeed, it is only in the last hundred years that the Thoroughbred has achieved its remarkable increase in numbers and has spread to all parts of the world.

In 1962 the world Thoroughbred population, within the racing and breeding world, was estimated by Franco Varolo in the magazine *Courses et Elevages* as 233,000. Now, some ten years later, it is probably approaching a number in excess of 400,000. In addition, of course, the Thoroughbred exists in quite large numbers outside racing. That a near-perfect racing machine has evolved over so comparatively short a period of time is tribute to the knowledge, judgement and enthusiasm of the generations concerned with its production.

Apart from the necessary quality of speed the Thoroughbred is the ideal riding horse. In movement the action is long, free, easy and fast at all paces and since action is dependent upon conformation that of the Thoroughbred is the nearest to perfection. Add to this the elusive factor of quality combined with balance, and

true symmetry of proportions, and the Thoroughbred is without doubt the aristocrat of the equine species.

In all these respects he far exceeds his progenitor the Arab, and still retains the latter's fire and courage. Generations of confined breeding, however, as well as other factors, have resulted in a loss of much of the inherent soundness that is a characteristic of the Arab horse. Many authorities would hold the practice of two-year-old racing responsible for so much wastage. Despite the precocity of the modern Thoroughbred, there is inevitably risk of overstrain or breakdown when weight has to be carried at speed on an immature structure.

This apart, the Thoroughbred is regarded as the ideal cross to produce hunters and jumpers when mated with either half-bred mares or with Arabs and Arab crosses.

THE ANGLO-ARAB

The Anglo-Arab horse, as its name implies, is the product of the Arab and Thoroughbred. Although in the strictest sense the Anglo-Arab cannot be regarded as a *pure* breed, since new blood, either Arab or Thoroughbred, is continually added, it is nevertheless recognised throughout the world as an established one, having its own well-defined characteristics.

The fusion of the two premier world breeds should in theory, and indeed frequently does in practice, produce a riding horse combining the

An Anglo-Arab in peak condition for being shown in hand.

16

A French Anglo-Arab stallion.

best qualities of both. The modern pure-bred Thoroughbred is not always entirely suited temperamentally to present-day activities; he may be too excitable and highly couraged for the disciplines involved in dressage training or for the precision required in show-jumping arenas. Moreover, the Thoroughbred cannot be said to have retained the inherent soundness of his Arab progenitor. He has, however, speed and jumping ability far greater than that of the much smaller pure-bred Arabian horse. These qualities, together with the Thoroughbred's natural balance and good riding conformation, when combined – not necessarily a straight first cross – with the intelligence, soundness and stamina of the Arab can result in a riding horse of the finest type, even if it is not quite as fast as the Thoroughbred.

The present-day Anglo-Arab is usually about 16 hands and rarely exceeds 16·2 hands. Its appearance is marked by a distinctive head, well-set and clearly defined withers, sloping shoulders, roomy girth, good limbs and joints and excellent hard feet. Endowed with intelligence, sobriety, scope, endurance, balance, weight-carrying capacity and no mean turn of speed this is one of the world's greatest all-round riding horses.

3 The horses and ponies of Britain

Great Britain has a unique heritage in her famous native breeds. Apart from the heavy horses, most of these are ponies which, while they share some characteristics common to all true ponies, have developed along different lines according to the conditions of their particular environment, the addition of foreign blood in their breeding patterns and the different uses to which they have been put.

The characteristics that all real ponies share have been developed for several reasons. In general, horse-breeding has been influenced by men to a greater extent than the breeding of ponies. Until recently, with a few exceptions such as the introduction of Arab blood into the island strain of Scotland's Highland breed, ponies have bred naturally, and nature's process of selection has led to superlative quality in

Pollyanna, a famous show pony of the 1960s and perhaps one of the most beautiful ponies ever bred.

each breed for the needs of that breed. Perhaps the most difficult pony quality to define, and that which essentially differentiates ponies from horses, is 'ponyness'. True pony character is the result of an independence and intelligence fostered by life in natural and frequently harsh environments, combined with an equable, sensible temperament. Far fewer ponies than horses 'hot up'; far more ponies than horses will find their way out of an apparently impenetrably-fenced field. There are, of course, plenty of horses with positive and individualistic personalities, but ponies do seem generally to have more character than their larger and better-bred relations. Part of the elusive pony character is to be observed in their expressions. Typically, ponies have short, trim ears on neat heads, giving them considerable alertness and a particularly intelligent and endearing expression. Even among the carefully-bred show ponies, some of them in many respects very different from the native pony stock on which they are founded, this essential quality of pony character is regarded as all-important. Without it, a pony can become just a smaller version of the horse.

There are also some physical features shared by pony breeds which are not always found in horses. They are tougher than many of the horse breeds, able to thrive in harsh conditions and to get themselves out of trouble. Centuries of having to fend entirely for themselves in order to survive at all in the mountain and moorland areas of Britain have sharpened their faculties and increased their hardiness, stamina and sure-footedness. Ponies are rarely ill, seldom go lame if properly looked after, are remarkably adaptable, and seem to have a tremendous sense of fun. Curiosity, a necessary part of survival in the wild, is just one characteristic typical of the pony in domestic surroundings which endears him to his human companions.

It is hardly surprising, in view of how much they have to offer, that ponies are now widely used in the breeding of horses, and that crossed with a quality blood horse—such as a Thoroughbred or an Arab—they provide the best of all foundation breeding stock. The quality of the British native pony has been widely recognised, and examples of all the breeds—in particular those from Wales—are now exported all over the world. The establishment of breed societies for each of the native breeds during this century has ensured the protection of the quality of the ponies and the maintenance of their traditional attributes.

Crossed strains of riding pony have also been developed, with superlative results. At their best, these ponies are full of quality while retaining their native characteristics.

Exmoor

The Exmoor, oldest of all the native pony breeds, is known to have existed in the Exmoor area of Devon and Somerset in prehistoric times. The moors are wild and solitary, the climate is harsh; there is little protection from the elements here. In order to survive, the ponies had to develop what is still one of their prime attributes—hardiness.

In addition, the Exmoor is known for its agility, quick-witted intelligence and considerable powers of endurance. The ponies are strong out of proportion to their size, and it is not unusual to see a diminutive though sturdy pony of about 12 hands carrying a large West Country farmer both during his shepherding work and behind hounds. Properly handled, the Exmoor is a good pony for children, too, though its primary value is considered to be for breeding.

Exmoor ponies should not exceed 12·2 hands, though the stallions may reach 12·3 hands. The short pointed ears of the breed enhance the kindly look typical of these ponies, with their wide foreheads and nostrils and large eyes. Exmoors, which are bay, brown or mouse-dun in colour, have the attractive mealy muzzle and 'toad eye' as well as being lighter in colour on their bellies and the inside of the thighs. The coat colour may not include any white.

A charming Exmoor mare and foal.

The strength of this breed is displayed in the deep, wide chest, powerful loins and clean legs, and the hardness of its feet ensures its surefootedness even in difficult country. The winter coat of the Exmoor is extra thick and has no bloom, for it is unusually wiry in texture in order to protect the pony from the rigours of the winter climate on the moors. The foals are similarly protected, with a thick woolly undercoat covered by a waterproof top layer of long hairs.

Dartmoor

The Dartmoor pony, neighbour of the Exmoor, has had to learn to withstand similar climatic conditions, and has developed some of the same characteristics as a result. The moorland environment has not only produced hardiness and surefootedness in the breed; the Dartmoor is a valuable pony for many other reasons as well.

One of the advantages of the Dartmoor is its versatility. These ponies are remarkable jumpers for their size—they do not exceed 12·2 hands—and are much appreciated as foundation

A champion Dartmoor filly.

stock in the breeding of larger all-round ponies and top-class quality riding ponies. Their value in this respect has been shown by the fact that a part-bred Dartmoor register has been formed.

The Dartmoor pony is strong, well-made and good-looking. It should have a small, well-bred head and an alert expression, strong shoulders, back and loins, a full mane and tail and particularly well-shaped feet. The typically good front and relatively high head carriage makes Dartmoor ponies feel specially safe to children. To all these physical advantages the Dartmoor adds its intelligence, an ability to think for itself, a kind, sensible character and a particular liking for children.

New Forest

The New Forest pony is to be found all over the extensive woodland and open heath of the New Forest in Hampshire. The Forest has been the home of this breed since the days of King Canute in the eleventh century. As stock of other breeds was turned out to run in the Forest from time to time, the blood of the native ponies has become rather mixed. The breeding was affected by deliberate attempts, made at the end of the nineteenth century, to improve the breed by the introduction of other bloodlines; when these efforts were limited to the introduction of other native pony breeds all went well, but alien blood was also brought in and at one time the breed was in danger of losing its hardiness.

The ultimate result has been that there are now great variations in type of the New Forest pony. Its size varies between 12 and 14 hands; with the increase in height one finds an accompanying increase in sturdiness and overall size.

A New Forest mare and foal on open grazing near Lyndhurst, Hampshire.

The larger ponies are ideal as all-round family riding ponies. The New Forest pony is intelligent and quick to learn, has an aptitude for sporting events, is very useful in harness, and is thoroughly reliable.

The ideal New Forest pony should have a conformation enabling it to perform as the best type of riding pony. The head should be well set on, there should be a good length of rein, a short back, strong loins and quarters. These ponies must carry a substantial amount of bone, a good forearm and second thigh, short cannons and healthy feet.

Welsh breeds

The ponies of Wales are widely recognised as being among the most beautiful in the world. In addition to this, they possess to such a remarkable degree all the other desirable pony qualities that almost all children's riding ponies today carry a percentage of Welsh blood in them.

The Welsh Stud Book caters for all four of the distinctive Welsh breeds. The first and most important of these is the Welsh Mountain pony (section A). The Welsh Mountain pony may not exceed 12 hands, and is at best one of the supreme examples of all that a pony should be. It combines in its character intelligence, courage, gentleness and endurance. Its exquisite, concave face is set on a graceful neck, it has a deep, sloping shoulder, short, strong back, a tail set high and proudly carried, short limbs with dense, flat bone, and hard, small feet.

The Welsh Mountain pony has always been bred out among the hills of Wales, and as a result has the most hardy constitution. The action is typical of a quality pony accustomed for centuries to moving over rough ground. It is sure-footed, quick and full of action, moving with the utmost freedom at all paces. These ponies are natural jumpers, and very adaptable, being equally at home ridden or in harness.

Section B of the stud book caters for the Welsh pony, which inherits many of the characteristics of the Welsh Mountain but is bred more specifically as a child's riding pony. The emphasis is placed on quality, bone and substance, hardiness, constitution and pony character. The Welsh pony may be up to 13·2 hands in height, and makes an ideal show and performance pony. Like all the other Welsh strains, these ponies may be any colour other than piebald or skewbald.

Welsh ponies of cob type and the Welsh Cob, covered in sections C and D respectively, are similar, though the former may not exceed a height of 13·2 hands, while the latter are over that height, averaging 14·2 to 15·1 hands. The cob ponies are sturdy, active and strong, with considerable substance; a quality head is important, as they should still display true pony character. Free, true, forceful action is essential in both types, accompanied by considerable presence and zest, two typical characteristics of the breed. The larger type makes an excellent hunter, being a natural and clever jumper and with considerable staying power, while the smaller one is unsurpassed for trekking, now a very popular holiday activity in Wales and elsewhere in the British Isles.

Fell

In the northern counties of England some rather different breeds have developed. The Fell pony, native to Cumberland and Westmorland, is descended from the Celtic pony. During the seventeenth, eighteenth and early part of the nineteenth century it was greatly valued as a pack pony, principally being used to carry lead from the mines inland to the port towns on the north-east coast. To be able to carry a sizeable load the Fell pony had to be powerfully built and with considerable stamina; it is a graceful as well as strong pony, with a compact, muscular body, strong, squarely-set clean legs with plenty of bone and open, hard, round feet. It has the typical charming head and prick ears of the pony, carries its tail high and has an overall air of gaiety and liveliness. Great emphasis is placed on the importance of straight and active movement at all paces. Fell ponies should not exceed 14 hands; they are usually black, dark brown and bay in colour, though an occasional grey can be found.

In the past the local farmers organised trotting races between their ponies when the pack work had been finished for the week. The Fell also used to be the all-round work pony on the north country farms, being used for riding, shepherding, pack work and light haulage as well as being

The versatile Fell, though a pony in stature, can easily carry an adult.

called on to pull the family trap. Now the ponies, which stand at between 13 and 14 hands and are still very strong, are used for all sorts of different activities. They make excellent riding ponies, are still used for shepherding in the more remote areas, and their stamina stands them in good stead in competitive events such as long distance rides and combined training events.

Dales

The Dales pony is in some respects similar to the Fell, for it originally sprang from the same stock. It is found principally in County Durham and Northumberland, to the east of the Pennine range. Like the Fell, it has great hardiness and can thrive in spite of the cold, harsh climate of this part of the country.

The Dales pony is the largest of the native pony breeds; it is also the heaviest and strongest of them, capable of carrying a full-grown man all day on the fells. In the past, Dales ponies were used for all kinds of farm work, and after suffering a decline when motorised transport and machinery became generally available, they are now increasing in popularity again with the growing demand for ponies suitable for trekking. They are ideally suited for this work, being hardy, quiet, sure-footed and above all sensible.

Great emphasis is again placed on the importance of sound limbs and clean, healthy feet where the Dales is concerned. Straight, true action is also demanded–action which should give an impression of rhythmic movement and power. In spite of its size and strength the Dales should show no sign of coarseness. A neat pony head with no suspicion of thickness of jaw or throat is expected; the body should be compact, with a short back and powerful loins, well-sprung ribs, depth through the girth and well-developed quarters. The ponies should not exceed 14·2 hands, and their colouring is again limited to blacks, bays, browns and a few greys.

Shetland

The charming and lovable Shetland pony is also a native of Scotland. It comes from the Shetland and Orkney Islands off the north coast. This diminutive pony is of ancient origin and until very recently has been the only means of transport for people and for goods in the islands. Strongest of all the native breeds for its size–the Shetland is a tiny 10·2 hands–it has a small, refined head which is frequently almost hidden beneath its abundantly protective mane. The weather in the northernmost parts of Britain is extremely unpleasant, wet and cold, and the Shetland needs all the protection it can get from its double winter coat, profuse mane and thick, long tail.

The Shetland gets its strength from its short back, depth of girth, sloping shoulder and well-sprung ribs. The hard, short legs and small open feet give a surprisingly airy action for one apparently so stocky in appearance. Of an independent and sometimes headstrong mind, the size of the Shetland makes it ideal as a pet and a child's pony, but it needs firm, though kindly, handling if it is not to get above itself.

Highland

The Highland ponies of Scotland used to be divided into two types, though the mainland strain has achieved general recognition throughout the Western Isles as the older and more pure-bred strain. The mainland ponies are larger than their island cousins, standing at about 14·2 hands, while the island type can be as small as 12·2 hands.

Highland ponies have traditionally shared the life of the crofters, being used as general utility ponies in the craggy uplands of Scotland. They are capable of carrying great weights, and combine this strength with remarkable agility and sure-footedness.

The famous strength of the breed is coupled with an attractive appearance and true pony character. The remarkable strength is to be found in the quality of bone: stallions should carry between nine and ten inches and mares well over eight inches. Neat heads and kindly eyes, a solid, deep and powerful body, muscularly well developed, and short strong legs are all combined in Highland ponies. Their natural paces are the walk and trot, for a turn of speed has never been required and has seldom even been practicable in this sort of country.

Highland ponies are most frequently found in one of the many shades of dun colour–ranging from golden-brown to silvery-blue. It is usual to find the dark dorsal eel-stripe in almost all pure-breds except for those predominantly black, grey-black and brown.

Connemara

There is one native breed of pony in Ireland, the Connemara. As its name suggests, it comes from the area of western Ireland known as Connemara. These ponies are a very old breed and a very hardy one. They should stand under 14 hands and are usually dun-coloured or grey, though occasional brown ponies are to be found. The mountains of Galway and Mayo have ensured that they are remarkably sure-footed and with an ability to survive on very little food. They also show a marked ability to jump. There is a very active breed society for Connemara, which maintains records and a stud book. Connemaras are primarily used as children's ponies, though they are also used for farm work. Breeding experiments to improve the quality of the breed by crossing with small Thoroughbreds and Arabs have been notably successful.

Cleveland Bay

The Cleveland Bay is another British native to be found in the north of England. The Cleveland is the only native horse–as opposed to pony–

that does not belong to the heavy horse group. It has been known since mediaeval times.

Before ironstone mining became general in Yorkshire and thus provided pack and haulage work for the horses, there was plenty of work for them to do in other ways. Until the mechanisation of agriculture, the Cleveland Bay was a real all-purpose horse. The long back and strong loins typical of the breed made it ideally suited to all kinds of pack work, for it was able to carry larger and heavier loads than the neighbouring Dales pony. These same qualities came in useful, too, for carrying the farmer's family – to market or to church – before the improvement in road surfaces led to the introduction of the gig.

As well as facilitating the family's movements, the Cleveland was used for agricultural work, was ridden to hounds and, when carriages became fashionable, was adopted as the most popular carriage horse.

The Cleveland adds other characteristics to those which have earned it a reputation as a valuable work horse. It has excellent hunter qualities, frequently being a natural jumper, up to a great deal of weight, with the courage to go all day and a cleanness of leg and strength enabling it to move 'over the top' rather than through heavy going, as most horses up to weight – themselves of the heavyweight sort – must do.

The Cleveland is usually a bright bay in colour with black points, though brownish bays are also seen. Standing at between 15·2 and 16 hands, the Cleveland has a large, well-made body with hard, short, clean legs and some nine inches of bone. Its back is still relatively long and its withers unpronounced, and it has a fairly large head on a long neck. Clevelands have considerable stamina and are usually long-lived. Their prepotency is greatly valued by breeders.

An elegant pair of Cleveland Bay carriage-horses parading in the show ring.

BRITISH HEAVY HORSES

The heavy horse breeds in Britain today fulfil a rather different role from those of their forebears. Originally horses of considerable size and strength were needed by mediaeval horsemen as chargers to carry them and their weighty armour into battle. In days when agricultural work and transport relied entirely on the horse the heavy breeds to be found in Britain flourished in most parts of the country. With the advent of increasingly mechanised equipment for farming during the present century there has been less and less demand for these horses, but recently interest in them has been increasing again, and splendid examples of these noble breeds can be seen at shows all over the country. There is also a lively international interest in the British heavy horse breeds; Clydesdales have for a long time been exported to countries both throughout the Commonwealth and also to others where their value for haulage has been recognised; and the equally famous Shire horse is also appreciated, particularly in the North and South American continents.

Clydesdales, named after the area of Scotland now centred in Lanarkshire – the Clyde valley – have a long history. The breed comes from a region always regarded as the best horse-breeding land in Scotland. It was here that the majority of horses required to carry Scottish knights were bred. Edward I of England was the first of many English kings to impose a ban on the export of horses of military value north of the border, and as a result stock was mostly drawn from Flanders and also from Denmark. The rural horse stock of the south-west area of Scotland therefore probably carried a fairly high proportion of the famous mediaeval 'Great Horse' blood. The 'gig mares' of those parts were covered by Flanders stallions in the late eighteenth century to produce the modern Clydesdale horse.

Clydesdale

The Clydesdale is a handsome, powerful animal standing at about 17 hands, and combines great stamina with strength and gaiety. The amenable disposition of the Clydesdale makes it

A Clydesdale mare and foal at Stirling in Scotland.

an easy horse to manage, while the emphasis placed on the quality of its legs and feet has made it an outstanding horse for both farm work and haulage in town conditions. The typical well-built Clydesdale is an attractive and almost elegant horse as well as a strong and energetic one, with an open, flat-profiled head, and straight legs planted well under its close-coupled body. Clydesdales are dark brown or black in colour, often with a white-striped face and white hind shanks. They carry a good deal of shaggy feather, which shows off their active paces to great advantage.

Shire

Shire horses were founded by mares supplied from the stock of the Old English Black horse bred on the east coast to the north of East Anglia. Like all the heavy breeds it was originally used for military purposes, and its origins can be traced back at least as far as Tudor times. Originally, as its name implies, the Shire was to be found in the Shires, in particular the counties of Leicestershire, Staffordshire and Derbyshire, though it is now more often found in the northern counties, in East Anglia and in Wales.

In both height and weight the Shire is the greatest of the heavy horses, and it has played a major part both in achieving more efficient agricultural cultivation and in helping the movement of heavy loads from one part of the country to another.

The Shire has all the qualities needed in a

A splendid Shire horse.

draught animal: strength, constitution and stamina. It is an immensely powerful horse of commanding appearance, the stallion sometimes standing at as much as 18 hands, and weighing anything over a ton. Wide-chested, with legs well set under the broad, muscular body, the Shire, like the Clydesdale, is remarkably docile. It is characterised by white markings and heavy feather against a body colour of black, bay or grey.

Suffolk Punch

As the name indicates, the Suffolk Punch breed originated in Suffolk, though it has for a

A pair of Suffolk Punches displaying their strength.

long time been considered native to the whole of East Anglia. The breed has been mentioned as far back as 1506. It is possible that the foundation stock may be a legacy of the Viking invasions hundreds of years before this time: the Suffolk Punch bears a marked resemblance to the Jutland horse which faces it across the North Sea. In the sixteenth and seventeenth centuries stallions of the Flanders breed were used on Suffolk mares.

The Suffolk Punch shares qualities of stamina, strength and docility with the other heavy horses of Britain. To these it adds unusual longevity and an ability to thrive under poor feeding conditions. The average height of the Suffolk is 16 hands – less tall than the Shire horse, but its equal in weight, for many Suffolks also weigh over a ton. Rather large-headed, the Suffolk is characterised by the depth of its neck in collar, its deep, round-ribbed body and short cannon bones. Typically, it too is tremendously well-muscled and impressively powerful. Suffolks are always chestnut, though there are seven acknowledged shades ranging from a dark to a bright chestnut. They carry noticeably less feather than the other heavy breeds, and less white is found on the face.

Percheron

The Percheron, a native of the La Perche region of France, is also a familiar sight in England. It was introduced into the latter country in 1916; it is perhaps the most widely dispersed heavy breed in the world. Its qualities are discussed in the chapter on French horses.

The maintenance of quality has always been of prime importance to breeders of heavy horses, and each breed has its own society to encourage breeding standards. Heavy horses are much admired even in this mechanised age, and they can also still be found at work both on the land and, particularly, in use with drays of the big brewery companies. The efforts of the breed societies have been largely responsible for the recent renewal of interest in these magnificent animals, and their breeding is encouraged. They are a familiar sight at all the major shows, beautifully decked out and carrying themselves proudly on parade.

BRITISH TYPES

The hunter

The word 'hunter' could with justification be applied to any horse used for the purpose of hunting. Like show-jumpers, hunters may come in all shapes, sizes and, indeed, colours, since they are not a specific breed.

In practice, however, the word refers to the *type* of horse best calculated to carry riders of various weights safely, expeditiously and comfortably over a country during the course of a season's hunting. That is the criterion by which a hunter is judged, but it has to be borne in mind, also, that the type will vary according to the country in which it is to be used. For instance, in the Shires – that part of the Midlands including Leicestershire, Rutland, Warwickshire, Northamptonshire and a part of Lincolnshire, which is regarded as the best English hunting country – the type best suited to the big, strongly-fenced pastures is the Thoroughbred or near-Thoroughbred. Size, speed and scope in full measure are needed if a horse is to remain in touch with hounds over this sort of grass country where scenting conditions will nearly always be good.

Conversely, such a horse might be a liability in a rough, hilly country, in ploughland or an area of small enclosures and big woodlands such as are to be found in the 'provinces' – a disparaging term originally used by those fortunate enough to hunt in the Shires when referring to hunting countries outside their own. In such countries the big-striding, bold Thoroughbred horse, so well suited to galloping over grass, is inhibited and likely to become increasingly frustrated when asked to 'creep' a trappy place or to pick his way up and down rough, stone-strewn moorland combes. His courage is then a disadvantage, his speed an unimportant factor, while the slow business of finding and hunting a fox in and over poor scenting land may be altogether too much for his volatile temperament. In these circumstances a short-legged, compact sort of little horse, possibly carrying a percentage of native pony blood and the temperament that goes with it is the type needed.

In plough countries, like those of East Anglia, speed is again not a vital factor, since

A champion hunter stallion shown in hand.

the arable lands constitute 'cold' scenting conditions. It is frequently thought that a big, strong, common-bred horse is the sort to be used here; in fact, this is not so. The old maxim that 'an ounce of blood is worth a pound of bone' is just as applicable to plough countries as elsewhere. A Thoroughbred would not usually be considered a good choice here, although there will always be the exceptions, and the ideal is possibly the good stamp of active, short-legged half- or even three-quarter bred with enough scope to tackle the wide ditches and enough common sense to cope with them when they are 'blind' in the early part of the season.

No discussion of the hunter could exclude the Irish variety, bred on the limestone and rich pastureland that are eminently suitable for breeding stock, and having the advantage of the mild Irish climate.

Ireland is traditionally a horse-breeding country, and even today many Irish farmers continue to keep mares and breed youngstock. At one time the market for their produce was almost entirely confined to England. Today, while the English are still substantial buyers, the market is international and the prices, for successful entries in the hunter classes at the Royal Dublin Society Horse Show, are little short of astronomical. Many of the best types of Irish hunters are bought for show-jumping and eventing by the representatives of continental countries and not a few have dominated the international arenas, particularly those bought by the Italians – The Rock, for example.

The Irish hunter was frequently bred out of

an Irish Draught mare – a big, roomy sort, not exactly beautiful, but possessing excellent limbs and great bone – and by a Thoroughbred stallion, whose pedigree was often not exactly definitive. The resulting progeny were big, galloping horses, up to weight, admirably balanced, usually temperate and as clever as cats over any kind of country. Their ability to jump was virtually in-bred by the practice of leading or long-reining youngstock over banks and ditches at an early age, and then riding them quietly to hounds in a snaffle and on a long, even loose, rein. In this way the young horses learnt to look after themselves and most of them developed that invaluable 'fifth leg' which keeps a good hunter on his feet in situations where the more impetuous land on their expensive noses.

In England the encouragement of hunter breeding is largely in the hands of the Hunters' Improvement and National Light Horse Breeding Society, founded with the object of improving and promoting the breeding of hunters, as its title implies, as long ago as 1885. This Society maintains a list of recommended hunter judges, publishes a Hunter Stud Book, and puts on two shows a year, one for stallions and the other for youngstock. The principle activity of the Society, however, is to make available suitable Thoroughbred stallions for the purpose of producing the most desirable type of hunter, an animal which in these days may also be successful in point-to-points, National Hunt racing and eventing.

Clearly, the HIS Premium stallion has a considerable influence on type, but the greatest factor in setting the standards that should be aimed for by breeders is the show-ring, or more specifically the show hunter classes and the judges appointed to officiate in them. The show hunter, which is the ideal, is Thoroughbred or nearly so, and is judged on conformation, action and on the ride he gives. That such horses may never go hunting, most of them being too valuable to run the risk of disfiguring blemishes, is immaterial. The show classes are there to provide the pattern of horse who, by virtue of his make and shape and the action that should accompany near-perfect conformation, will fulfil the requirements of a top-class hunter – namely, to carry a rider throughout a season safely and comfortably at a good hunting gallop with the minimum of effort and the least risk of incurring physical strain.

The show hunter must, therefore, be well

A winning show hunter, mature, fully developed and in the peak of condition.

proportioned; in fact, nearly perfectly so, since good conformation not only results in a balanced ride under saddle but is also less likely to lead to the unsoundnesses that are inherent in a badly made horse. The structure of back, loins and quarters must be powerful and the quarters capable of great propulsive effort, while the shoulder must be well sloped and in no way straight or loaded. The horse should give an impression of substance and power ('blood weeds', often pretty and elegant, are not hunters) and the body, showing a deep girth to allow unrestricted use of the lungs, needs to be set on good limbs, having clearly defined, clean joints, short cannon bones and a good measurement of 'bone' beneath the knee. It is this last measurement, combined with the quality of bone, that together with the general proportions of the animal determines its weight-carrying capacity; an important point in any hunter.

Few hunters of any worth will have less than eight inches of bone, while those intended for carrying heavyweight riders (above 14 st. 7 lb.) may well have more than ten inches. Measurement of bone by itself is not, however, sufficient; its quality also matters. Thoroughbred bone is of greater density than that found in common or cart-bred horses and will carry, inch for inch, a greater weight. Twelve inches of poor quality bone with a wide central core encompassed by only a thin wall is obviously a structure of less strength than bone of a lesser overall circumference with a smaller central core surrounded by a thicker proportion of denser bone.

However, while conformation is of the utmost importance it would be of no value unless the action of the horse were equally good. A hunter must walk and trot freely and straight, but the gallop is the pace at which he must excel. The stride should be long, low and effortless and devour the ground. Wasteful knee action and going 'into the ground' instead of over it are faults to be heavily penalised.

Good manners, an equable temperament, a kindly disposition and a good mouth are also necessary requirements in the show-ring. Gassy, tearaway horses that career away, fighting and fretting and almost out of control, do not make for comfortable or safe rides, however fast they may gallop.

Outside what might be termed the 'beauty' classes are the very popular competitions for working hunters, in which considerable emphasis is laid on performance. Judging is carried out on the basis of 40 per cent for jumping ability, 30 per cent for conformation and presence and 30 per cent for ride and action.

The hack

What is a hack? Today one thinks of a hack only in terms of the show ring, but to get it in its proper perspective one should really go back a hundred years, to before the days of motor cars. This was the age of the hack.

There were, in fact, two types of hack: the park hack and the covert hack. The former was the kind of horse on which ladies and gentlemen of leisure went riding, either in their park at home or in the public parks in the towns. In the latter case the horseman or horsewoman was exposed to the gaze of the public, and so it was essential that the whole appearance should be pleasing to the eye. Consequently, the park hack had to look very elegant, move beautifully and be perfectly turned out. In addition, of course, it had to have perfect manners, as did the hack used in the country; and also be a really comfortable ride. The emphasis, therefore, was on elegance, movement, manners and comfort. It is exactly the same today, or should be.

The covert hack was slightly different. This was the animal on which a man rode to the hunt while his hunters were hacked on at a steady jog by road. On his covert hack the hunting man tittuped across country at a fair pace, only getting onto his hunter at the meet. It was, of course, again essential that the horse should be thoroughly comfortable and well-mannered, but looks were of slightly less importance, while in conformation the covert hack was probably rather tougher than the more elegant park hack.

In considering the hack now one should never lose sight of its prototype, the hack of a hundred years ago. And so a judge today will look first and foremost for quality. The show hack should be a delight to look at and, of course, a pleasure to ride. The hack exhibitor is always striving to find the animal with these two attributes.

To me, personally, real quality means Thoroughbred. There can, perhaps, be a little Arab blood creeping in. Small hacks tend to have it more than large hacks, because obviously it is more difficult to find a small Thoroughbred horse. Often pony blood is also present, but on the whole one finds that the champions are pure Thoroughbred with just a touch of Arab.

Once one has bought a hack, young and with good potential, the next step is to produce it.

The production of a hack is an extremely specialised art, because although one might have the best-looking horse in the class it does not follow that it will win if it does not go correctly, or if it does not give the judge a good ride. To produce a hack is a more specialised job than producing either a hunter or a pony, as perfect manners and a good ride for the judge are so absolutely essential.

Recently there has been a most encouraging increase in the popularity of hacks. A few years ago they seemed to be dwindling. Many people thought that the hack class was being replaced by dressage, and that the dressage-trained horse would soon swamp the hack altogether.

In fact, there is a great difference between the two. The hack may, today, be considered a little old-fashioned, but basically it is the elegant riding horse, to be enjoyed both as a ride and in appearance. What more can one ask? It is really not surprising that each year it is increasingly popular.

Suppleness and obedience mark the quality hack. This Anglo-Arab became a successful dressage horse.

A charming example of a show hack.

The cob

In days gone by the cob was as much used in harness as under saddle, and was ideally suited to this dual role. Essentially, the cob was the mount of heavy, elderly riders who wanted a comfortable ride without any fireworks and who appreciated his lack of inches when mounting and dismounting. This does not mean that a cob is necessarily a slug. In the show ring he is expected to walk, trot, canter and gallop, and much emphasis is laid on his ability to cover the ground comfortably and expeditiously at all these paces. Very necessary attributes of the cob, however, are his temperament and good manners. He should be able to gallop flat out without hotting up and at all times he should come easily back to hand. Most cobs have equable temperaments, are inherently sensible, and nearly all are great characters. They are in fact intensely interesting horses, generally having exceptionally good balance and being anything but stodgy rides, even though they are often classed as 'confidential' and designated by clever dealers as 'gentlemen's gentlemen'.

The Welsh Cobs are an established breed; there are, however, many cobs that are not Welsh but are nonetheless of a well-defined type. The word cob refers to a strong, stocky animal, large in the body and carrying himself on powerful, short legs. Ideally, the head should show as much 'quality' (fineness) as possible and be well set on to an elegant but powerful neck. The body must be of exceptional depth at the girth and the back short and strong. In height the cob does not exceed 15·3 hands, though the limit set in the British show ring is two inches less than that, i.e. 15·1 hands. In the show ring it is also stipulated that cobs should be capable of carrying 14 stone.

Today, when there is no demand, or very little, for harness cobs of the sort that were once a familiar sight in the big cities drawing milk floats and tradesmen's vans, really good riding cobs are not so easily found; even so, good classes can still be seen at major British shows.

The hackney

A good deal is known about the origin of the modern Hackney, but it would be extremely difficult for anyone to attempt to decide exactly how the breed was evolved. It can, however, be proved that the ancestry of the Hackney on the sire's side dates back to the Darley Arabian and about 1704, though horses known as Hackneys were used in this country for centuries before the Darley Arabian arrived on these shores, and the trotting horse was recognised as a separate and valuable breed.

By the nineteenth century the Hackney had become firmly established as a riding horse and pack horse, being the means of transport used by many farmers, and it was as a riding horse that the first Hackney made its name.

The introduction of the railway system reduced the demand for the Hackney as a riding horse, as it became customary for farmers to

The cob—sturdy and reliable.

use the railway to go to market. But in spite of this, its popularity as a harness horse increased. The improved roads and much improved carriages in the second half of the nineteenth century demanded a lighter, faster type of horse than was used up to that time and the Hackney soon became the most fashionable harness horse as it combined good looks, action and courage.

The popularity of the Hackney encouraged a number of breeders to establish a register of the breed and, as a result, the Hackney Horse Society was formed in 1883. The first stud book was printed in 1884, at a time when the breed was beginning to attract increasing notice from horse breeders far outside its native eastern England. At that time there was a rapidly growing demand for light horses for many purposes and Hackney stallions were particularly sought by overseas breeders to produce the types of horses most needed.

By the turn of the century the Hackney had firmly established itself in Britain and abroad as the finest harness horse in the world, and has since maintained its world-wide popularity. This overseas demand for Hackneys for breeding purposes reached a peak in about 1906, when the Society's records show that horses were shipped to many foreign countries, with Canada and the United States taking the largest number. Today there is a considerable market for Hackneys to Argentina, Australia, Brazil, Canada, Denmark, France, Holland, Italy, Japan, Mexico, New Zealand, Portugal, South Africa, Spain and the United States.

The Hackney Horse Society has guarded jealously the interests of the breed and its type. This and other contributing factors have resulted in the development of this unique harness horse which has a reputation reaching far beyond the British Isles.

Here is a brief description of the breed. The Hackney should have a small convex head, with a small muzzle; large eyes and small ears; longish and well-formed neck; powerful shoulders and low withers; compact body with great depth of chest; tail set and carried high; short legs and strong hocks, well let down; well-shaped feet; fine silky coat. The most usual colours are dark brown, black bay and chestnut.

Both in action and at rest the Hackney has highly distinctive and readily observable characteristics. Shoulder action is free and progressive, with a high, ground-covering knee action, the foreleg being well thrown forward, not just up and down. Action of the hind legs is the same to a lesser degree. In a good Hackney the action must be straight and true. At rest the Hackney stands firm and foursquare, forelegs straight, hind legs well back, so that it covers the maximum of ground; the head is held high, ears pricked, with a general impression of alertness.

With its extremely high action and almost volcanic personality, the Hackney stands alone in the show ring as the personification of beauty and elegance. At the same time it continues to prove its stamina, courage and versatility. It is outstanding for private driving purposes, as can be seen in many of the marathons organised by the British Driving Society, and today Hackneys compete with great success in the new FEI Combined Driving Competitions, which consist of a dressage test, a marathon of well over twenty miles and an obstacle driving test.

A demonstration of the extravagant, showy action for which the hackney is famed.

4 The Americas

NORTH AMERICA

Man and his progress through the centuries owe much to the horse. It is on his back that armies travelled; that conquests were made; that different cultures and civilisations met and mingled. The horse has been valued as friend and companion; used as transport in quests for new territory; even revered as a god by the Aztecs when, in the sixteenth century, Cortez and his *Conquistadores* rode into old Mexico bringing Spanish dominion with them, destroying old cultures and imposing their rule and religion on the New World of the Americas. Without the horse, the *Conquistadores*' ravages into the interior would have been well-nigh impossible, a fact fully realised by Cortez when preparing for his expedition. Sixteen horses, eleven stallions and five mares, left Spain for the New World. It is from the survivors of this band, and the many that followed, that the vast herds of America grew, and from the subsequent importations of bloodstock from England, Europe and the East, that the breeds of America took shape.

The Quarter Horse

Formally recognised as a breed in 1941, the Quarter Horse has a long history dating back to Colonial days in America, when horses descended from old Spanish stock were crossed with blood imports from England. Among the most famous of these was a Thoroughbred imported in 1756. Named Janus, he was a grandson of the Godolphin Arabian, and is considered the ancient foundation sire of the present Quarter Horse breed. Today his name figures as head of nine of the twenty-four main 'families' of Quarter Horse.

Now to be found all over the USA, in Colonial days the breed was centred mainly in Virginia and the Carolinas, and it was here the breed

name originated. Freed from weekday work, farmers, land and plantation owners indulged in their favourite Sunday pastime–match racing their fleetest horses down the Southern towns' main streets. It was a rare town that could boast a street longer than a quarter of a mile, and from this the stocky, fast-starting little horses took their name.

Naturally, those fortunate in possessing match race winners found their horses in demand as breeding stock, thus ensuring transmittal of the Quarter Horse's prime asset—early speed. Nowadays, through selective breeding, the Quarter Horse is the fastest horse on earth over his distance, the quarter-mile.

However, speed alone is not the only factor ensuring his popularity. He has a more than equable disposition, is generally easily handled and broken, and when trained lives up to the typical but descriptive American phrase of 'a kid-broke horse'. He is also rated supreme as a working cowhorse, combining intelligence with muscular build and superb conformation that enables him to perform with ease manoeuvres calling for incredible agility.

The average Quarter Horse stands at between 14·3 and 15·1 hands, and weighs between 1100 and 1300 pounds at maturity, which with this breed tends to be somewhat earlier than with some others. A good Quarter Horse should possess a short head with small muzzle, foxy ears and the well-developed jaw so characteristic of the breed. His neck is of medium length, joining the shoulder at an angle of approximately 45 degrees, neither heavily crested nor too light of muscle. Good shoulders slope also at about 45 degrees, making for a smooth ride. The chest is wide and deep, allowing for the generous heart room so vital for this active horse. Forelegs are heavily muscled but without coarseness. The back is short-coupled and very strong, especially across the loins. Ribs are well sprung and very deep

Some exquisite Lippizaner mares at stud in Austria

An impression of the powerful, agile Quarter Horse.

through the girth. Hindquarters are very broad and heavy with powerful muscles, especially in the thigh and gaskin. Unlike other breeds, who tend to narrow here, the Quarter Horse's stifle is wider than the hips. It is from these tremendously powerful quarters that he gets his quick acceleration and the ability to stop rapidly, throwing all his weight onto his hindquarters. Hocks are well let down, and cannon bones short. Medium length pasterns and hooves are set at an angle of 45 degrees which, coupled with a good shoulder, increases the horse's durability as leg concussion is thereby minimised.

Within the breed there are distinct types, raised with a view to the work they will be called upon to perform, yet every good Quarter Horse retains the breed's hallmark of muscular strength coupled with refinement. Hence we find that the stockier 'bulldogger' type, for all his muscle and greater body size and weight, retains the refinement so apparent in his elegant brother, the 'racing' Quarter Horse, and the agility of a cutting horse. In this sphere, where inborn cow-sense and agility are called for, the Quarter Horse reigns supreme, and it is in racing that he shows his lightning burst of speed, scorching the track with fantastic twenty-second times for the quarter-mile.

Year by year the number of horses registered outnumbers that of all other breeds in the USA. The uses to which the Quarter Horse is put are legion, but first and foremost he excels as a working horse, having taken the highest honours wherever he competes in cutting and roping. He is also in great demand in every other Western sphere. Throughout the USA there are Quarter Horse shows, where the cream of the breed competes for points in pleasure, reining, trail, barrel racing, pole bending and working cowhorse classes. In addition he is also used under English saddle in pleasure, jumping, working hunter and polo classes. At the year's end the horses accumulating the highest number of points are awarded the American Quarter Horse Association's Championships and Register of Merits. Quarter Horses also figure largely and successfully in open shows, where many breeds show in the same classes.

Since the Quarter Horse is by far and away America's most popular breed, being versatile, easy-going and tough, horsemen in other countries have become eager to buy that blood, and Quarter Horses are widely exported.

The Paint Horse

Closely allied to the Quarter Horse is his colourful cousin, the American Paint. Formed as recently as 1962, the American Paint Horse Association is dedicated to upgrading the quality of this increasingly popular breed. From the initial year's 250 registrations numbers have now leapt past the 22,000 mark, amply substantiating the APHA's claim to be the fastest growing breed registry.

Modelled along stockhorse lines, and because of heavy infusions of Quarter Horse

John Kidd on Maple Signalla at Hickstead

An American Overo Paint.

blood, the ideal conformation of the Paint Horse is closely allied to that of the Quarter Horse. The Paint breed falls into two basic categories of colour pattern: the Tobiano—a predominantly white animal with large patches of colour, especially on head, flanks and chest, with white often spreading unbroken across the back; and the Overo—a solid-coloured horse with white splashed mainly on the mid-section of his body, and rarely with white spreading across the back. The Overo's legs are frequently dark-coloured, and in contrast to the Tobiano he will often be bald-, apron- or bonnet-faced according to the amount of white. Overos frequently lack the extra clear-cut demarcation lines between colours that are to be found in Tobianos— there is often a blurring of shades where the colours meet. In addition to the white, the accepted body colours of paints are black, bay, sorrel, dun, palomino and roan. Some Paint characteristics are blue eyes, white above the hocks and knees, variegated manes and tails, a pink skin under the white hair, and a bluish tinge where the dark and light skins meet.

One facet of the breed is that no horse is so highly individualistic as a Paint. Though they will be either Tobiano or Overo, no two horses carry the same markings, each animal being distinguished by his own Paint pattern—a real safeguard these days when horse-stealing still happens, as reference to horse journals proves.

One of the reasons for the breed's rapid growth in America is the Paint's versatility. Predominantly a Western horse, he figures largely in open shows where he is certainly an eyeful of colour. With his legacy from Quarter

Horse blood he competes on level terms in the many events open to Western horses—pleasure, reining, roping, cutting, speed events, trail—as well as the English divisions in jumping and pleasure. He also earns his share of the prize money in the action-packed rodeo arena, where it is not the style he displays that counts but the sheer speed and co-operation with which he places his rider ready for a throw in calf-roping, or moves up close to the steer for the bulldogger rider.

Currently gaining favour and becoming more numerous and valuable are races for Paint horses. These are run on the same lines as the Quarter Horse races, and the infusion of Thoroughbred blood lends enough speed to make the colours blur down the straightway.

The Standardbred

The foundation stock of many American breeds was imported from Britain, and the Standardbred breed is no exception. It was a grey Thoroughbred stallion named Messenger, foaled in 1780 and imported into the United States in 1788, who was the breed's foundation sire.

In those days, particularly in the eastern states, harness racing was popular at country fairs. It was at these gatherings that owners with fast horses competed. In the early days race winners were determined by holding several heats, the horse winning most being the overall winner. This tough method resulted in the elimination of weaker animals, only the horses 'in the money' being rated best breeding stock. Although Messenger was used extensively and successfully as a sire of Thoroughbreds, it was when crossed on these harness horses that the ability to trot at racing speed resulted in his offspring. From these small beginnings the Standardbred breed took hold, receiving a tremendous impetus with Messenger's famous greatgrandson Rysdyk's Hambletonian, who gained such lasting fame as a racer that the name Hambletonian became synonymous with Standardbred. All present-day Standardbreds trace back to Rysdyk's Hambletonian, and through him to Messenger.

The breed name originated because when the breed type was being fixed and the American

Trotting Register was started in 1871, horses were accepted for permanent registry only if they could trot or pace a mile in a standard time. For the trot it was 2·30 minutes, and for the pace 2·25 minutes.

At first glance the Standardbred horse reminds one of the English Thoroughbred, to whom he owes so much, but comparing the two one sees that the Standardbred is a heavier-boned animal, longer in the body and with a flatter rib-cage, and quarters sloping to a greater degree. The muscles of the quarters, particularly in the thigh, are powerful and long, and this, combined with the extra slope to the quarters, gives the Standardbred such impetus in his racing gait. In keeping with the heavier bone, the head is not so refined as that of a Thoroughbred, often being straight or very slightly convex, but with a good generous eye. The nostrils are capable of immense flaring, necessary for oxygen intake when at speed. The ears tend to be rather on the long side. The neck is somewhat shorter and straighter. The most predominant colour is bay, followed by browns, chestnuts, blacks and a few greys. The manes and tails grow profusely and very long, with the mane being extremely fine in texture. The average height ranges between 15 and 15·3 hands, though some horses go over 16 hands.

Although Standardbreds started their career as country fair racers, going on to increase in numbers and achieve a phenomenal popularity after the second world war on recognised race-tracks mainly in the eastern states, Pennsylvania, and on the west coast, they also appear in many other guises. Top-class shows always include classes for roadsters, which are 'driven to bike' and with the driver wearing racing colours.

The Walking Horse

America has developed many breeds, and one of the most distinctive of these is the Tennessee Walking Horse. It gained official status when leading breeders met in May 1935 and formed the Tennessee Walking Horse Breeders Association.

The beginnings of the Walking Horse breed trace back almost two centuries, when the rich farmlands of central Tennessee started attracting settlers who brought horses of Standard-bred, Thoroughbred, Morgan and Saddlebred breeding with them. From crosses of these four breeds came the foundation stock of the present-day Walker. Each breed transmitted its prime asset – Morgan tractability; Saddlebred elegance; Thoroughbred quality; and the substance of the Standardbred, which also strongly influenced the development of the Walker's gaits.

In early days the Walker was bred primarily as an all-round working horse, equally at home in harness, under saddle, or earning his keep on the land, but it was as a saddle horse that he really excelled. Because of his remarkably smooth gaits, the Walker was in demand on the vast cotton and tobacco plantations of the southern states, where landowners and their overseers, who spent hours in the saddle, needed a horse capable of giving a supremely comfortable ride. Hand in hand with comfort went looks, as southerners took immense pride in the quality of the horseflesh they raised. Before long these smooth, gliding horses became known as 'plantation horses'.

Many prepotent sires figured in the breed's formation, but it was not until the early 1900s that the horse considered as the foundation sire of the modern Walking Horse began to have such an impact on the breed. Black Allan, a direct descendant of the great Standardbred, Hambletonian, was foaled in Lexington, Kentucky in 1886 and was originally intended for the trotting tracks. However, he showed a predilection to pace and remained unraced. Many of today's Walkers are inclined to pace or trot early in life, a tendency which is curtailed early on as the trainer induces the correct walking gaits.

Some breeds have many characteristics in common, but the Walking Horse's conformation is unique and unmistakeable. Average height ranges from 15·2 to 16 hands, and his frame is very compact and full of substance. The head is rather long, with the profile straight and with narrow pointed ears. Carried high, the head joins the neck at approximately 90 degrees. The neck is fairly long and powerful, moulding into a sloping shoulder that contributes so much to that smooth ride. The back is extremely short, while the quarters slope slightly. The profuse tail is carried high. The legs are fine, with the forelegs set slightly forward and the hind legs set with the hocks well away from the body. Colours are sorrel, chestnut, black, roan, white, bay-brown and occasionally yellow, and white markings are often very prominent.

The Walking Horse is synonymous with comfort. In all his gaits—gaits possessed by no other breed—he gives a ride completely devoid of any jarring. These gaits are the flatfoot walk, a true four-beat gait in which the horse seems to glide over the ground, all the while exhibiting a slight nod of the head; the running walk, a much faster and very spectacular version of the flat-foot walk in which the hind feet overstride the front—with exceptional Walkers by as much as fifty inches. The running walk is again accompanied by the nodding head, only now much more pronounced. The Walking Horse's canter, often referred to as a 'rocking chair' canter, is very distinctive, as the horse elevates his fore-hand in a rolling, forward motion, while the action of the hindquarters remains relatively level. The hind legs in all three gaits are carried well underneath the horse, creating impulsion and drive and also enabling the horse to achieve his remarkable smoothness. I have heard it said, and can quite believe it, that a good Walker in a canter can balance a glass of water on his quarters and not spill a drop.

Walking Horses come in two categories— show Walkers and pleasure Walkers. The show Walker is always shown with a set tail, and his gaits show more defined action, particularly in the running walk. To encourage greater action the front hooves are often weighted, mercury sometimes being inserted in the tip of the shoe, and the hooves themselves are built up with several layers of leather pads. In fact the horn of the hoof is pared very little in comparison with that of other breeds, and it is a matter of great concern to the owners of show Walkers if any part of this extra long hoof breaks away. A farrier shoeing Walking Horses has to be exceptionally skilled and the cost of shoeing a Walker is about twice that of ordinary saddle horses.

Pleasure Walkers are bred from the same stock but usually lack the potential of their more showy brothers. Their training is not taken to such a high degree, and though they perform in basically the same manner there is none of the high-powered drive and action of the show Walker. At all good-sized shows there are classes for show Walkers and others for pleasure Walkers. Show Walkers are invariably trained by professionals, sometimes being shown by their owners but more often by their trainers. Pleasure Walkers are usually owner-trained and ridden.

The Morgan

Durability and stamina are just two of the characteristics that hallmark the Morgan breed. Now rated as one of the foremost of America's many horses, the Morgan breed began in Springfield, Massachusetts, with the birth of a bay colt named Figure in 1789.

Most breeds evolve over a period of time, as various horses, bloodlines and existing breeds are crossed and recrossed before a breed type is established, but with the Morgan it happened in just one generation—the time it took for Figure to get his first crop of foals on the ground. Coming into the ownership of the local school-master, Justin Morgan, in Randolph, Vermont in 1793 in payment of a debt. Figure stood at stud to local mares as well as working as an all-round saddle, harness, racing and draught horse. In those early days much land still had to be cleared for homesteads, and Justin Morgan's tough bay stallion excelled in snaking heavy logs out from clearings. Today's Morgans still prove their strength in the show ring pulling a heavy stone boat—the only breed that has to show both as harness, show and draught horse.

Taking his new name from that of his owner, Justin Morgan's successes in match-racing, pulling contests, and as a trotter in harness, when pitted against all comers, meant he was in steady demand as a sire. Even when put to quite ordinary mares, the resulting foals were born inheriting their versatile sire's compact and very robust frame as well as his elegance and kind disposition. All these qualities, combined with inherited versatility, made him one of the most successful sires in history. Over the ensuing years, until Justin Morgan died at the ripe old age of thirty-two, he continued to stamp all his offspring in the same way, so that well before his death the breed had become established and very popular.

As well as being a famous breed in its own right, the Morgan has largely influenced the formation of three of America's best-known breeds—the Standardbred, the Saddlebred and the Tennessee Walking Horse. Many present-day Standardbreds have Morgan blood in their ancestry. The Saddlebred, too, owes much to this tough breed, gaining its short coupling and rounded barrel from Morgan conformation as well as its docility of temperament. The Tennessee Walking Horse has been directly and strongly influenced by the Morgan.

Predominantly bay, the average Morgan stands between 14 and 15 hands. His conformation is robust but very refined—a rare combination. The head is small and dry, with neat ears and a large expressive eye. The neck is of medium length and carries a proud, heavily-maned crest. Well sloped shoulders enhance his smooth ride. The back is short, and the barrel rounded and deep. Loins are strong and the croup level, with the long and profuse tail carried high. The limbs are very fine and strong. The general carriage of the Morgan is alert and gay. He is also a thrifty keeper—a great asset in these days of high-priced feedstuffs.

In the past the Morgan was used mainly as a utility or working horse on the farms, in the family buggy, and as an all-around saddle horse. Today he still shows his innate versatility, but more along the lines of the family pleasure

This Morgan stallion is being driven to a Meadowbrook cart in Rhode Island.

horse, taking readily to any aspect of equine activity that is asked of him.

Set on the road to popularity by its prepotent founder, this very versatile breed gained swift recognition in the 1800s, followed by a tremendous increase in numbers, particularly in the northern and eastern states, although Morgans were to be found all over the country. Later on, they were used largely in New York when tramcars relied on horses rather than horsepower. With mechanisation their use, and therefore the numbers bred, declined. However, many still see service in the north as police horses, as their tractability, courage and ease of handling make them ideal in the welter of city activity. Now that the horse is enjoying a popularity boom there is a resurgence of interest in the Morgan, his particular attraction being that he can honestly be said to be an all-round performer.

The American Saddlebred

Most of America's breeds of horses originated east of the Mississippi, and the American Saddlebred is no exception. Hailing from Kentucky, this elegant animal was yet another of the breeds developed by the settlers staking homesteads in the early days of American independence. As people drifted further west and deeper into the south looking for new land tracts to support the increasing population, their horses played a vital part in the success of their enterprises. Once settled and becoming

prosperous, Kentuckians began evolving a new breed particularly suited to their own needs from their original stock of Thoroughbreds, Morgans, Standardbreds and Carolinian Nara-gansett Pacers. By crossing the best of these breeds the American Saddlebred was born.

The Saddlebred foundation sire was a Thoroughbred named Denmark, and most modern Saddlebreds trace back to him through Gaines Denmark, the result of a mating between Denmark and a pacing mare. It is from the Gaines Denmark line that the easy gaits evolved.

Combining the best of all the foundation breeds, the Saddlebred presents a picture of extreme refinement and elegance. One of America's taller breeds, he stands between 15·2 and 16·2 hands, with occasional individuals over or under this height. The predominant colour is a rich coppery chestnut, often accom-panied by a flaxen mane and tail. Other common colours are bay, black and grey, and lately there have been a considerable number of palomino-coloured horses registered.

The typical Saddlebred is a close-coupled, proudly alert horse with high head and tail carriage. The head is refined, dry and rather narrow, topped by narrow mobile ears. The eyes, set wide apart, are extremely large and lustrous, enhancing his intelligent appearance. The neck is elegantly long, running into moderately high withers that hold a saddle well. Well sloped and powerful shoulders make it possible for the horse to achieve smoothness, while his short back and rounded barrel give strength. A level croup and rounded quarters give thrust to his gaits. Limbs are long and fine with tendons clearly defined. Mane and tail hair is silky textured and very fine.

Originally a utility horse destined for general farm and saddle work, his ability to perform at five distinct and smooth gaits combined with overall beauty made the Saddlebred a natural for the show ring when easier times meant horsemen could ride for relaxation instead of out of necessity. Consequently the modern Saddlebred, which is the product of intensive breeding to enhance all the finer qualities of gait and conformation, is primarily a show and pleasure horse. As such he is eminently success-ful, being shown as either a three-gaited, fine harness or five-gaited horse, as well as intro-ducing children to the show ring via the equitation classes.

Although capable of tremendous collection and animation, coupled with the eagle-proud head carriage brought on by intensive training, the Saddlebred not destined for the three- and five-gaited show events remains a much more relaxed horse that is eminently suitable for the more normal facets of pleasure riding. He is also being used quite considerably as a jumper, though high head carriage and action is a defi-nite handicap, and some Saddlebreds even find their niche as working ranch horses.

The Appaloosa gained its name from the Palouse river in the lands of the Nez Percé Indians. The breed, which is now becoming increasingly popular throughout the United States, is descended from Spanish stock. The Appaloosa Horse Club was formed in 1937 to promote recognition of this special type of spotted horse.

LATIN AMERICA

Although there are a considerable number of breeds of horses to be found across the length and breadth of Central and South America, all but a few of them are descendants of one original breed – the Andalusian of Spain, which arrived in Latin America as the mount of the *conquistadores*.

The characteristics held in common by many of these breeds are the distinctive *paso* gait and the proud bearing inherited from the original Andalusians. While the Peruvian Paso has been the breed to make the biggest impact outside Latin America (principally in the United States), there are also paso-type breeds in Puerto Rico, Colombia, Cuba, Venezuela, Brazil and the Dominican Republic. And although the fiercely-nationalistic devotees of each breed fervently maintain its absolute supremacy, in fact all of them are remarkably similar both in appearance and in gait.

Interestingly enough, the North Americans have been the first to take a measured overall look at the situation, and accordingly have formed the American Paso Fino Horse Association, which takes in all the so-called Paso Fino breeds and is working towards blending the best of all of them to mould an ideal mount of this type.

The North American society employs the slogan 'The gait is the birthright of a Paso Fino', and this is, indeed, what really sets it apart. Basically the horse's movement is lateral, with the two legs on one side first being used, and then the two on the other. However, while somewhat similar to a normal pacing gait, the *paso* is actually performed in four steps, two by two, the two of each lateral pair being very close in timing. It could perhaps be described as a 'broken pace', with the hind foot touching the ground a fraction of a second before the front foot. This unique high-stepping action eliminates the jarring effect of a true pace, and so the Paso Finos offer a very smooth ride indeed which, allied to their proud bearing, amenable temperaments and considerable stamina, is why they are becoming so well known in the United States.

Representative of the *paso* breeds, and certainly the best-known, is the Peruvian Paso.

Mature animals of this breed measure from 13·3 to 15 hands in height, with the average being around 14·2 hands, and they weigh 950 to 975 lb. Colours to be found are grey, white, chestnut, bay and black, and many of the horses have white markings on head and limbs. Palominos also occur. However, piebalds and skewbalds are rare, since they are most unpopular in Peru, and mares with these markings are normally taken well away from the band of brood mares and used for suckling mule foals.

Peruvian breeders have been steadily developing the breed for more than 300 years, from the time when the original imported Andalusians were putting their great hearts into covering vast distances over Peru's high and rugged mountains, through her parched deserts and in her humid, green jungles. These demanding conditions gradually produced a super-tough trail horse, chockfull of stamina and able to perform on a minimum of forage. Since the Peruvian riders were in the saddle for many hours at a time over some really punishing terrain, they paid the closest attention to the smooth purity of their horses' natural *paso* gait, and they also looked for, and only bred from, animals with proud but very docile temperaments.

However, while the Peruvian Paso still retains much of the great pride, almost amounting to arrogance, of the Andalusian, the many hundreds of years in a very different environment have wrought considerable alterations to his conformation. He has become smaller and more wiry, and his legs in particular have altered to become so fine that a good Peruvian Paso looks very light of bone. However, the breed's bone is remarkably dense and tough, and the Peruvian Paso's legs stand up to an enormous amount of hard use, gliding him over the steep, rocky trails of the soaring Andes all day or eating up miles through burning sand in the featureless deserts.

The Peruvian Pasos have steeply-sloping quarters and low-set tails, and the cannons of their hind legs are often sloped forward so that they are somewhat sickle-hocked. The rear legs move with a minimum expenditure of effort in a smooth gliding action which imparts very little motion to the hindquarters. In the natural *paso* gait the front legs of the Peruvian Paso, moved from the shoulder, reach far forward and are lifted to between a foot and sixteen inches above the ground. The knee and fetlock joints are flexed at the same time, and the feet are thrown six inches or more to the side in a unique 'dishing' motion which is greatly prized by the South American horsemen, and which is in fact essential to the smooth, fast regularity of the horse's forward progress.

As well as the normal *paso* gait, the Peruvian Paso also performs the pace and the so-called 'marching *paso*' and can trot, canter and gallop as well. However, no self-respecting Peruvian *caballero* will ever allow his mount to perform anything but one or other of its *paso*-type gaits. The 'marching *paso*' is very similar to the pace, but the supports last longer than the suspensions, giving an impression that the horse is 'marching'. The print of the back hoof falls ahead of the corresponding front hoof but less than it does in the pace.

The other best-known of Latin America's breeds, Argentina's Criollo, also descends from the redoubtable Andalusian. This very strong, stocky, tough and agile horse is the pride of his homeland, where he carries the picturesque *gauchos* after cattle on the wide-flung *estancias* of the Pampas.

The Paso Fino is noted for its characteristic *paso* gait. This stallion is performing the *paso corto*.

The Criollo stands some 14 hands, is short-backed and has very strong legs with short cannons. Most Criollos are dun in colour, but there are also piebalds and skewbalds. They are remarkably tough and long-lived, and two famous Criollos which were ridden the 13,350 miles from Buenos Aires to New York, crossing Andean mountain passes and Ecuadorian deserts in the process, lived until they were in their mid-thirties!

Today's Criollos owe their origin to the importation in 1535 by Pedro de Mendoza, founder of Buenos Aires, of some hundred Andalusians from Spain. When Argentina's fledgling capital city was attacked and sacked by Indians, many of the horses escaped into the Pampas. There they multiplied so quickly that within fifty years their wild descendants were numbered in thousands.

Harsh winters and scorching summer droughts ensured the survival of only the fittest, however, as did determined hunting by the Indians, who had acquired a taste for horse-flesh. When taken from the wild herds by the moustachied *gauchos*, the tough, agile Criollos soon proved their worth as cattle horses, and also as strong, enduring pack animals.

However, about a century ago the breed was nearly ruined by crossing many of its members with stallions from Europe and the United States. The use of these imported sires produced speedier and more elegant animals, but it quickly whittled away the inherent toughness and stamina of the Criollo, not to mention his hard-won native sagacity, which could often be very useful on the large unfenced ranges of the time. Fortunately, before it was too late and the good qualities of the Criollo had gone for ever, a number of alert breeders became aware of the dangers that existed in crossing the native cattle horses with imported stallions, and they made a forceful and concerted effort to produce the old-style Criollo. Severely selective breeding from the best remaining specimens of the breed was a crash programme that worked, and in 1918 an association was formed to foster and to promote the Criollo breed.

Argentina is also famed for the excellent polo ponies it produces, which are not only models of speed, agility, balance and courage, but are often schooled to a very high standard by their expert Argentinian trainers. The polo pony of Argentina is a specialised Thoroughbred type whose origins lie in the crossing, in the early years of this century, of Thoroughbred stallions on native mares. A continuous effort to upgrade the polo pony stock was made over many years, with today's splendid results.

5 Europe and Scandinavia

FRANCE

The history of the horse in France has been greatly affected by changes in breeding policy and classification, and the appearance of most breeds has altered accordingly. There are two notable exceptions: the English Thoroughbred and the pure-bred Arabian.

The Anglo-Arab originates in the cross-breeding of English Thoroughbreds and pure-bred Arabians, though under special conditions the stud book has been opened to the progeny of part-bred Anglo-Arab mares. The Anglo-Arabs currently registered there result from breeding Anglo-Arabs to English Thoroughbreds or pure-bred Arabians, English Thoroughbreds to pure-bred Arabians or Anglo-Arabs to Anglo-Arabs. The name of any Anglo-Arab included must indicate the percentage of Arab blood the horse contains, the minimum allowed being 25 per cent.

The Southern part-bred, resulting from the cross-breeding of pure-bred Arabians or English Thoroughbreds with native mares already strongly impregnated with Arab blood and whose ancestry could be traced, was eventually also bred to Anglo-Arab stallions.

The principal breeding country of France has always been the south-west, particularly the Plain of Tarbes and the Limousin around Limoges. Anglo-Arab stallions have for some years been used similarly to English Thoroughbreds for the upgrading of the quality of other breeds. For example, the progeny of Selle Français mares bred to Anglo-Arab stallions are classified under the denomination of their

A Selle-Français stallion from Normandy.

44

dams or, if the mare is without pedigree, simply under 'Selle'. The general description of Selle Français has replaced that of Demi-sang, which was formerly used to describe any horse other than an English Thoroughbred, a pure-bred Arabian or an Anglo-Arab.

The name of Selle Français, or French riding horse, can be applied to any horse with a pedigreed sire and dam.

The Demi-sang Normand or Anglo-Normand is probably the best known of these, as Normandy has always been famous horse country, even before the seventeenth century, when Louis XIV's enterprising minister, Colbert, imported Arabians to improve the native breed.

The Vendée, Charente, Loire-Atlantique and Deux Sèvres, all départements in western France, bred horses in the nineteenth century of a popular riding horse type to Anglo-Norman English Thoroughbred and Anglo-Arab stallions, producing the prototype of a highly-bred, rather tall, powerful horse of fine conformation known for its jumping ability.

The Charollais came from the centre of France, an ancient native breed up-graded by Anglo-Norman and English Thoroughbred blood. Raised on excellent grassland, it had plenty of bone and quality and produced fine hunters.

The Limousin was a remarkable horse: full of quality, averaging about 15·2 hands, extremely refined, supple and light in its paces, ideally suited to dressage work. Additions of English Thoroughbred and Anglo-Norman strains made it an even more excellent ride.

The Camarguais lives, as is well known, in the Camargue. The climate and soil in and around the Rhône delta combined with Arab and Berber origins to produce a small (13·2 to 14·2 hands), extremely robust horse used by the 'gardians' for herding cattle. Nature continues to be responsible for the horses in this area, and their breeding is not controlled.

The French Trotter originates in Normandy, where native mares were bred to English Thoroughbreds and a few American sires. In 1836 trotting races were instituted, and since 1858 only those stallions who have proved themselves on the racetrack have been recognised by the authorities. The stud book,

The small, tough horses of the Camargue are an indispensable part of the life of this region of France.

opened in 1922 and closed in 1941, is reserved for the offspring of previously registered trotter sires. Some of them, in spite of their conformation (their straight shoulders, for example) have been successful in show-jumping.

There are many draught horses in France, the four principal breeds being the Boulonnais, the Percheron, the Ardennais and the Breton. The Boulonnais is raised in the northern départements of Pas-de-Calais, Somme and Oise, with a division into large and small horses. The large one can reach as much as 17 hands, and is sturdy with a short head and wide forehead, massive arched neck, straight back, short loins and double croup. It is used for heavy draught work in farming and transport. The smaller type, averaging 15 to 16 hands, is a fast trotter and was popular with city tradesmen. Some large black horses can be found, but the breed is typically grey in colour. It has been improved by the addition of Arab blood.

The Percheron, also infused with Arab blood, is raised in the area west and south-west of Paris. The breed originated with mares of the Parisian basin bred to Norman, Danish, English and German stallions. The large horses stand well over 17 hands; the smaller type, more har-

The French Percheron.

monious in build, is known as the Percheron Postier.

The Ardennais, bred in north-eastern France, was formerly a highly-strung, agile and resilient animal, making an excellent heavy artillery horse. After early nineteenth-century cross-breeding with pure-bred Arabs, English Thoroughbreds and part-breds this breed was modified to a horse some 16 hands, today used principally in farming. Very deep-chested and showing little daylight, its colours are chestnut, bay and roan.

The Breton, though it has its own history going back to the Middle Ages, has received since the eighteenth century English, Arab and Norman blood, resulting in the two principal types seen today: the heavy one, with a wide, short, dish-faced head, barrel-shaped body, double croup, a lot of bone and feather; and the light draught horse, better known as the Postier Breton, as robust and sober as his heavier cousin but somewhat more elegant, standing from 15 to 16 hands, with a nice shoulder and good withers. This lighter type, formerly used extensively for work with light artillery, is now a useful farm horse. The most usual colours for the breed are roan and grey.

This horse is a splendid example of the lighter type of Hanoverian now being bred in Germany.

WEST GERMANY

In the Federal Republic of Germany there are today three principal breeds of warm-blood horses. Local provincial strains have been created by using stallions of these breeds, Holstein, Hanoverian and East Prussian (Trakehner)—principally the last two—plus the Thoroughbred. Some of them are also breeds of long standing, such as the East Friesian, with 1,360 registered brood mares, founded in 1715, and the Oldenburg. These strains share the same stallion lines and are based on the Dutch Friesian. Other breeds are the Westfalen, Kurhessen, Württemberg, etc. Altogether, in 1970 there were 252,000 horses in West Germany.

The Holstein is not as popular as it used to be, nor is it bred in such numbers. As well as Schleswig Holstein, Kurhessen has a small breeding centre, though in the seventeenth and eighteenth centuries stallions of the Holstein breed were used in many provinces. The horses were originally bred in the maritime climate of the marshes of the mouth of the Elbe and neighbouring rivers. They were then big strong horses with convex heads, high action and noble outlook, like their Neapolitan and Spanish

A superbly matched team of high-class Holsteiners during a driving marathon.

Power and pride—a fine team of Jutland horses from north Germany.

ancestors. Later, Yorkshire Coach (Cleveland Bay) and Thoroughbred blood was introduced, and thus horses with jumping ability evolved for the show ring. The first stud orders were issued in 1680, and in the Royal Stud at Esserom the famous white horses were first bred. The Electress Sophia of Hanover, granddaughter of James I, is said to have been responsible for the creation of this white or cream breed of horses, of which the Holstein stallion Mignon was the founder. Her son, George I, introduced them to Great Britain, where they were used in the royal mews and at Windsor.

The Hanoverian is a true 'son of the soil' and his native land covered most of north-west Germany: Brunswick, Mecklenburg, Pomerania and Brandenburg. The original mares were native and were crossed with Mecklenburg, Thoroughbred, Cleveland Bay and East Prussian stallions. In the different districts coach horses, artillery and agricultural horses as well as saddle horses and warm-blood racehorses were bred. The last two decades have seen a change in conformation to a lighter, more elegant saddle horse which commands a high price at the auction sales at Verden, held twice a year.

The East Prussian or Trakehner horse is a refugee from East Prussia. The breed is now chiefly in private hands, though the Trakehner breed Society has a stud at Rantzau in Schleswig Holstein, and selected colts are raised, together with Hanoverian colts, at Hünnesruck stud in the Solling. During the second world war, this breed was almost decimated.

The Noriker or South German cold-blood horse is bred in Bavaria, Württemberg and Baden. It is a short-backed, strong horse and is used for draught work and in agriculture. In Austria the breed is divided into two types, the other being the famous Pinzgauer spotted horse. The evolution of the Noriker can be dated to the period of the former Roman province of Noricum and therefore to the Roman occupation of nearly two thousand years ago.

The Schleswig and Jutland cold-blood horses of north Germany and Denmark share the same family tree. The breed is partly descended from mediaeval war horses and was at one time used for draught work, especially for omnibuses and trams.

One of the best Arabian studs in Europe is Marbach an der Lauter which, in 1932, took over the breeding of the Arab horse from Weil stud. It is a state stud, the only one in the Federal Republic, founded by Duke Ludwig of Württemberg in the sixteenth century to breed hardy horses. This policy has now resulted in the modern Württemberg warm-blood horse.

The Haflinger of southern Germany is found in the Bavarian mountains as well as the Austrian Tirol and its native south Tirol. It is above all a sturdy mountain pack pony able to carry heavy loads on its back. The breed is also of extreme antiquity and may be descended from the small Noriker pack pony, a breed which was later improved by the introduction of Arab blood.

The Trakehner, widely used as a riding and harness horse.

Horses being watered in the plains of Hungary.

AUSTRIA AND HUNGARY

From the earliest historical times the vast *puszta* country that is now known as Hungary was the habitat of wild equine populations. It was also the home of one of the earliest of the horse-breeding peoples—the people of the Tripolje civilisation.

The native horse of Hungary was small, very fast and had plenty of stamina, and it formed the basis for several very hard warm-blood breeds.

The largest stud in Europe in 1774 was the Austro-Hungarian state stud Radautz in Buko-wina, now part of the Ukraine in the USSR.

The task of these huge state studs was to breed remounts and cavalry horses. In 1889 the stud Babolna was added, to breed entires for agricultural purposes.

The state stud Babolna breeds some of the finest Arab horses in the world, although much valuable material was lost during the last war. A particularly successful cross of Arab stallions on native mares has resulted in the beautiful Shagya Arab breed.

The famous Lippizaner is bred not only in Austria but also in Yugoslavia and Bulgaria. These horses have made the Spanish School in Vienna famous with exhibitions of high-school dressage. The breed was founded in 1585 by the Archduke Karl, at Karst near Trieste. It was here that the old Karst horse, used by mediaeval knights, had been bred. The Spanish Jennet (descendant of Spanish-born Barb horse) the heavier Villanos from Castile, and the Italian Neapolitan with its high action, all helped to create the splendid Lippizaner.

The chestnut Haflinger with its flaxen mane and tail is of old lineage and originated in the Tirol for mountain and pack transport. It still brings hay down the mountainside on its back. This is one of the breeds which is on the increase today, and Haflingers are bred in other countries as well.

49

These Yugoslavian Lippizaners are competing in a team dressage event.

The Dutch Gelderland horse is used both in harness and under saddle.

BELGIUM AND HOLLAND

The equestrian Low Countries can be divided into several areas. The heavy Ardennes horse, bred in the Ardennes, has been known from Caesar's time, while Brabant is the home of the heavy Brabant horse which helped to sire several heavy breeds. Friesland is where the magnificent Dutch black Friesian horse is bred; and Gelderland is the home of the lighter saddle and harness Gelderland horse, which may be seen in many horse shows in Holland. In age and type peculiar to locality the Friesian runs the Ardennes a close second and since the Middle Ages has been the best known.

Both Holland and Belgium breed blood trotting horses for racing. Modern European trotters have evolved from three distinct breeds: the American Standardbred; the Russian Orlov; and the French Anglo-Norman. These three breeds have evolved on different lines but the Standardbred would seem to be the superior in speed. From the Standardbred crossed with the Orlov, a new, and it is said faster, horse called the Métis has evolved, while from the Standardbred crossed with the Norman, the Noram breed has been created. Trotting as a sport is immensely popular in most of the countries of Europe.

SPAIN AND PORTUGAL

The great contribution of the Iberian Peninsula to the world's horses has been the famous Andalusian of Spain. For many centuries this horse was the most sought-after mount in Europe; and at one time exportation of breeding stock from Spain was even forbidden, on pain of death and confiscation of property.

During the great years of Spain's 'golden age' the horse from the far south of the peninsula made history in both Europe and the Americas. In Austria in the sixteenth century the Andalusian laid the foundation of the Lippizaner of the Spanish Riding School of Vienna; the breed played a sterner role at this time across the Atlantic by providing the mounts of the *Conquistadores*, those few valiant mounted men who explored and annexed so much of North, Central and South America for the Spanish Crown. Hernan Cortes, who led a handful of riders to overthrow the Aztecs and capture Mexico for Spain, proudly proclaimed, 'After God, we owed our victory to the horses!' Andalusian blood lives on in the Americas in the Quarter Horse, the Appaloosa, the Saddle Horse, the Palomino, the Pinto and the Mustang in the United States and Mexico, the Peruvian Paso in Peru, the Criollo in the Argentine, the Colom-

A colourful parade, Western style

bian Paso in Colombia, and the Paso Fino in Puerto Rico.

The classic Andalusian continues to thrive in Spain—in fact its popularity is greatly on the increase. In latter years, good quality Andalusians have been exported to many countries, including Australia. In Spain itself there is also a growing demand for these fine horses from the newly-affluent in the country's developing economy.

The Andalusian is a most impressive sight, with his sculptural beauty, proud bearing and natural high action. The horse is strongly built and yet extremely elegant; naturally high-stepping and yet with catlike agility; while he presents a picture of spirited animation under saddle or led in hand, he is at all times perfectly amenable to the will of the person controlling him, and has a friendly, docile temperament. The Andalusian's beauty lies in the balanced symmetry of his noble proportions, and he was for centuries used as a model by sculptors of Europe. The head is majestic, with large, kind, well-set eyes, a broad forehead and well-placed ears. The neck is reasonably long, broad yet elegant, and well-crested in stallions. Well-defined withers precede a short back from which stems the Andalusian's notable agility; the quarters are broad and strong. The croup is gently rounded, being neither horizontal as in the Arabian nor steeply sloped like that of many

The Spanish Andalusian.

Andalusian stallions, harnessed in Jerezano style, being driven in *media potencia* to a four-wheeled Spanish brake.

Working farm horses can still be found today

Quarter Horses. The tail setting is rather low, and both tail and mane are luxuriant and silky and worn long. The horse's shoulder is long and sloping, the chest splendidly broad and the body well ribbed-out. The legs are of medium length, clean-cut and elegant, yet more than strong enough to support the robustness of the body. Andalusians average around 15·2 hands, weigh something over 1,000 lb., and are white, grey or bay in colour. Blacks and roans also exist.

The Andalusian's temperament is exceptional; his calm, good temper and ease of handling is to be found even in serving stallions of the breed. But though the Andalusian is so docile he is no slug, and he moves with a tremendous amount of elegant animation.

Andalusians are also crossed with Arabians and Thoroughbreds to produce excellent general riding horses; a successful blending of all three breeds, known as the Hispano-Anglo-Arab, is particularly highly prized.

Closely related to Spain's Andalusian is the Lusitano of neighbouring Portugal. However, while some strains of the breed are of very high quality, the Lusitano tends to be longer-backed and longer-legged than the Andalusian, and is consequently less agile. Their heads are often rather unattractive, too long, with Roman noses and too-large ears. It would appear that the Lusitano is in fact descended from a cross of the Spanish Andalusian on heavy, rather coarse mares.

Another horse containing a fair dash of Andalusian blood is Portugal's Altér, a tall, impressive bay horse with high action, powerful quarters and broad chest which is used for high-school displays. There are not a lot of these horses, and a really good individual is greatly prized.

Both Spain and Portugal have a number of Arabian studs, with some very good stallions and mares being owned by the government stud farms. Spain's Arabian population is much bigger than that of Portugal, with most of the

A Portuguese
Lusitano performing
the *haute école*
Spanish Walk.

The troika, a traditional driving style favoured by the Russians.

animals concentrated in the southernmost region of Andalusia. The environment there is said to be exactly the same as that of the best Arabian-breeding areas in the Middle East, and certainly Spain produces some magnificent-looking Arabians—lean-bodied and stylised, with excellent steel-tendoned limbs and hard feet, and with exquisite heads showing the much sought-after quality of 'dryness'. The parent stock of Spain's Arabian population was drawn from a number of sources, principally the desert, Poland and Hungary.

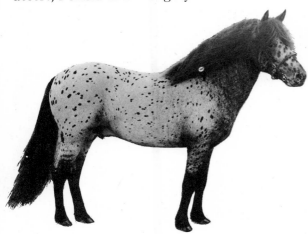

The Knabstrups bred on this stud in Denmark are exported to circuses all over the world.

THE USSR

Since the USSR consists of fifteen republics covering an area of over 8½ million sq. miles (17·1 million sq. km.) of desert, steppe, mountain, forest and tundra, it is scarcely surprising that a great number of breeds is to be found within the USSR.

These breeds include, just as naturally, desert, steppe, mountain and heavy breeds of horses. In the far north-east, between the rivers Kolyma and Omolon, there are also said to be wild horses with pony characteristics.

Most of the pony and steppe breeds are descended from the Tarpan, *equus przewalski gmelini Antonius*, and are therefore counted among the native primitive stock of the district in which they are found. The Panje pony, which is also found in Poland, belongs to west Russia as does the Lithuanian Imud, which is both large and small in type, and the Zeimatuka, with its pronounced dorsal stripe, which has been crossed with other breeds. There is, too, the strong Klepper which is not so much a breed as a type, obtained by crossing Arab and Ardennes, and which in turn has been used to improve the Obwa draught breed.

Going further east, there is the 14 hands Kirghiz pony, which has been used to form the slightly larger New Kirghiz by crossing with Don and Thoroughbred stallions. The Bashkirs of the Ural Mountain district have a strong all-purpose draught and saddle pony known as the Bashkir. In the north of the Urals around Archangel there is the 14 hands Viatka, which is often palomino or chestnut in colour with the dorsal stripe. The same strain is found in the Obwinski and in the Kasanski breeds.

In the Baltic states there are also some heavy-weight harness draught breeds of horses. These are the Toric, the Lithuanian and the Latvian. Very widely spread throughout the Ukraine, Udmut, Kirovograd, Archangel and Vologda provinces is the small but powerful Russian Heavy Draught horse whose average height is only 14·2½ hands, and the Vladimir Heavy Draught horse, bred up from Ardennes, Percherons, Suffolk Punches and Cleveland Bays.

Two breeds of mountain horses, separated by more than 1,500 miles but with a distinct similarity of conformation, are the Kabardin from the northern Caucasus and the Lokai from Tadzhik in central Asia.

The Moshua collective farm at Ashkabad breeds the Turkmene desert horse. Desert horses were bred at Ashkabad in 1000 BC and were even then mentioned as racehorses. The Turkmene is therefore one of the oldest *breeds* of horses known. King Darius of Persia, born in 522 BC, had a cavalry bodyguard of 30,000 Bactrian horsemen, mounted without doubt on the same type of Turkmene horse which is being bred today. The Turkmene, which has influenced almost every light horse breed throughout the world, is herded in *tabuns* on the steppe in the care of mounted herdsmen.

The Akhal-Teké is a direct descendant of the Turkmene (the Jomud is another) and is bred in Turkmene, Kazakh, Usbek and Kirghiz. This is a genuine desert horse of almost unbelievable stamina. One test of endurance covered 2,580 miles, of which 600 miles were over a trackless sandy desert without water. The distance was covered in eighty-four days. The Akhal-Teké is described as occasionally spotted or striped and of a golden dun colour. Like the Turkmene, these horses often have a metallic glint to their coats.

The Don breed of horse originated during the eighteenth and nineteenth centuries in the steppes and plains bordering the river Don. It was originally a small, tough, active oriental type of horse which was known as the Old Don breed. These horses were crossed with Orlov trotters and Orlov-Rostopschin, a saddle breed which originated in the Orlov and Thoroughbred. Don horses are very hard and are used for agriculture and riding. Their endurance test consisted of covering a distance of 160 miles in twenty-four hours.

The Bujonny, named after Marshall Bujonny, who improved the breed, was bred in the Rostow district from a cross with the Don and Thoroughbred. It rapidly became a fixed breed and stallions were subsequently used to improve the native horses of other republics. The Bujonny has real jumping ability and makes an excellent saddle, harness and draught horse. The champion stallion Sanos covered a distance of 185 miles in twenty-three hours excluding rest pauses.

An Akhal-Teké mare of the Komsomol Stud in the Turkmenian SSR.

Gerwazy, owned by the author of this chapter, is one of the most outstanding Polish Arabs.

Of all the Russian breeds perhaps the Orlov trotter is the best known. As so often happens, it was the genius of one breeder that was responsible. In this instance it was Count Orlov-Tschmenski who founded the stud in 1775.

POLAND

The very important place held by Poland among the horse-breeding nations of the world results first of all from sheer numbers. In spite of a considerable decline in recent years, there are still nearly three million horses in Poland, which places her second in Europe only to the Soviet Union.

The largest regions are that of the 'Wielkopolski', a warm blooded half-bred hunter type with Trakhener blood, and that of the 'Malopolski' in the south, comprising rather lighter and smaller horses of traditional east European bloodlines of Arab half-bred and Anglo-Arab origins.

The modern Wielkopolski horse has emerged as a breed embracing several older breeds once prevalent in central and western Poland. These include the Poznan and the Masuren. The Wielkopolski is a big and handsome horse equally well suited to riding or driving work. The Malopolski is believed to be nearest in type to the original Polish horse. It displays several typical characteristics of Arabian bloodlines in its soundness, stamina, elegant movement and stamp of quality. Other regions in Poland specialise in heavy horses, such as the Slaski in the south-west, and ponies, for example the Hucul.

The Ministry runs its own government studs, each specialising in one or two breeds. At present there are over thirty of them, including seven for Thoroughbreds and two for Arabians. The purpose of these studs, equipped with a nucleus of élite breeding stock and excellent conditions, is firstly to breed stallions for the Ministry's stallion stations. They also produce the cream of Polish horses for performance and for export.

The Arab horse in Poland has a history of over 300 years, and is recognised as the great improver of other breeds. The pure-bred Arabs suffered severely in both world wars and the present stock owes its existence largely to the restoration to Poland of those horses which found their way into British hands in Germany. Numbers have been built up only very gradually, owing to a strict policy of quality control and culling. Particular attention is paid to the preservation of true desert type and to fertility and temperament. Racing is used as a test of soundness. The first post-war export of Arabs to a Western country was made to Britain in 1958, and Polish Arabs are now valued highly

SWEDEN, NORWAY AND DENMARK

The present-day Swedish warm-blood horse is descended from native mares whose ancestors had been brought to Sweden during earlier centuries, and perhaps also from an older native strain. To improve these horses as a breed, Hanoverian and East Prussian stallions were introduced with great success in 1916. The Swedish warm-blood breed had been founded, and so successfully that for the past thirty years only home-bred horses have been used in the Olympic Games, most of them of the East Prussian bloodline. The state stud is at Flynge; a number of top-class horses have been exported from there under the direction of the well-known breeder, Dr Aaby-Erikson.

There are no small native ponies in Sweden itself. The native North Swedish horse is descended from an old Scandinavian strain and resembles a light draught or cold-blood horse. The breed was almost lost towards the end of the nineteenth century, but around 1890, with the help of the Norwegian Döle and Belgian stallions, the breed was revived. The best types are found in Jämtland, Dalecarlia and Värmland, and along the Verboten coast. The colour is often dun with black points, dark brown and black, and although in conformation these horses may resemble draught horses, their lively temperament and energy are characteristics of a warm-blood breed. They are exceptional trotters and are raced, have strong hard legs and joints and considerable stamina, and are well-muscled and hard. Apart from trotting races, the North Swedish horse is used in forestry work and agriculture.

The island of Gotland, which belongs to Sweden, lies in the Baltic Sea. The native Gotland or 'Skogsruss' horse stands at about 12 hands and is the living representative of a very early primitive strain which lived wild in the forests. It is a typical descendant of the Tarpan, *equus przewalski gmelini Antonius*. The colours are brown, black, chestnut, dun, palomino and grey. These ponies are renowned for their stamina and speed and for a primitive contrariness.

Very similar in conformation and characteristics is the Norwegian Northlands pony, but of all the Scandinavian pony breeds the sturdy dun Norwegian Fjord or 'Westland' is best known. This breed is native to Rofaland, Hordaland, Sogn og Fjordane and More og Romsdal. The Fjord has been exported to the Canadian Rockies and many European countries, where it is used in harness, as a draught pony and sometimes as a riding pony.

The Fjord is thought to belong to an ancient primitive breed which was native to Norway before the period of the Vikings and was used by them, since they were able if rough horsemen. In colour they are always mouse dun or yellow dun, with black points, a pronounced dorsal stripe and silver and black mane and tail. The mane is often cut to an upright position. The Fjord is very hardy, long-lived, economical to keep, robust in disposition and fertile. It stands at 13·1 to 14·1 hands. They are genuine ponies capable of great effort and hard work.

The Döle–Gudbrandsdal is a popular heavy draught horse and forms about two-thirds of the total equine population, which has decreased from 237,974 in 1946 to 142,247 in 1956 as a result of motorisation. This horse has hard legs and is very active. Its action has been created by crossing the native strain with Danish (possibly Fredericksborg) and Thoroughbred stallions. The black or brown Döle horse is used in city transport, in agriculture and forestry. Stallions of this breed, and all other Continental breeds of horses, have to undergo a severe test of endurance, stamina, health and willingness.

The Scandinavian countries are counted among the foremost countries to breed racing trotters based on American blood. The

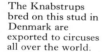

The Knabstrups bred on this stud in Denmark are exported to circuses all over the world.

A display of skill
given by the Royal
Danish Hussars.

Standardbred crossed with Anglo-Norman and Norman is well known for its speed and stamina. In 1953 the famous Swedish-bred mare, Frances Bulward, created in Norway a European record.

The oldest breed of horse in Denmark is the Fredericksborg, founded in the sixteenth century. They were then regarded as the best parade and school horses in Europe, and were in great demand at all the courts of Europe. The Fredericksborg had basically Spanish Andalusian and Italian Neapolitan blood, though crosses of both Arabs and Thoroughbreds were introduced. The royal stud was disbanded about a hundred years ago and the Fredericksborg became a native breed of Seeland. The horse is now used for light harness work and as a draught horse, as well as for driving and riding.

The spotted Knabstrup is a lighter type of the Fredericksborg strain, and these horses are very popular for circus work.

6 Australia

The Australian horse world is a vigorous and expanding one. Many of the world's breeds are represented and the country boasts several indigenous types as well.

Most famous of the Australian horses, an animal with a far-reaching and well-deserved reputation for toughness and endurance, is the Waler, which reached the peak of its worldwide fame during the last century and the earlier part of the present century. Its heir is the Australian Stockhorse.

The origins of the Waler are rather obscure, but the type that is called by this name, and its principal attributes, are easy to identify. The Waler is a hardy horse standing 15 to 15·2 hands, close-coupled, with an excellent sloping shoulder, a good length of rein, a sensible head, and very good limbs and feet. Carrying much blood from smaller Thoroughbreds, he has a deep chest and plenty of heart-room, and he is a speedy long-strider who grew up the hard way, ranging the huge spaces of the outback.

The Waler of today, recently designated the Australian Stockhorse, is very popular for working cattle on the huge stations of the outback, and has also shown up very well in endurance riding competitions, where his stamina, toughness and persistent will to win have all stood him in good stead. An official Register has been formed for the purpose of transforming a definite type of horse into a distinct breed.

The stocky, fast-starting, agile and very even-tempered Quarter Horse of the United States has been imported into Australia during the last few decades, and has become increasingly popular for certain types of cattle work. However, many ringers (Australian cowboys) feel that when it comes to racing for miles after fast wild cattle in heavily-timbered bush, there is nothing to equal the long, steady, ground-consuming stride and stamina of the Waler-type Australian Stockhorse.

Another horse of the Australian bush is the Brumby, a wild horse living in free-ranging bands. Descendants of domesticated horses which strayed, or former saddle stock gone wild, they too are tough, and very wily: they are as sharply-alert to danger as deer, and it is very difficult indeed to sneak up on them, let alone to catch them. However, there have always been hard-riding 'Brumby runners' who have made a living from capturing the wild horses by driving them into skilfully-concealed temporary stockyards, and then selling the best of them for saddle horses.

The American Quarter Horse, already mentioned, has arrived in Australia to stay, and there have also been a number of importations of the spotted, stockhorse-type Appaloosa from the United States. The high-stepping, peacock-necked American Saddlebred is another United States import, used mainly for breeding purposes.

The breeding of Thoroughbreds is an increasingly important activity in Australia, where racing is a major passion. There are now a number of high quality Thoroughbreds being bred in Australia, and several Australian sires have done well at stud in the United

The Australian Waler, first bred by the early settlers.

60

A herd of brumbies.

States during the last few decades. Virtually all the Thoroughbreds in Australia are descended from parent stock imported from the British Isles.

Topping a new peak of popularity in Australia today is the Arabian. This breed is used mainly by the 'hobby rider', in many activities ranging from testing endurance contests to colourful costume classes in the show ring. Much of the parent stock of these Arabians came from Britain, which still supplies most of the imports of the breed, though increasing interest has recently been shown in American Arabians, generally of Egyptian bloodlines.

There are other popular imports from Britain. Hackney horses and ponies have been brought in for many years, and there are also general-purpose driving animals used in show ring classes. Heavy horses are not much in demand, for Australia's agriculture is highly mechanised, but a few enthusiasts do breed the big animals, mainly to show them; the attractive and active Clydesdale is particularly popular.

British native ponies have long been established in Australia, with the Welsh pony most in demand. Shetlands are popular, too, and recently a great deal of interest has developed in the Connemara, a number of people suggesting that its qualities would be useful additions to the Stockhorse.

Australian ponies are attractive and handy animals themselves, with their own stud book. They too are descended from various British native pony breeds, and probably also have a strong dash of Timor pony, from the Island of Timor in the Indian Ocean.

New Zealand has many of the breeds and types of horse found in Australia, and in fact much of New Zealand's original stock not surprisingly came from here. New Zealanders specialise in trotters and pacers, breeding them to a very high standard. The Thoroughbred is at home in the two islands as well, and a number of authorities think that New Zealand's excellent green pastures and temperate climate provide an almost ideal environment, superior to that of Australia for the breeding and raising of Thoroughbreds.

New Zealand horsemen are very interested in hunting, and as a result breed very good hunters. There is also a typical type of hardy cow pony to be found there. The product of a blending of various bloods, he stands about 14 to 14·2 hands, and is tough and agile, with exceptional stamina. New Zealand, too, with its great open spaces and timbered backblocks, has its wild horses. Large bands run free in the Lake Taupo district, and thrive there.

Part 2
Care and management

1 Aspects of management

The first thing to decide when buying a horse is how, and where, you intend to keep it. The most natural environment for a horse, obviously, is to be outside at grass, browsing. However, this does presuppose the availability of a large area of good-quality land; it is not enough to put a horse out in half an acre of poor, over-grazed land and expect it to do well. While horses do adapt themselves quite equably to the more closeted life of the stable, certain character traits need to be borne in mind in this connection, such as the need to avoid boredom and loneliness on the part of the horse.

Perhaps the best solution to the question of which method to use for keeping a horse is the combined system, where the horse is partly stabled and partly put out to grass. This method is particularly useful for horse owners who do not have enough time to give their horses a great deal of exercise every day, and who also wish to save time by eliminating some of the work involved in keeping a horse stabled for the whole twenty-four hours. Perhaps more important than this, though, is the fact that the horse which is allowed out for a few hours a day is closer to its natural way of life. It will be less likely to develop bad habits, to become bored, bad-tempered and over-full of itself than the horse which is cooped up all day except for its exercise period.

Horses and ponies kept at grass need more care and attention than is sometimes appreciated. They need, first of all, enough grass for grazing and of the kinds which they find most palatable. About two to three acres of land per horse should be allowed for, and this should be rested at intervals.

The pasture should be given its own share of attention. The land must drain adequately; on sandy, chalky or gravelly soils this will happen naturally, but where the soil is of clay drainage must be assisted by the provision of ditches or even of piped drainage. It is also a good idea to have the soil analysed, especially if the pasture is old, so that deficiencies can be made up. Lime, phosphates and potash are all needed and can be added to the soil if necessary. The pasture should contain a variety of leafy grasses, including a good proportion of clovers, and be as free of weeds as possible. If the quality of the pasture is really poor, it is advisable to re-seed it.

The land will benefit by being fertilised, too. Liming need take place only once every few years, and the same applies to the application of phosphate fertilisers. Pasture from which a crop of hay is to be taken should be treated with stable manure in the autumn; a nitrogen treatment given in February promotes good growth of grass in the spring.

The maintenance of good pasture is also helped by harrowing and rolling. The former helps to aerate the soil and to spread droppings which, if left in heaps, sour the ground. Rolling will firm the topsoil, which becomes loosened by frosts and heavy rain, and thus helps to provide the right conditions for good plant growth. Because horses are selective feeders, it is a good idea to have the pasture grazed by cattle from time to time, as the latter will eat the longer grasses—horses prefer shorter growths—and the grass level will be kept even.

Apart from the quality of the grazing land itself, there are other important considerations for horses kept at grass. They must have a proper water supply, which is best provided by piping it to a trough in the field. The trough should be cleaned regularly so that the water remains fresh. Water for horses should never be allowed to stagnate.

There should always be adequate shelter for horses at grass. Ideally, this should be provided by trees and thick hedges, giving protection from prevailing winds and heavy rain in winter and from sun and flies in the summer. Failing this, a shelter must be erected, sited so that it will give maximum protection.

Before a horse is turned out to grass the field should be carefully inspected to see that it is safe. The fencing should be strong and solid. Hedging is ideal, but where fencing has to be put up posts and rails—the best, though most expensive, method—or heavy gauge wire strung tightly between posts should be used. Chicken mesh wire and barbed wire should not be used. Any potentially dangerous objects, such as stakes, large stones, old rusty nails, discarded tins, and so on, should be removed, as should all poisonous plants and shrubs.

A horse out at grass cannot be left entirely on its own. It should be visited several times a day even when no extra feeds are being given, the water supply checked and the horse itself inspected. A horse ignored for several months will be very much less friendly and co-operative than one which continues to be handled.

With the exception of a horse not being given any work, and out at grass in the late spring and early summer when the grass is at its best—being both abundant and nutritious—almost all horses will need some extra feeding. This is particularly true of those animals, generally ponies, which are kept at grass but which are expected to do a fair amount of work at the same time. Ponies, in particular, tend to become over-fat if left out all day to feed, and it is generally a good idea to bring them in for a few hours each day in order to avoid this. They can be fed a small quantity of hard food during this time. Ponies with a lot of native blood in them will require rather less care and attention than the Thoroughbred blood horse, which needs more preparation and conditioning if it is to perform satisfactorily.

The mental state of a horse is important to its well-being, and this should particularly be borne in mind when stabling is being considered. Loose boxes are preferable to stalls as a form of stabling, for a horse that is tied up all day with only a wall to look at will inevitably become bored. It is not always necessary to have stables built from scratch; existing buildings can often be satisfactorily converted as long as some of the basic requirements can be fulfilled.

Loose boxes should be generous in size, light and airy. As horses are happier in company, boxes should if possible be grouped together so

Saddlery and other equipment should be well cared for.

that horses can see each other, and also be situated so that the occupants can survey their surroundings and watch the various activities of the household—equine or human—going on during the day.

There are three essential elements of proper stabling: drainage, insulation and ventilation.

If existing buildings are converted into stables the draining factor can present a problem, and it is sometimes a good idea to have the stable area re-floored. At one time stable floors were drained by having a channel running through them. This is now not common practice; it is better to have the floor very slightly sloped towards the door, and to have a drainage channel running outside the door of each stable. Many stables have no constructed drainage system at all, and this does not matter as long as the horse's bedding is scrupulously removed and replaced. Specially constructed floors—with or without drainage channels—are usually made of concrete, but in many parts of the world floors of hard-packed earth are to be found. Less satisfactory from the drainage point of view, they nevertheless provide better warmth and insulation and are less likely to cause injury.

Insulation is important to the well-being of a stabled horse. Stabling should be so constructed that it keeps out the cold in winter and the heat in summer, and draughts should be avoided. Wooden stables should be lined in some way to achieve this, and the roofing should be completely waterproof and draught free.

At the same time, plenty of ventilation is necessary. If the top half of the stable door is left open, adequate ventilation will automatically be provided, in addition to allowing the horse to look out and take an interest in what is going on. If the box has a window, it should be placed in the same wall as the door in order to avoid cross-draughts, and should open upwards and inwards so the current of air goes over, rather than on to the horse.

Safety is an important part of stable management. The box should not contain any projections—such as old nails—on which the horse

can injure itself. Windows should be covered by a metal grille, and electric light switches fixed to the outside of the stable wall. The light itself should be situated well out of the horse's reach. The horse should have plenty of bedding, not only for warmth and comfort but also for protection. Certain fittings are necessary, but these too should be constructed with the safety element in mind. Mangers, for example, should be built into the corner of the box and set at breast height. Mangers need to be cleaned regularly, and for this reason it is just as satisfactory to use heavy feed tins which can be removed after the horse has eaten.

Water must be freely available to the horse at all times, and the simplest way to provide it is by using buckets. It is possible to equip stables with self-filling water bowls, though this is really only economically practicable in a large stable.

Many old stables have hayracks, generally fitted high up on the wall. These should not be used, as horses feeding from them get seeds and dust in their eyes. Hay should rather be fed from nets, which should be tied to a ring in the

Horses travelling by box need to be properly protected from injury: careful rigging up and bandaging is important.

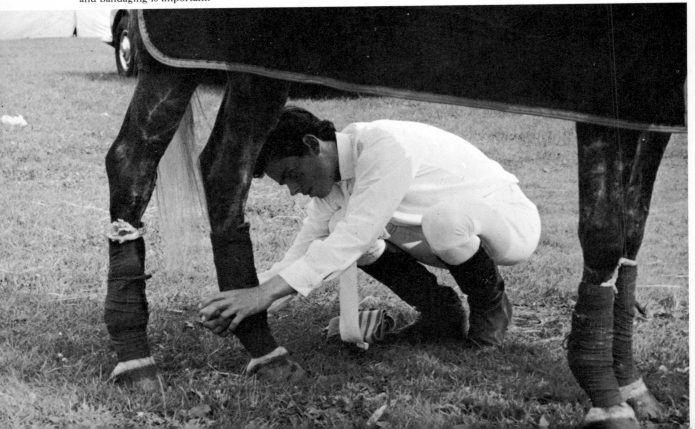

wall at a height that prevents a pawing horse from getting its foot caught in the net. It is also much easier to calculate how much hay is being given to a horse if it is fed by this method.

Mangers, buckets and the stable itself should all be cleaned out so that they remain fresh. The treatment of bedding depends to a certain extent on what kind of bedding is used. Wheat straw is the most satisfactory form of bedding, though oat straw (which some horses tend to eat) and barley straw are also available. Bracken, sawdust, shavings and peat moss are also used. Opinion varies, but it is usual to clean out straw beds daily, and to pick up droppings and wet straw at intervals during the day. When the bed is remade, straw should be well banked up round the sides of the box for warmth, comfort and protection, and the floor covered in a generous layer. The deep-litter method, where straw is put down to cover earlier layers and the stable cleaned out only when the bed becomes inconveniently high, provides extra warmth and is a great labour-savour, but it does have other disadvantages.

Good stable management relies to some extent on the right tools and equipment. An adequate number of buckets, feed tins, haynets, etc., are an obvious necessity, as are proper stable tools. A barrow, two-pronged pitchfork, four-tine fork, stable shovel, broom and skep are all essential. A piece of sacking in which to carry straw to the stable is also useful and prevents wastage.

The storage of food is also important. Hard foods should be kept in damp-free, mouse-proof containers; hay should if possible be kept indoors (the stable loft is ideal), but if this is not possible it should be stored off the ground and covered. The cover should, however, be removed as often as possible to allow air to reach the hay.

As well as the grooming kit, there are other items of equipment that contribute to the comfort of the horse. A stabled horse should be clothed in a light linen sheet before it is clipped. Once clipped, it is necessary to provide heavier rugs. The essential clothing consists of a top rug, made of jute or canvas and fully lined with wool, and a large woollen blanket. An open-mesh sheet is also extremely useful, providing extra warmth by insulation in cold weather and

It is a good idea to teach a horse how to box quietly and without fuss.

keeping the body cool when the weather is hot. It also helps to prevent horses from breaking out into a sweat when travelling, after exercise or through nervousness. When one of these rugs is used in conjunction with the top rug, sufficient warmth will be provided in all but really cold weather, when the blanket can be added. A day rug, made of wool and bound in a contrasting colour, is not strictly necessary but is rather an attractive addition to the horse's wardrobe. A horse kept on the combined system, particularly if it has been partially clipped, will need a really well-fitting, top-quality New Zealand rug for use when it is turned out.

Rugs are kept in place by rollers or surcingles. Rollers can be made of leather or of webbing, and care must be taken to see that they are properly stuffed on either side of the spine or a sore back will result. Rollers should not be fastened too tightly. Surcingles are made of web and are sewn to the canvas of the top rug. Here again, the padding is important to ensure that no pressure is applied to the backbone. Rugs and rollers or surcingles should be fitted with as much care as other items of saddlery.

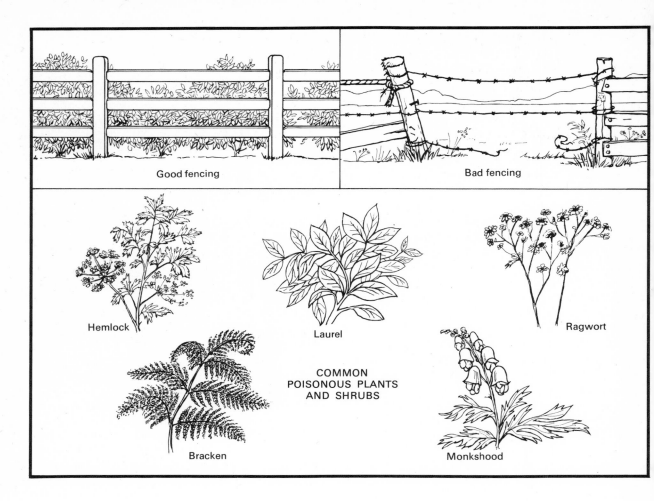

Good fencing

Bad fencing

Hemlock

Laurel

Ragwort

Bracken

**COMMON
POISONOUS PLANTS
AND SHRUBS**

Monkshood

Stable and exercise bandages should also be available. The former, which are intended to give extra warmth, cover the leg from just below the knee to below the fetlock joint; the latter give support and protection from knocks, etc., during work, and leave the fetlock joint free. Gamgee tissue should be wrapped round the leg before the exercise bandage is put on.

Boots, pads and other protective items which prevent the horse from damaging itself or being damaged, should be bought as they are needed. For horses with a tendency to over-reach, to brush or to knock themselves, these can be invaluable, but they should not be used indiscriminately.

2 Foods and feeding

No horse, or for that matter pony or donkey, can remain healthy and give of its best unless fed correctly. Every horse must be treated as an individual as far as its feeding is concerned, and it is essential to study each horse's temperament, its likes and dislikes, and its ability to digest certain types of food; for what will suit one horse could well disagree with another.

When feeding horses it is essential to choose only the best quality food. Poor quality food, besides having little feeding value, can be extremely harmful if it is mouldy or musty, as food in this condition will cause serious upsets to the digestive system. Dusty food can also prove harmful to the wind and lungs and cause respiratory troubles.

The nutrients required to keep a horse in good health are not unlike those required by humans: water; carbohydrates; fats; proteins; vitamins and minerals – all of which will, according to how they are fed, determine the horse's performance, health and appearance.

Clean, fresh water must always be available to a horse at all times, and in a clean container – either a bucket or a trough. Horses are fastidious creatures, and they will not drink stale or dirty water; before long they will start to lose condition if no fresh supply is provided. If water is not constantly available, the horse must be offered a fresh drink at least three to four times a day and before every feed. Never give water to a horse after feeding or when it comes in very hot from work – colic can follow if one does. If a horse has a fresh bucket in its box, then it may take a short drink during or after a feed. This is all right; it is only if a horse consumes a whole bucketful after having been fed that there may be trouble.

Stable buckets should be washed out every day, and refilled four to five times during the day – the last time being on one's final evening visit to the stables. Field troughs need to be scrubbed out about once a week if they are large – both automatically-filled ones and those filled by a hose; small troughs and buckets need daily cleaning, and must also be refilled frequently.

Owing to the formation of the horse's stomach it prefers to eat small amounts of food at frequent intervals. The horse at grass, living on its natural food, will eat most of the time. The stabled horse should be allowed to follow this pattern of nature as closely as possible. It is far better to feed three or four times a day than only once or twice. It is also necessary to provide some form of bulk feed to assist the horse's digestion.

In summer, when the grass is at its best, a horse can live on grass alone if it is of good quality, sweet and fresh. Grass by itself will not, however, provide the necessary proteins and oils for horses carrying out strenuous work, or for those feeding young or for growing youngsters except where the grass is exceptionally good. In an ideal year May, June and July will see enough good grass to support a horse, but come August the goodness starts to go and for many extra feeding in the form of either concentrates or hay will be necessary.

A horse fed on grass alone will be in soft condition, and to become fit and hard will require – as well as adequate excercise – either oats or some other form of concentrate in addition to its hay or grass. All horses should have some fresh grass every day during the summer, being either turned out to graze, led out on a long rein to pick the grass along the roadsides or provided with cut grass in the stable. If cut grass is fed, care should be taken to ensure that it is not allowed to heat and start fermenting, which can be dangerous. Lawn mowings are not suitable fodder, even when fresh, as they can ball up inside the horse and cause a blockage.

Grass land needs attention to keep it right, and it is essential to 'top' paddocks frequently to about four inches to ensure a sweet growth, and to collect droppings to prevent the infestation of the paddock with worms, which cause serious harm to horses grazing there. Harrowing is the alternative to picking up droppings and with large paddocks is more feasible; small paddocks must have the droppings picked up once or twice a day or the horses will never thrive, however well fed.

Hay, the means by which we provide bulk to help the horse's digestion in winter and for those stabled all the year round, is made from grass either cut from permanent pasture – meadow hay – or cut from specially seeded pasture – seed hay. The former can be upland hay, which is of good quality, or lowland, which is generally poor and unsuitable for horses. Seed hay can be a mixture of good grasses and clovers or vetches, and also sainfoin which is a member of the trefoil family. Good hay, cut when the sap is still running and well saved (dried and baled or ricked when really dry), should be sweet-smelling, crisp to touch and free from all forms of must, mould or dust. It is best fed in nets or racks, provided that these are set low so that seeds cannot fall into the horse's eyes, or from the ground, though this is wasteful. It is always advisable to shake up the hay first to make sure that no bad patches are sandwiched in the parcel of hay from the bale and to remove loose seeds and dust.

A big horse will need between 14 lb. and 16 lb. of hay a day in winter, or, within reason, as much as it can eat. Smaller horses normally require 12 lb. to 14 lb., depending on how much concentrate they are being fed as well. Chaff or 'choppy' is merely hay that has been passed through a special machine to cut it up small; when in this form it is mixed with the short feed to form bulk and make the horse chew its food properly. The protein content of hay varies from 5 per cent to as much as 15 per cent in top-quality hay. The vitamin and mineral content varies, too, but is only present to any valuable extent in hay under two years old and cut young.

During the winter months all horses and ponies running out at grass, as well as those stabled, will need to be fed. Hay will provide much of the necessary extra feeding, but youngstock, mares in foal and older horses and ponies will also require concentrates to

create the body warmth needed to keep them healthy.

We now come to the energy foods. These are needed to provide the body heat that goes either to keep a horse warm or to enable it to become fit enough to do strenuous work without detriment to its health. The principle energy foods are those containing carbohydrates, which include sugars, starches and cellulose. Oats, barley and maize contain about 60 per cent sugar and starch, while cellulose is found in the fibrous parts of the oat and barley hulls (the outer case covering the grain) as well as in bran, which is the outer part of wheat. For this reason oats, barley and maize are classed as concentrates – one needs to feed only a relatively small quantity as compared with bulk foods to provide energy.

Fats are necessary in the horse's diet to enable it to absorb certain fat-soluble vitamins, but in their natural state fats are not easily digested by the horse so a means of supplying them has to be found. Linseed, with its very high oil content, is extremely useful. Soaked overnight, then brought to the boil and simmered for a day, it is mixed with either a bran mash or into the evening feed. It is excellent both for putting on flesh and for maintaining it throughout the winter, and for sick horses, as it is easily digested in its cooked form. It also gives a good gloss to the coat, and it is valued for its high protein content.

Protein is the all-important feeding factor in producing fit, healthy horses. It is essential to build muscle, its prime use being in the formation and repairing of tissue, besides being largely responsible for sound and healthy bone, blood, skin, hair and hooves. Insufficient protein leads to weak frames and lack of bone; and hearts incapable of withstanding the rigours of training – as hearts are, after all, only lumps of muscle that act as pumps for the circulation of blood round the body. Those horses needing extra protein are the young, the very old, breeding stock and those in work.

In order to provide the required protein for our horses we can feed either cereal foods – oats, barley, maize and linseed; or the modern compound feeds – horse or cattle nuts (pencils, cubes or cake). The former is the traditional method of feeding, the cereal being mixed with bran, choppy and any extras that might be required, while the latter is the modern method, and is fed on its own. Both require hay in addition to provide bulk. Alternatively, a mixture of cereals and nuts can be fed to form the concentrate ration.

Nuts vary in their protein content and also in their oil and fibre content – the higher the protein, the lower the fibre (composed mainly of dried grass meal, which provides protein as well as fibre). Every bag carries a label giving the percentages of these elements. Horse and pony nuts normally carry 10 per cent protein and anything from 15 per cent to 17·5 per cent fibre, whereas the 14 per cent protein nuts carry only 8 per cent or 9 per cent or less of fibre. The former are excellent for children's ponies and for horses in light work; the latter are essential for those in hard work like hunting, jumping, eventing and racing. Those carrying are higher percentage still are supplementary nuts to be used as a booster. The cattle-rearing nut, carrying 16 per cent protein and a high oil content, comes into its own as a booster nut for horses in hard work. There is also a 12 per cent protein nut, which is good for ponies in hard work and for horses needing more than the standard 10 per cent nut but who are – probably because of temperament – unable to accept the 14 per cent nut.

There are also nuts made for a special purpose. Stud nuts are specially designed for breeding stock and youngsters, for they carry the right ratio of calcium and phosphate, besides other vitamins and minerals; transit nuts should be fed to horses travelling long distances or ones that are confined to the stable through injury, as they are very low in protein.

All nuts have one disadvantage: though easy to feed it is impossible to give variety to the feed. This applies in particular to the 'complete' nut, a nut containing even the hay ration. It can be useful in some cases and for a limited period of time, but it can lead to boredom and stable vices if fed for too long.

One disadvantage of nuts fed on their own lies in their nut form. Should the horse require medicine there is no base to mix it in, and it is very difficult to adjust each horse's intake of, for example, vitamins or minerals as the nuts are fully vitaminised and mineralised.

Pound for pound with oats the high protein nuts need feeding at a slightly lower rate, whereas the low protein (10 per cent) nuts need feeding at one-third more for the same value.

Oats – still the best of the cereal foods – can be fed whole, bruised, cracked or crushed, and though they are heating and are therefore inclined to make some horses hot up, they are excellent for those in hard work. Their protein content varies, which is why a high protein nut is useful to boost the ration. Work and high protein foods must match – more work, more food; and the rider, too, must be capable of coping with a fit horse. Oats should be clean, sweet-smelling and rattle in the hand.

Barley is growing in popularity and if cooked – soaked overnight and then cooked till it forms a jelly – is useful for putting on flesh and tempting shy feeders. It can also be fed crushed. Barley is fattening, though, and should be fed with care.

Maize – corn in the United States – is fed flaked and is an excellent source of protein. These cereals, together with linseed and other sources of protein and oils, form the bases of nuts. Beans, which are fed cracked, are a source of protein but should only be fed to horses in very hard work as they make those in normal work far too excitable. Molassine meal – a good source of sugar – gives feeds a pleasant smell and taste, horses usually love it and it is very good for them. Bran is rather hard to find, but is very necessary for mashes and to aid digestion; $\frac{1}{2}$ lb. in each feed is enough, but it must be damped. For a mash, 2–3 lb. should be mixed with boiling water till well moist but not running wet, and then left to cool. It is useful for sick horses and for others once a week as a laxative. Sugar-beet pulp is often used to form bulk. It is usually supplied mixed with molasses, thus also providing sugar, but it must be well soaked overnight and should always be fed fresh.

Modern farming methods mean that much of the natural vitamin and mineral content is lost before we ever buy our feeding stuffs, and supplements are needed to make up the deficiency. There are supplements with a limited vitamin and mineral content and those with a comprehensive one. The latter are best. Some are based on honey, others on cod liver

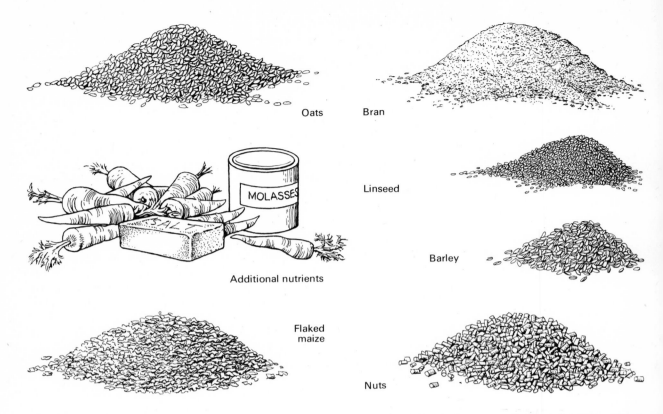

Oats

Bran

Linseed

Additional nutrients

Barley

Flaked maize

Nuts

oil or a mixture of cod liver oil and linseed. Seaweed is another source of vitamins and minerals favoured by some. Whatever we choose to feed in the way of supplements we must stick to one brand – more than one and an imbalance will result. No vitamin or mineral supplement should be necessary if a full ration of nuts is fed; extra salt, however, should be supplied to all horses, however their food ration is made up, and can be given either in the form of a lick or in the feed at the rate of an ounce a day.

Roots are another source of vitamins for the horse, and carrots – sliced lengthways – are an excellent addition to the winter diet of stabled horses or those kept out; so, too, are mangels.

Whatever one feeds, some rules for feeding must be followed: water before feeding; feed at regular intervals and little and often; feed plenty of bulk food; do not work a horse until at least an hour after a feed; feed according to the work demanded; do not make sudden changes to the diet; make sure all food is of the best quality, and wash out mangers, feed tins and buckets once a day; never guess the amount of a feed – weigh food carefully to ensure that the horse is getting its due ration, and mix the feed carefully. It is also important to see that the horse's teeth are in good order and do not require filing; bad teeth will lead to a loss of appetite. Lastly, the horse must be kept free from parasites – worms and lice – as to feed unwanted visitors is a waste of money and no horse can do well if he is acting as host to them.

3 Conditioning the horse

In order to get the best out of a horse, and for both horse and rider to enjoy the activities they perform, it is necessary for the horse to be properly conditioned. There are many different levels of fitness in a horse. For example, a racehorse needs to reach a peak of fitness different from that required by the hunter; this again is different from the level suitable for a hack which will only be used for gentle rides at slow paces. It is obvious, though, that no horse can perform effectively, efficiently and safely if it is not fit enough.

The aspect of safety is an important one. A horse that has not been properly conditioned is more likely to suffer from strains and other ailments than one which has undergone a careful training and conditioning programme; a horse with inadequately developed muscles will be less well balanced and weaker than one in which the muscles have slowly been built up by suitable exercise. As a result, where the fit horse will be able to make an extra effort when required – as, perhaps, when jumping a big or tricky fence out hunting – the unfit horse will not be able to do so, and is very much more likely to get into trouble.

The conditioning of a horse divides into three parts: exercise, feeding and grooming. These parts are closely related and must to a certain extent be considered together. A horse that has just come up from grass, and is therefore fat, with soft muscles out of tone, cannot be successfully conditioned just by a change of diet from grass to hard foods and by strenuous grooming. The conditioning process is one of gradual progression, where adjustments to diet, the amount of exercise taken and the grooming given are all an integral part of the process.

There are two other important general points to be borne in mind. The first is that the condition of rider and horse should be advanced side by side – a well-developed, fit horse will generally prove to be a considerable handful to a rider who is himself out of condition. The second point is the physical state of the horse before a conditioning programme is embarked on: a horse that is very fat will need to be given an initial period of very gentle exercise before it is able to cope with more strenuous work; equally, a horse is out of condition if it is too thin, and it must be allowed to put on flesh before being given any substantial amount of work to do. However it is fed, a thin horse will only go on getting thinner if it is asked to do a lot of work.

The exercise given to a horse being conditioned should vary in order to keep the horse interested, to build up its muscles and develop them for the different activities it is going to perform. The amount of exercise should be built up gradually over a period of many weeks. Work at slow paces in the initial stages should include lungeing, loose schooling, work in the *manège*, road work and hacking over different kinds of terrain. Walking and trotting are the two most beneficial paces; the horse should first be worked in the loose school and on the lunge so that its muscles can begin to develop before it is asked to carry the extra weight of the rider. These exercises should be continued even when ridden work has begun. Slow road work will harden the legs, and the horse should be both walked and trotted at this stage. Slow trotting uphill is excellent for the improvement of wind; both uphill and downhill work improve the balance and muscular development of the horse. Balance is also improved by riding the horse over uneven ground.

Schooling should not be entirely restricted to the school. The horse should be prepared to perform some of its schooling lessons while out on exercise, for as well as emphasising the lessons themselves it will keep the horse interested. Short periods of collection, variations of pace, even, perhaps, a few strides of half-pass on a quiet road – all are good for improving the horse's concentration and obedience.

It is difficult to generalise about a training programme for developing a fit horse, but there are certain basic rules to apply. For the first week or two the horse should be given about an hour's exercise a day, the work period being divided between lungeing and slow hacking at the walk and trot. After this initial period the time should be increased to, say, an hour and a half, during which time the horse will be lunged for about fifteen minutes, have about thirty minutes at school work on the flat and again spend the remainder of the time hacking at slow paces. By this time the muscles should be developed enough for the speed to be increased, so that short periods at the canter and some school work over cavalletti are within its capabilities. Towards the end of the second month the overall exercise time can be increased to two hours, and should include at least an hour and a half hacking, with some steady cantering and an occasional short gallop.

In order to remain fit once a reasonable level of fitness has been reached, as it should have been by nine to ten weeks of work, the horse must obviously continue to be given an adequate amount of exercise. It is not enough to expect a horse to hunt one or two days a week and on the other days just to give it a short hour's work. At the same time, a horse that is asked to perform really strenuously—hunting is again a good example—at regular intervals should be allowed a certain amount of rest as well, or its physical condition will begin to deteriorate.

Feeding and grooming should be considered with as much care as the exercise programme, and in conjunction with it. The right food will build up the horse's body and supply it with the material it needs for making muscle, as well as producing the necessary energy. It is perhaps useful to emphasise here that while fat is reduced and muscle improved during the conditioning process, fat is not turned into muscle. It is important to bear this in mind when considering a horse's diet: the excess fat will not itself be turned into muscle by training and exercise, it can only be eliminated while muscle is at the same time built up by the gradual increase in work and development of the diet.

Because horses vary in temperament and their physical ability to use food, each horse will need to be treated individually as far as diet is concerned. A horse that is a 'good doer', one whose body utilises the energy foods to maximum effect, will need less of the body-building, energy-supplying foods than one which is prone to lose condition easily. An excitable horse will need to be conditioned on a diet containing a lower proportion of oats than that suitable for a horse that is naturally lazy or calm and does not hot up.

The amount and kind of food given will again vary depending on what work is to be expected of the horse. For a reasonably well-bred, 16-hand horse with a sensible temperament, the average will range between a diet of, say, 4 lb. of oats, 2 lb. nuts, 2 lb. bran, 1 lb carrots, and 18 lb. hay, fed at intervals during the day in three feeds, for a horse that has just begun its conditioning programme, to that of a fit horse being given a considerable amount of work, which might receive about 10 lb. oats, 3 lb. nuts, 2 lb. bran, 1 lb. carrots and 11 lb. of hay a day. It will be seen from these examples that the amount of hard food (e.g. oats) is increased in proportion to a reduction in the feeding of bulk foods such as hay. Most horses also benefit from being given one bran mash a week and by their diet being altered from time to time. Horses vary in their tastes, but additional foods such as apples usually make a welcome change in diet, and it is also a good idea to allow even a really fit horse to graze for a few minutes each day.

The feeding of ponies is a rather different matter. Many of them either live out at grass all the year round, or are only partly stabled. A high-quality show pony will have different requirements from a hardy native animal used to fending for itself. Oats should be fed to ponies with circumspection, particularly if the rider is not an expert, but there are plenty of other foods available which will help to keep a pony in good working condition. Ponies should not be allowed to become over-fat on very lush grass, as apart from getting very out of condition their susceptibility to contract laminitis will be increased. During the winter a pony at grass should be fed an average of 10 lb. of hay a day, and at least 3 lb. of nuts and 1 lb. of bran should also be given. A pony being given a lot of work should have some bruised barley added to its diet as well.

Grooming, and the general care of the horse, are both important factors. Grooming will develop and tone muscles, and also cleans the body so that it can work most effectively. Grooming removes the natural grease from the horse's coat, and a stabled horse, which does not have to withstand long periods out in the rain and other natural elements, can therefore be groomed to improve its condition because it is protected by being indoors. It is, however, more likely to catch a chill. The stabled horse should not be brought home sweating but should rather be walked the last mile home in order to be given a chance to cool off, though in wet weather it should be kept warm by being brought back at a brisk trot and then thoroughly rubbed down and dried when it reaches home.

The skin is cleaned and stimulated by being groomed; this is not, however, the only benefit of it. Massage, hand rubbing and wisping also play their part in conditioning a horse. A horse or pony out at grass—and it is possible to produce a reasonably fit animal when it is not stabled—should not be over-groomed, because of the loss of the natural protection its coat gives. The stabled horse, however, should first be thoroughly groomed after morning exercise, and then be given wisping and massage later in the day.

The various items used in grooming each has a different function to perform. The dandy brush is most useful for cleaning muddy horses, though because it is stiff and hard it should be used with caution on ticklish horses and on the tender parts of the body. It should not be used to excess on horses out at grass, except for removing mud from the outer surface of the coat.

The body brush is soft-bristled and is used both on the body and on the legs and for brushing the mane and tail, the hairs of which would split were the dandy brush to be used. The bony parts of the horse should be brushed gently with the body brush only, particularly the head. Horses should always be treated considerately during grooming: do not bang them, particularly in the loin area where damage to the kidneys can result from rough treatment. Patience should be exercised with a horse that is head shy—it will almost certainly mean that the horse has been roughly handled in the past. Other standard items of grooming equipment include the water brush, mane comb, hoof pick and stable rubber. Rubber curry combs are replacing the old metal combs, and are generally much more satisfactory, and 'ready-made' hay wisps are now also available.

Most horses enjoy being groomed and quickly learn to co-operate, to move over when they are asked, to pick up their feet for them to be cleaned out and to put up with their more

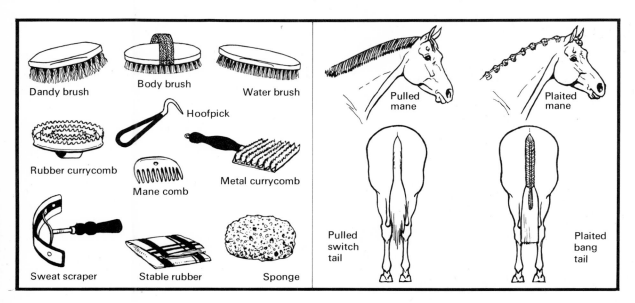

Dandy brush

Body brush

Water brush

Hoofpick

Rubber currycomb

Mane comb

Metal currycomb

Sweat scraper

Stable rubber

Sponge

Pulled mane

Plaited mane

Pulled switch tail

Plaited bang tail

ticklish parts being touched. When a horse is wisped for the first time, the wisping action should be relatively gentle, though the amount of energy applied can be increased with time.

Wisping is a very important part of conditioning. It develops and hardens muscles and improves the horse's circulation. The traditional wisp is made out of a rope of hay, though a chamois leather bag stuffed with hay is just as satisfactory. Wisps should be damped before use, and should only be used on the muscular parts of the horse's body: the quarters, shoulders and neck. They should not be used on the loins, head, belly or legs.

There are other aspects of conditioning linked to grooming. The heavy coat provided by nature to all horses in an environment where winter conditions are more severe than those in summer is a hindrance to peak conditioning. A heavy coat will make a horse taking a lot of exercise sweat to such an extent that it will begin to lose condition. It is for this reason that horses are clipped in winter, the warmth of the heavy winter coat being replaced by rugs.

There are various methods of clipping, the clip used on any particular horse depending on its type, the work it is to be expected to do and the conditions in which it is kept. A full clip involves removing the entire coat, while the hunter clip removes the coat from the body, leaving a saddle patch on the back, but not from the legs. A very fine-skinned horse will probably benefit from the extra protection given to its skin against galls or scalding and against cuts, cracked heels and chills from the legs. A horse with a very heavy coat, however, is probably better off if it is given the full clip.

The blanket clip, suitable for Thoroughbreds with fine coats, leaves the area of the body approximately covered by a sheet, as well as the legs, unclipped, while the trace clip removes hair just from the belly, the flanks and the sides and underneath of the neck. This last is useful for ponies kept at grass which are nevertheless expected to perform energetically during the winter, and for harness horses.

When clipping a horse it is advisable to have an assistant. The horse should be clean, the blades of the clipper sharp, and particular care should be taken to accustom the horse to the noise of the machine and to keep the animal calm so that it does not fidget. Neither mane nor tail should be clipped; if the legs are to be left unclipped it is usually a good idea to trim the heels using scissors and a comb.

The horse's appearance is generally much improved if its mane and tail are kept thinned, though in horses with very fine hairs, such as Arabs, they are not trimmed. Both manes and tails should be thinned a little at a time or the horse's skin will become sore and it will probably object to the next thinning session. Between sessions, the tail should be damped with a water brush and a tail bandage applied to encourage the hairs to lie flat and to give the tail a good shape. Tails can either be left as a switch or can be banged—cut off straight at the bottom, at a level about a hand's breadth below the point of the hock when the tail is carried at its natural level. A thinned mane should be about five inches in length. Once mane and tail have been thinned it is worth keeping them in good shape by thinning them just a little at regular intervals.

Manes are frequently plaited for special occasions, particularly for show events, and for displays are also sometimes braided with ribbon. The number of plaits will vary on the length of the horse's neck and the thickness of the mane, though it is customary to have an even number of plaits along the length of the neck and an extra one on the forelock. Manes can be plaited either by sewing or by using rubber bands; the former method undoubtedly looks neater, but the latter is quicker and easier. Unpulled tails are also sometimes plaited; this is a specialised skill and one best acquired by watching an expert at work.

The most important point to remember where conditioning any horse or pony is concerned is that forethought—thinking about what you are going to want your horse to do, planning to work out the best method of arriving at a suitable level of conditioning, and then applying your knowledge consistently and carefully, will repay all the extra effort.

4 Bitting and saddlery

There are an enormous number of different patterns of saddles and bridles on the market today. Firstly, some understanding of the construction of a saddle is necessary to the appreciation of the difference between a good and bad saddle, or of one well suited to any particular purpose.

The inner framework of the saddle is its tree, traditionally made of beechwood. The tree can vary in shape and size. The head and gullet are strengthened with steel, and a steel plate on the underside of the tree acts as a reinforcement. Laminated woods are now used, and experiments have also been made with other materials. So far only the use of fibreglass for very light racing saddles, a variety popular in Australia, has proved satisfactory. Modern spring tree saddles incorporate two light pieces of steel set on the underside of the tree, giving it greater resilience. Trees vary in length; the spring trees give a greater dip in the seat and need not, therefore, be so long as the rigid variety.

The stirrup bars are fitted onto the tree and are an important part of its structure. Good quality saddles always have forged rather than cast bars. The setting up of the seat is also important to the overall construction of the saddle. Pre-strained webs are stretched along

A famous firm of saddlers: the Giddens factory.

the length of the tree, a piece of canvas is stretched over them, tightly stretched serge is then stitched over this to form the seat shape and the space between it and the canvas stuffed lightly with wool. The pigskin seat, with the skirts covering the bars welted into it, is finally stretched on.

The saddle flaps and panel are also attached to the tree. The panel is an important item, for it affects both the comfort of the horse and the correct position of the rider in the saddle. There are four different basic shapes of panel: full, short, Saumur and Continental patterns. The full panel, the oldest type, prevents close contact between horse and rider, and for this reason the introduction of the short panel was an advantage. As trends in equitation emphasised a more forward seat, the Saumur and Continental panels evolved. The former, cut much further forward, is narrower in the waist for extra contact with the horse, and has an extension to support the knee; the latter is similar in some respects, but is also a much fined down version of the old full panel.

Panels are either made of felt and covered with leather, or are stuffed with wool covered by leather, serge or linen. A leather covering is much the most satisfactory, and well worth the initial extra cost.

The construction and the fitting of saddles are closely linked. Ideally, a saddle should be made specially for a particular horse, though this is not always possible. It is also best to use a saddle only on one horse, for with time it will mould itself to the shape of a horse's back. Again, though, it is not always possible to restrict one's use of a saddle in this way.

Careful fitting of a saddle is important if soreness to the horse's back is to be avoided; adjustments to a saddle which does not fit are seldom satisfactory. Trees are made in different widths, and great care should be taken to see that the tree fits the horse's back properly at

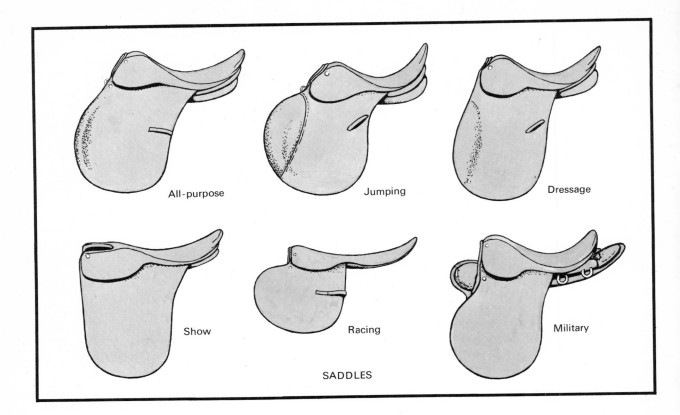

All-purpose

Jumping

Dressage

Show

Racing

Military

SADDLES

the outset. The length of the saddle, too, should be suited to the length of the horse's back.

The saddle should clear the withers, and both the length and breadth of the backbone. The saddle should be constructed so that the panel bears evenly on the back, thus ensuring an even distribution of the rider's weight. It is important to maintain the regularity of shape and the resilience of the panel.

Most horses change shape according to their condition, and with use over a long period a saddle may alter in shape too. It is essential to keep an eye on the fit of a saddle and to make sure that these criteria are always fulfilled.

The modern saddle, generally known as the spring tree saddle, has become universally popular in recent years and is now used for most riding activities. Its construction encourages the rider to sit in the correct position, allows maximum contact with the horse and is more comfortable, both for horse and rider, than many old-fashioned rigid tree varieties.

The saddle has a long, resilient tree which, because of the 'springs' incorporated in it, gives it considerable flexibility and allows the use of the seat as an aid, transmitting the seat pressure to the horse. The tree is shaped to conform with the shape of the horse's back, thus bringing the rider into close contact with it, and also giving him as narrow a grip as the shape of the horse itself permits. This advantage is maintained by other aspects of the saddle's construction which further eliminate bulk under the thigh, such as the recessed stirrup bars and narrowed panel waist. The saddle carries a strong forward roll on the panel which supports the rider's thigh. This, and the sloped back head, allow the stirrup bars to be positioned further forward than used to be possible; the resulting hang of the leathers helps the rider to hold his lower leg correctly. Another advantage of this saddle is that the girth straps hang relatively far back, so that if a girth of the right length is used the buckles are not felt.

There are two varieties of this saddle, one for general use and one modified for show-jumping. The latter is cut slightly differently to allow for a more forward seat and shorter leathers.

Besides these, however, and other saddles different in details of design but produced with the same aims in mind, there are many other kinds of saddle still to be found.

The English hunting saddle, though still widely used, is perhaps the antithesis of all that the modern saddle tries to encourage, and it is probable that its popularity will decline. In some respects it resembles, with its flat seat and straight-cut flap, the show saddle. The show saddle is designed to display to advantage the horse's conformation, in particular its shoulder. It is cut with a completely straight, i.e. vertical, flap and also has a flat seat. This design makes it difficult for the rider to sit correctly, and as both horses and ponies being shown are seen by the judges stripped of their saddles, the value of the show saddle is small.

A good dressage saddle, on the other hand, does have advantages. At first these were just adaptations of the straight-flapped show saddle, but with the increase in popularity of dressage since the war and a clearer understanding of what it tries to achieve, valuable modifications have been made. As in the jumping saddle, the tree is deep, but it is shorter and is straight rather than being sloped back. The stirrup bars are thus positioned further to the rear; this, and the relatively straight cut of the flap, demand an increased length of leather. The position of the leg permits much less grip, but does free the lower leg, placing it so that a finer degree of control and application of the aids can be obtained.

One of the advantages of the modern all-purpose saddle is that it encourages the rider to sit over the centre of the horse's balance. This is also true of the dressage saddle: the balance of a dressage horse moves increasingly to the rear with the necessity for collection and lightness in the forehand, and with a correctly designed saddle the rider is able to assist rather than to interfere with this shift in balance.

Racing saddles are made with some very different criteria in mind. The first is weight. A very light flat racing saddle may weigh only ounces; a weighted steeplechase saddle may have to total some thirty pounds, though when a lot of extra weight has to be carried it is advisable to use a weight cloth. The very light saddles do not use stirrup bars (the leathers are

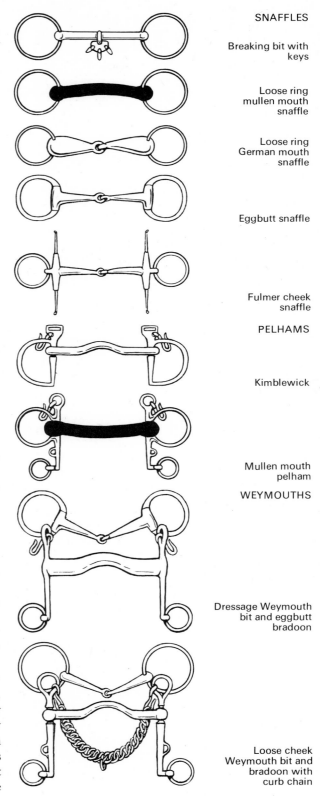

SNAFFLES

Breaking bit with keys

Loose ring mullen mouth snaffle

Loose ring German mouth snaffle

Eggbutt snaffle

Fulmer cheek snaffle

PELHAMS

Kimblewick

Mullen mouth pelham

WEYMOUTHS

Dressage Weymouth bit and eggbutt bradoon

Loose cheek Weymouth bit and bradoon with curb chain

looped through a slot round the tree) and the panels are covered in silk or nylon. The heavier saddles generally have serge-stuffed panels, and stirrup bars can of course be used. Recently, Australian styles of saddle have been copied elsewhere, using leather for the panel covering and with very lightweight trees. The trees in all racing saddles are relatively fragile, and these saddles therefore have only a short life. Weight is saved in the size, shape and substance of the flap and in the thickness of the panel, which is reduced to a minimum. Trainers use a heavier, stouter version, known as the race exercise saddle, for exercising purposes.

Various special saddles are made for use by children, beginning with a cheap pad of felt, sometimes the only solution when a compromise must be found between a very small child and a very fat pony. The smaller version of the all-purpose spring tree saddle is much the best and helps children to develop a good seat. It is possible to find saddles that incorporate some of the important advantages of the spring tree saddle, such as a good deep seat and generously forward-cut flaps, but which do not cost quite so much.

Girths are made in several different materials and to a number of different designs. Leather girths, except perhaps with horses that are very soft and out of condition, are much the most satisfactory. There are three kinds: Balding, Atherstone and three-fold girths. These should all be kept clean and supple. Girths are also available made of webbing, sometimes with elastic inserted, of elastic, lampwick, tubular webbing and nylon cord.

Breastplates are useful with horses whose conformation makes saddles slip to the rear. They are widely used in the racing world, and are also valuable in very hilly hunting country.

Stirrup leathers should always be of good quality, and as most people ride slightly unevenly, with more weight on one side than the other, the leathers should be alternated. Stirrup irons should be made from stainless steel or a good metal mixture such as Eglantine. They should always be too big for the foot rather than too small. There are various different designs available, such as the plain iron, Kournakoff, bent top, peacock safety iron, and so on.

It is worth considering in some detail the objects of the bit. It is an extension of the hand, and acts as a regulator for the energy or impulsion created in the quarters of the horse by the rider's seat, back and legs. It is not, or should not be, a means by which a head carriage is imposed on the horse. The origin of the head carriage (and, indeed, of direction) is in the quarters.

As the hind legs become further engaged under the horse's body, so the head is held higher. The bit is only a means of indicating the required position of the head. Should the bit be used to force a particular head position before the horse is physically able to assume it he will react by evading or resisting its action.

The lower jaw, and particularly the bars of the mouth, are the areas most closely associated with the action of the bit, though it also affects other parts of the head. In addition to the bars, the corners of the lips, the tongue, the curb groove, the poll, the nose and the roof of the mouth are all subject to pressure according to the type of bit used.

In the selection of a bit examination of the mouth is essential. The shape of the bars and jawbones, the height of the palate, the size of the tongue and the depth of the declivity in which it lies are all factors that should influence the choice of bit. The bars may be more or less thick and heavily covered; on the other hand, they may be sharp, vee-shaped and lightly covered. The first disposes the mouth towards being less sensitive, the latter towards greater sensitivity. It should be remembered, however, that there is no such thing as a hard-mouthed horse until man has made it so. If the tongue appears to be too large and to overlap the bars, certain problems will arise in the fitting of a curb bit, which will be prevented from acting on the bars. The shape of the jaws will also restrict the types of mouthpiece which will be effective. Careful fitting of bits and bridles is just as important as the correct fitting of a saddle. Not only will the action of the bit be affected by a badly fitting bridle, but chafing and discomfort to the horse will result, and encourage further evasive habits. The width of the bit used and its position in the mouth are both particularly important.

There are innumerable kinds of bits, which is perhaps why excessive emphasis is sometimes still placed on 'finding the key' to a horse's mouth. A bit will assist – or hinder – training and performance; no bit can replace training or achieve what training should achieve.

There are five groups of bits or bitting arrangements: the snaffle, the Weymouth, the Pelham, the gag and the bitless bridle. The basic construction of the bridle applies to all these groups, though the details of design vary according to the purpose for which any particular bridle is designed. A bridle consists of the headpiece and throatlatch, cheekpieces, browband, cavesson noseband and reins. With curb bits, curb chains of various kinds and lipstraps are also used.

An all-purpose bridle or one used for hunting, for example, will be made of plain, fairly substantial leather, while those used for showing will be much lighter and finer, the noseband frequently adorned with extra stitching. The bit and reins can either be stitched on or fastened with studs, billets or buckles. A sewn bridle is both the neatest in appearance and in some ways the most safe; other types of fastening are easier to dismantle and to clean.

The snaffle is the simplest kind of bit, basically consisting of one mouthpiece which acts on the corners of the mouth to produce an upward effect, raising the head. The mildest snaffle is a rubber mullen mouth, or half moon, one. Eggbutt snaffles, with a jointed mouthpiece and fixed rings, are perhaps the most popular. Dee cheek and eggbutt snaffles both developed from the cheek snaffle, one of the oldest kinds. The Fulmer (or Australian loose ring cheek) snaffle also used to be popular, though there are fewer of these bits in use today. Snaffles with loose rings allow a greater play of the bit in the mouth; fixed ring bits cannot pinch the corners of the mouth and the horse cannot evade their action by sliding them through the mouth.

There are many other varieties of snaffle available, such as eggbutts with slots in the rings; German snaffles, which have thick – and therefore comfortable – mouthpieces; the Dick Christian, which has an additional link in the centre of the mouthpiece; and the French bradoon, with a 'spatula' central link.

There are also stronger snaffle bits, such as the twisted snaffle, those with rollers set round or across the mouthpiece, Scorrier or Cornish

bits with four rings instead of the usual two, Y-mouth or W-mouth and spring-mouth snaffles.

The Weymouth or double bridle is the most advanced form of bitting. It consists of the bradoon, or snaffle, and the curb bit. It encourages the correct position of the head by the combination of a raising of the head caused by the snaffle and a lowering and nearly-vertical positioning of it produced by the action of the curb. In a horse that has been properly trained in a snaffle, the double bridle will help to achieve a head carriage which gives most effective control.

There are also several varieties of double bridle, though the number of these has been reduced with the increasing popularity of the snaffle. The best known are the slide cheek and fixed cheek Weymouths, the dressage Weymouth and the Banbury.

The Pelham bit attempts to combine in one mouthpiece the action of the snaffle and the double bridle. Though this is, of course, not really possible, many horses do seem to go well in Pelhams. There is a confusing variety of them, the best known being the mullen mouth, arch mouth, Hartwell, Hanoverian and Scamperdale. The Kimblewick, adapted from a Spanish jumping bit, has rapidly become popular and is now frequently seen.

The gag bridle uses a bit similar to the snaffle, but a cheekpiece is passed through the top and bottom of the bit rings and attached to the reins, thus accentuating the upward head-raising action of the ordinary snaffle. The gag is another form of bridle that should only be used by experts, for it tends to stiffen the head carriage. It is best used with an extra pair of reins, attached to the bit rings in the normal way, which can be used when the horse is carrying itself correctly, the gag reins being reserved as a corrective aid.

Bitless bridles are less common than the others. They achieve control by acting on the horse's nose rather than its mouth, and are most useful with horses that for some reason cannot be ridden in a normal bridle. In its simplest form it applies pressure to the nose, the curb groove and, to a lesser extent, the poll. It is also useful when training a horse to jump, as the possibility of the horse being pulled in the mouth, causing pain and a loss of confidence, is avoided.

The choice of reins is largely a matter of personal preference. Plain leather reins are the simplest, and should be nice and narrow. They do, however, slip in wet weather or when covered in sweat, and rubber-covered reins or plaited leather ones are a satisfactory alternative.

Nosebands and martingales are designed to help the action of the bit and to counteract evasive measures of the horse. Properly used, these extras can be very useful; wrongly applied, they can do considerable damage.

The most popular noseband is the drop noseband, which has two important functions. It alters the limited action of the snaffle, making flexion of the lower jaw and poll possible. Its second function is to close the mouth, thus preventing the horse from crossing its jaws, opening its mouth or getting its tongue over the bit, all common evasions.

It is extremely important that a noseband should be correctly fitted. It should lie about 2½ to 3 in. above the nostrils, with the rear strap, which passes under the bit, fitting into the curb groove. It should be fastened snugly but should never be too tight.

There are other nosebands which act on the same principle, that of applying pressure to the nose. The Flash noseband combines the cavesson and drop noseband in one, and can therefore be used in conjunction with a standing martingale. Grakle nosebands have two straps, one fastening above and one below the bit. Pressure is exerted on one point only, where the straps cross over in front, and it is perhaps stronger than the ordinary drop noseband as a result. The Kineton or Puckle noseband is the most severe, consisting of two metal loops with an adjustable connecting nosestrap. It does not close the mouth, but any pressure on the bit is transmitted to the nose.

All martingales are used in order to lower the horse's head and increase the rider's control. The most common is the standing martingale, a single strap which attaches to the noseband at one end, and—like other martingales—to the girth at the other. It is kept in place by a neckstrap. It increases control by exerting pressure on the nose. Standing martingales should be fitted with care, as if they are adjusted too tightly they hamper the horse when jumping.

Running martingales divide in two where they pass through the neckstrap, each end being attached to the reins by a ring. They thus act on the mouth rather than the nose. The action of a running martingale is severe if it is tightly adjusted, and this amount of extra control should only be used by experienced riders with sympathetic hands. If used with a double bridle, the martingale rings should be attached to the curb rein. Leather or rubber stops should always be put onto reins when a running martingale is in use, to prevent the rings from sliding forward.

Various other martingales are also available. The bib, which has an action like that of the running martingale, has a piece of leather between the two branches as a safety precaution. Irish rings, also known as Irish martingales, are not really martingales at all: they only affect the direction of rein pull. The combined martingale acts as both a standing and a running martingale. The pulley martingale resembles the running martingale but consists of a cord, with the rings at either end, that passes freely through a pulley on the main strap and allows the horse greater lateral freedom.

The Market Harborough martingale, also known as both the German rein and the English rein, consists of two straps which are attached to the reins at one end and pass through the bit to be attached to the martingale body at the other. The straps are slack while the horse holds its head correctly, but exert a downward pull on the bit as soon as the head is thrown upwards. Though it is the subject of considerable controversy, the Market Harborough martingale has its advantages, one of which is that it does not restrict the horse's ability to extend while jumping.

Part 3
The horse's health

1 Indications of sickness and health

'The eye of the master maketh the horse grow fat.' Regular observation of horses is essential if they are to be kept in the best of health.

A healthy horse is alert, stands squarely on its legs (resting one hind leg is normal and is not a cause for anxiety, but resting a foreleg indicates disease), its attitude is of awareness of its surroundings, its ears are pricked or moving and it turns its head to see any person who comes near. It is ready for its food at mealtimes and eats its full ration steadily and without quidding. Its droppings are well-formed and moist with no parasites or mucus visible in them, without strong offensive odour, and sufficiently firm to break when dropped to the ground; urine is passed several times a day in amounts of a quart or more and is light yellow and rather thick. The eyes are bright and free from dull spots or blemishes and without discharge. The coat shines, lies flat and is freely movable over the underlying tissues; the dock area is clean and shining and free from worm eggs. The legs are not puffy and the bones, tendons and ligaments are clearly defined. The horn of the hoofs is not cracked or ridged; the frog is large and in contact with ·the ground and there is no offensive odour or discharge from the cleft; the horse is not lame. Temperature and pulse are normal and breathing is regular and unhurried.

Before examining a horse in detail one should approach quietly and observe from a distance. This is the time when one notices if the animal is resting a foreleg, observes the nature of its breathing, its posture and movements, and looks at the facial expression. Not until one has obtained a general impression of the animal and its condition and surroundings should a closer approach be made.

Temperature

The temperature is taken from the rectum using a clinical thermometer—the stub-ended, half-minute type being best. The mercury should first be shaken down well below the normal temperature and the instrument lubricated with oil, soap or other suitable substance. The tail is quietly raised and the thermometer inserted gently into the rectum; at first the horse may keep the sphincter tightly closed so that there is difficulty in inserting the bulb, but with steady pressure and slight twisting movements a well lubricated thermometer usually slides in easily. The thermometer should be directed to one side so that it is in contact with the lining of the bowel and not just in the faeces—there is a marked difference in the two temperatures. The normal temperature is 100–101°F, but it may rise a degree or so after exercise or in hot weather and is up to half a degree higher in the evening than in the morning. In infectious diseases a rise in temperature is often the first symptom, and during an outbreak regular temperature-taking enables horses in the early stages of infection to be detected, and thus taken out of work and treated without delay. A rise in temperature is part of the phenomenon of inflammation or reaction to infectious disease and helps the animal in its fight against the bacteria or viruses. Although pyrexia (as a high temperature is called) may make the patient uncomfortable it is usually undesirable to reduce the temperature without taking other steps to overcome infection. An exception is heatstroke, when there is a failure of the heat-regulating mechanism.

Markedly sub-normal temperature is a grave symptom of ill-health.

Pulse and heart

The pulse is a guide to the condition of the circulation. When the heart contracts it drives blood through the arteries—this wave is felt as the pulse. The common sites for observing the pulse in the horse are at the angle of the jaw and

84

inside the forearm; in both these places the artery being felt is under the skin and lies against bone. There is one pulse for each beat of the heart, and the rate and nature of the pulse show how the heart is behaving. The heart beats about forty times a minute but increases with exercise, excitement and when the digestive organs are replete. There is an increase in the rate in the primary stages of fever and when there is inflammation of the abdominal organs. The type of pulse reflects the action of the heart. Thus what is known as a quick pulse, in which the number of beats per minute remains normal but the duration of each pulse is shorter, indicates that there is some heart disease causing the cardiac muscle to contract rapidly. A slow pulse, in which the pulse is longer than normal, may be associated with resistance to the flow of blood from the heart such as occurs in narrowing of the great arteries. Congestion of the lungs leads to a full pulse in which the arteries carry more blood than usual. A hard pulse occurs when the arterial walls are contracted and the vessel becomes less compressible against the underlying bone – this is one of the symptoms of laminitis, in which disease the pulse is also quick, full and bounding.

Sometimes the pulse is intermittent, a beat or beats being missed. The omission may be regular (occurring at, say, every fourth beat) or irregular (occurring at varying intervals). Intermittency may be compatible with apparent health and is more likely to be of consequence when it occurs after exercise. In this condition, knowledge of the individual horse is valuable.

Skin

The condition of the skin at any time is a good indication of a horse's overall state of health. It should be glossy and blooming, not harsh, dull, staring or ragged. Nor should it be hidebound – i.e. tightly adherent to the underlying tissues – but should move freely when the flat of the hand is run down the neck and over the ribs. A hidebound animal may be suffering from malnutrition or a chronic wasting disease such as worm infestation. The condition also occurs in acute illness and when there has been a loss of water from the body, as in diarrhoea.

In acute fever the skin feels hot to the touch; localised heat may indicate inflammation.

Common skin conditions are, firstly, louse infestation, causing rubbing and ragged coat and perhaps louse eggs on the hairs; mange causes stamping and bald patches on the back of the legs, with crust formation; bot eggs can be seen stuck on the leg hairs; ringworm shows as patches of broken hairs with scaly skin; and sweet itch leads to rubbed mane and tail.

Mucous membranes

The unpigmented tissue of these membranes (a 'skin' lining the eyes, mouth, nostrils, vulva, etc.) allows the colour of the blood in the capillaries to show through and thus indicate the condition of the blood. In health the mucous membranes are salmon pink, moist and glistening. If an abnormality is found in one portion of mucous membrane and not in others it points to localised disease. Pallid membranes are paler than normal, indicating a reduced flow of red blood, such as occurs in bleeding or in infestation with blood-sucking parasites like lice. The nature of the pulse may help to ascertain the cause of pallid mucous membranes. An injected membrane (deeper red than normal) indicates inflammation and is an early sign of bacterial or viral infection and raised temperature. When bile pigments are broken down (as in some liver diseases) the yellow pigment they contain circulates in the blood stream and turns the tissues yellow. This is most easily seen in the mucous membranes and is called jaundice. When the blood lacks oxygen, as in diseases of respiration and of the heart, the mucous membranes turn a leaden blue colour and are 'cyanosed'.

Eyes

Discharges from the eyes tend to be watery at first, and in general infection later change to a sticky fluid. When only one eye is affected it is likely to be a localised illness in that eye, but when it occurs in both eyes, systematic changes are probably indicated.

Eyes sunken in their sockets show that fat has been absorbed from the back of the eyeballs, as occurs in chronic wasting disease or in old age.

Nasal discharges

Any discharge should be investigated. A thin watery discharge occurs in the early stages of some general diseases such as strangles and becomes purulent as the disease develops. If the discharge is from one nostril only it may be due to sinusitis from a diseased tooth or infection of the guttural pouch on that side. In health, tears flow from the eyes into the nostrils and watery eyes will lead to a thin nasal discharge. If the tear ducts become blocked then the discharge will run down the cheeks.

Mouth

The lining of the mouth should be moist and salmon pink. An offensive odour may come from diseased teeth or from wounds to the lining of the mouth (often due to sharp teeth); it also arises from alimentary disorders.

Ears

Disease of the ears is uncommon in the horse, but mites in them can lead to head-shaking. Blind horses have abnormally mobile ears: special attention should be paid to the eyes of a horse whose ears are always moving, particularly if it also picks its feet up high.

Lymphatic glands

Situated on the lymphatic ducts of the body, these act as 'sieves' in which invading organisms are held up and dealt with by the body defences. When this happens the glands often swell and become tender, and they may turn into abscesses which burst. This occurs with the glands under the jaws in cases of strangles. Tumour cells are also arrested by lymphatic glands, which then become enlarged. Any enlargement of the lymphatic glands suggests abnormality in the parts draining through them.

Respiratory system

The respiratory rate in a resting horse is about twelve a minute; breathing should be effortless. The rate is increased by excitement and exercise or by high temperature; it may be counted by watching the rise and fall of the flanks or steamy breath in cold weather. Any noise in breathing means that something is wrong. It may be due to laryngeal paralysis, stenosis or tumours. Difficult breathing is shown by dilated nostrils, head stretched out and exaggerated movements of the chest and abdomen; it is due to such things as nostrils or sinuses blocked with discharge, inflammation of the throat, pressure

from harness, disease of the lungs or pressure on the diaphragm from the abdominal contents.

If the chest is painful the animal will use its abdominal muscles for breathing and fix its ribs, causing a ridge, known as the 'pleuritic ridge', to appear behind the last rib.

Broken wind leads to a double expiratory movement, in which the flanks collapse inwards as the animal breathes out and then make a further expiratory movement to drive out the air from the lung vesicles, which have lost their elasticity and ability to collapse due to disease.

Coughing is a sudden forced expiratory movement by which undesirable matter is expelled from the breathing apparatus. This may be foreign material, such as particles of dust or hay, or it may be mucus due to inflammation. A cough can also be due to nervous irritability. In infectious diseases such as strangles the cough is harsh, dry and painful at first and then becomes soft, easier and less distressing as the disease progresses and more fluid is present. Harshness is due to the breathing passages being dry; when they are moist the cough becomes softer. A cough may also arise in connection with heart and lung disease as well as being due to local irritation and infection.

Abdomen

When the hind part of the abdomen is less in girth than normal the animal 'runs up' and is said to be 'tucked up'. This occurs in abdominal pain, debilitating diseases and also in exhaustion.

The normal noises made in the bowels are called 'borborygmi' and may sometimes be heard when standing away from the horse. They are sounds of health and can always be heard if the examiner's ear is pressed against the abdomen. The nature of the sounds differs with the area auscultated and only practice will enable the listener to detect the abnormal. Sounds may disappear in impacted colic. In addition to other symptoms, pain in the abdomen (colic) causes the horse to look round at its flanks and to paw the ground. Impaction of the bowel may cause pressure on the urinary bladder and make the horse strain as if to urinate.

Many symptoms of disease are related, and it is important that all the available signs are considered before any decision is made about an illness.

2 Diseases and ailments

The Skin

The common diseases of the skin are lousiness, ringworm, sweet itch, mud fever and cracked heels.

Lousiness—Horses readily become infested with lice unless well and regularly groomed. Infestation is most common in animals at grass, especially if in poor condition, and thus is most often seen in late winter and early spring, although summer cases are by no means rare.

Affected animals show bare patches from which hair has been rubbed due to the itching caused by the parasites. This may be so intense that the patient does not merely rub out the hair but causes a raw patch. The rubbed places occur on all parts of the body but most often on the quarters and sides of the neck. Most infected animals show apparent pleasure if scratched on the base of the mane and withers.

In Britain two kinds of lice affect horses: biting and sucking; differentiation is unimportant to the horse owner. The species vary in size, from being just visible to the naked eye up to $\frac{1}{16}$ in. long. While the large ones, especially on grey horses, may sometimes be seen from a distance of yards, in many cases prolonged and careful search is necessary before any lice can be found; they are slate grey in colour.

Effective proprietary louse powders and washes are on the market, and the washes are to be preferred. Where practicable, it is best to clip the horse before applying the dressing, as this provides less cover for the vermin and enables the dressing to reach them better. When a long coat is removed it is often found that the infestation is much greater than was at first suspected. The condition is contagious and as the lice lay eggs which stick on the hairs, the clippings should be burned or, if this cannot be done, buried deep in the dung heap.

As affected horses are likely to be in poor condition and may be anaemic, steps should be taken to build them up and to give them iron tonics if needed. A check should also be made to see if red worms are present.

Although lousiness is sometimes glossed over as 'a touch of the frost' it should always be treated seriously.

Ringworm—As the name implies this infestation commonly appears as a circular patch, but in the horse lesions may be of any shape.

The disease is caused by a fungus which grows on the hairs. In a typical case there are areas one to two inches in diameter surrounded by a crusty ring and with a scaly centre from which broken hairs protrude. Sometimes the places itch and make the horse rub raw patches so that sores and scaly areas appear side by side and the ringworm lesions may be overlooked.

Tincture of iodine is an effective and time-honoured treatment still satisfactory; it should be painted on to the affected places daily. In recent years medicaments have been developed which are given to affected animals by mouth, and the later ones are safe, effective and a convenient method of treating the disease, especially when numerous horses are involved or it is not feasible to clip the coat. Another hopeful modern approach to the disease is the development of a vaccine.

In the laboratory several forms of equine ringworm are recognised. They can also infest humans, and care should be taken to avoid contact of human skin with lesions on infected animals.

As ringworm is contagious, precautions should be taken to prevent it spreading from one animal to another by way of grooming kit, saddlery, rugs, and the like, The spores of ringworm are difficult to kill and can persist for years on stable woodwork against which infected animals have rubbed. Flaming with a blowlamp destroys the spores in buildings;

obviously great care is needed to prevent fire.

Sweet itch – This malady is not yet fully understood. It affects the long coarse hairs of the mane and tail and is accompanied by irritation which makes the animal rub itself until raw areas appear. The coarse hairs are broken and rubbed out and the underlying skin often thrown into large wrinkles.

Midges have been blamed for spreading the disease, and stabling susceptible animals during the evenings of the sweet itch season (summer and autumn) certainly reduces the frequency of attacks.

Administration of thyroid tablets throughout the month of February seems to relieve the severity of attacks and lessen their number in animals which in previous years have suffered from the disease. Soothing dressings, such as calamine lotion, are of help in treatment and benzyl benzoate is the basis of some popular proprietary treatments. Antihistamines and corticosteroids are also used by veterinary surgeons to control the itch.

Mud fever – Mud fever is a form of dermatitis most frequently seen on the skin of the belly and inside the limbs. It is associated with certain types of soil, and not all horses are susceptible. Prevention consists of washing off the mud if the horse is still wet after work and careful drying with a chamois leather or warm dry bran, avoiding friction; dry mud can be gently brushed off. After cleaning, soothing lotions are applied. Cod liver oil is a good dressing but rather unpleasant to use.

Cracked heels – Cracked heels resemble mud fever of the back of the pasterns. The condition is more often found on white heels than on those with dark hair. The condition can often be prevented by coating the heels with petroleum jelly or lanoline before work. Treatment is as for mud fever, and bandaging hot, oven-dried bran on the washed legs often helps.

Digestive tract

Sharp teeth, colic and worm infestation are the common alimentary ailments.

Sharp teeth – Before food is swallowed it is mixed with saliva and finely ground between the molars or cheek teeth. These teeth move from side to side, and to facilitate their grinding the upper jaw is wider than the lower, with the rows of teeth correspondingly farther apart. The result of this is that as the teeth are ground down the outer borders of the upper molars and the inner (tongue side) borders of the lower teeth are worn less than the rest of the surface and may become so sharp that they cut the tongue and cheeks. The pain from this will make the horse chew its food less before swallowing and it may eat less, too. Failure to masticate properly is shown by the presence of whole oat grains in the dung. Such interference with the chewing may lead to colic and to unthriftiness as nourishment is being lost in the faeces.

The sharp teeth can be felt by holding the horse's tongue and passing one's finger over the tooth margins. Care is needed to avoid being bitten by the horse or cut on the sharp edges of its teeth.

Treatment consists of filing away the sharp edges with a special rasp, and although painless this is often alarming to the horse.

Colic – The term colic is used to indicate abdominal pain and is usually associated with indigestion.

Spasmodic colic is the most common form. Pain comes and goes, with intervals of up to an hour between spasms. The horse looks round at its flanks, paws the ground, lies down and tries to roll, may stand as if trying to stale, and sweats. As the pain becomes more severe the horse assumes an anxious look and may groan. The pulse rate increases, and in severe cases the temperature rises.

Causes of colic include improper feeding, cooked feeds, sharp teeth, worm infestation, large feeds when exhausted, sudden changes of food, and watering after feeding.

Treatment consists of relieving spasm and pain and shifting any irritant from the bowel. In recent years several drugs have been synthesised which are a great step forward in the treatment of colic. Cases which do not respond to first aid will need professional treatment, and as it is important that the veterinary surgeon should know what drugs have been given it is as well that he should be asked to provide the colic drinks for the first aid chest.

Pain also occurs when the bowels are distended with gas (flatulent colic), a condition which may lead to rupture of the bowel. In another form the bowel becomes impacted with a dry mass of food. This causes dull pain and may need treatment for several days before it can be softened and shifted. Contraction of the muscular bands of the bowel wall can lead to telescoping of the gut, with fatal results.

Twist is a form of the ailment in which the mesentery (the membrane by which the bowel is suspended from just below the backbone) becomes twisted on itself, so cutting off the blood supply by pressing on the blood vessels which traverse the mesentery. It is unlikely that rolling leads to twist, as is popularly believed, and if an affected animal gains relief by rolling it seems inhuman to stop it doing so.

In the early stages of colic walking the patient is helpful, though care should be taken not to take it to places—such as public roads—where it would be dangerous or inconvenient for the horse to lie down, as it may be difficult to get it to rise. Nor should it be allowed to roll in a stable, where it might get cast under some fitting such as a manger.

Differentiation of the various forms of colic calls for an internal examination by inserting the arm in the rectum and palpating the bowels. For this, an expert knowledge of the anatomy and situation of the various parts of the alimentary tract is, of course, essential.

Worms—Horses are hosts to three types of worms in the bowel: tapeworms, large white round worms and strongyles (red worms).

Tapeworms seldom cause a problem and in many cases can be dealt with by giving half an ounce of freshly ground areca nut.

Ascarids, as the large white round worms are called, are more alarming in appearance than the other parasites. They are white or yellowish, $\frac{1}{4}$ in. or more in diameter and as much as a foot long. After successful treatment a horse may void a gallon of such parasites. Toluene is a commonly used drug.

Strongyles cause the most trouble and are a frequent cause of unthriftness and even death, especially in young stock. Red worms may be seen in the droppings of infested animals but some worms are so small as to be almost invisible. The worm eggs are numerous in the dung—sometimes many thousands to the ounce—but can only be detected with a microscope. The adult worms live in the bowel, but in the course of their life cycle migrate through the abdomen and may cause irreparable damage to the blood vessels; the worms also cause anaemia and weakness by sucking blood from the gut. The eggs in the dung hatch into larvae, which crawl up grass stems and are eaten by horses, leading to further infection.

Many effective red worm medicines are on the market, but control depends not only upon regular dosing of susceptible animals but upon preventing further infection by dosing horses before turning them out to grass. The collection of droppings from fields, or at least reducing the intensity of infestation by harrowing the dung so that it is quickly dried, is also necessary. When infestation of a pasture has built up over the years it is said to be 'horse sick'.

A worm called the oxyurid lives in the large intestine. The female lays her eggs around the anus, where they can be seen as waxy masses. These worms cause irritation and infested horses rub their tails sore and lose condition. There are effective proprietary remedies against these worms, and carbolic ointment may be used to allay the itching and to move the egg masses.

Systemic diseases

Horses are subject to numerous diseases, and so many viruses have been discovered in recent years that there are as yet no popular names for the diseases which they cause. The invisibility of viruses with orthodox microscopes makes their identification very difficult.

Influenza and some coughs are associated with viruses. Influenza sweeps across the country from time to time, often with years between epidemics. It is highly contagious, and although seldom fatal except in young stock can lead to permanent impairment of affected animals if they are not rested. Fortunately, effective preventive vaccines are now readily available. Affected horses often have a high temperature, they lose their appetites and develop a cough. The disease must run its course, but rest is essential and linctuses or electuaries can be used to relieve the cough.

There are other causes of cough against which there are as yet no effective vaccines. In the treatment of these coughs relief of the symptoms is aimed at, together with suppression of secondary bacterial infection with antibiotics or sulphonamides.

Strangles—This is an infectious and contagious disease mainly of young horses. It is widespread, and as hitherto isolated young animals are especially susceptible, cases are common in young stock which pass through markets or are conveyed in public transport.

Affected animals are off their food, have a high temperature and shiver, and then develop thick nasal discharge and cough. The lymph glands, which lie between the bones of the lower jaw, become swollen and tender. They may swell to the size of cricket balls or bigger.

These glands form abscesses full of pus. When the abscesses burst, pus escapes and usually there is a marked improvement in the patient's condition. The pus and all discharges are infectious and can transmit the disease to other horses, either directly or by contamination of the attendant's hands, clothing or other articles which may be affected.

Treatment consists of easing the nasal discharge by steam inhalations, fomenting the abscesses to hasten their 'ripening', warmth and fresh air and careful feeding. In some cases antibiotics and sulphonamides are used, but these drugs should not be administered

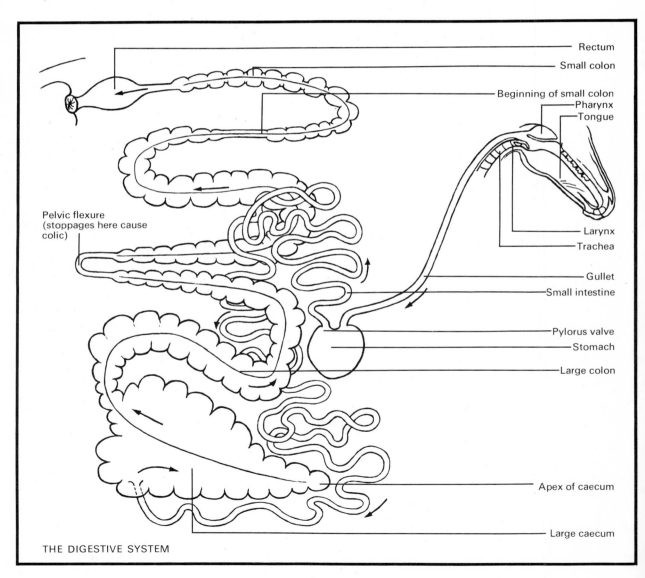

THE DIGESTIVE SYSTEM

indiscriminately. Usually the abscesses are confined to the glands of the head, but in some cases the abscesses appear elsewhere, sometimes with fatal results. Recovered animals have some immunity.

Tetanus–Also called lockjaw, because of the common symptom of being unable to open the mouth, tetanus is a widely-spread disease caused by a germ which occurs in horse dung. The germ will not grow in the presence of oxygen, and the disease is therefore associated with penetrating wounds such as those caused by a horse stepping on a nail. These puncture wounds heal at the surface, leaving the tetanus germs carried in by the nail without air. As horses' feet are usually contaminated with faeces, wounds of the feet are particularly liable to become infected with tetanus, but punctured wounds on any part of the body can provide entry for the disease germs. Large open wounds, because of exposure to air, are much less likely to lead to tetanus.

An affected animal is first seen to move stiffly. Sudden noise will cause the third eyelid to flick across the eye and the tail sticks out stiffly if the horse is moved back. The lack of co-ordination of gait increases hourly, and the patient may be unable to open its mouth to feed. In most untreated cases death follows in days or weeks.

Treatment consists of giving large doses of hyper-immune serum (blood from recovered horses) and such antibiotics as are effective against the tetanus germ. Nursing is important– the horse must be insulated from stimuli which might send it into muscular spasms. The stable should be darkened, nearby horses shifted and noise (even the rattling of buckets) stopped. Liquid nourishment is needed when the jaws are locked.

Immediate protection can be given to a horse at the time of injury by hyper-immune serum, but this protection only lasts for a few weeks. Immunity of much longer duration follows the use of tetanus toxoid, but the immunity is not immediate and this preparation cannot therefore be used in emergency.

Azoturia–Azoturia is one of the 'Monday morning' diseases, ailments which occur when horses are put to work after a period of idleness. It is most often seen in those animals which have been kept on full rations while resting. Symptoms show when the horse is working again: it is in great distress, sweats and trembles and shows muscular stiffness and hardening of the muscles, especially those of the quarters. If urine is passed it is dark brown from the muscle pigment excreted by the kidneys. It is essential that an ailing horse should be immediately rested and taken to a stable by horse-box even if there is only a short distance to go. Professional treatment is required and should be obtained without delay.

Broken wind or pulmonary emphysema–This is a dread disease of the lungs due to rupture of the microscopic alveoli in which the bronchioles terminate. The walls of these alveoli burst and the area of membrane available for gaseous exchange during breathing is decreased. This causes the animal to breathe more rapidly in order to get enough oxygen into its blood, but because the ruptured alveoli have lost their elasticity so an extra effort has to be made by the abdominal muscles to expel the contained air. As a result, the horse makes two movements of its belly when breathing out, and the tense border of the ribs forms a prominent arch which is characteristic of the ailment. As the disease advances more alveoli burst and the distressed breathing, at first only noticeable on exertion, occurs during light work and finally at rest. Coughing of a peculiar 'hollow' type develops and often flatus is passed with each cough. Circulation in the lung tissue is restricted, throwing a burden on the heart, which enlarges to cope with the additional load. The enlargement alters the valve seating in that organ and valvular disease of the heart adds to the horse's distress, because blood intended for the lungs is pumped back into the veins.

There are numerous theories about the cause of broken wind, and probably more than one exciting factor exists. The nature of the food given seems to play a part, and certain hay crops have been associated with a high incidence of the disease, possibly due to an allergy to some fungus on the hay. Horses showing severe symptoms have recovered when moved to other areas–these were probably cases of allergy rather than of true broken wind.

The drugs known as corticosteroids often reduce the symptoms, and careful management may enable lightly affected animals to continue work. Tests should be made to try to find if any food exacerbates the disease in a particular case, and care should be taken to ensure that affected animals are only worked when their stomachs are almost empty. The use of materials other than straw for bedding and the removal of hay from the diet often benefits the patient, as does cod liver oil and the damping of food to keep down irritant dust.

Roaring—Another respiratory disease is roaring or whistling. The names denote the type of noise made when the horse is breathing hard. The disease is associated with paralysis of the nerve leading to the vocal cord. It is nearly always that on the left that is affected, and the symptoms are seen most often in big horses such as heavyweight hunters. The paralysis allows the cord to impinge on the airway in the larynx and the horse cannot get enough air through the narrowed channel, so breathing becomes laboured when exertion is called for. The flaccid vocal cord vibrates in the current of air as the horse breathes in, causing a roaring or whistling sound. The cord is blown out of the way and does not impede the outward flow of air from the lungs, and the noise is thus heard only on inspiration.

The noise, especially in the early stages of the disease, may be intermittent and slight; whistlers may become roarers; cramping of the larynx by making the horse raise and flex its head may increase the disability. The harm in roaring results not from the noise but from the inability to breathe in enough air, causing partial asphyxiation.

Treatment is surgical, either by inserting a tube into the windpipe below the obstruction or by removing the offending vocal cord through an incision into the larynx. There are objections to both these techniques, although in most cases they do enable the patient to continue work. A new technique, in which an elastic prosthesis is attached to the vocal cord to pull it aside, holds promise.

Injuries—Injuries are of course common, and range from scratches to severe lacerations or even to severing a limb when barbed wire becomes wrapped around the leg of a frantically struggling horse. Terrible injuries are sometimes inflicted in motor accidents.

Harsh antiseptics and disinfectants have no place in modern treatment, in which the aim is to remove foreign matter and severely damaged tissue as gently as possible—generally by a fine jet of running water; to stop bleeding by pressure; to bring the edges of severed tissue together by suturing or bandaging; and to control infection with antibiotics or sulphonamides. Sedatives, tranquillisers and pain relievers are nowadays quite readily available and are used as needed to ease the patient and to prevent interference with the wound.

Minor infected wounds are poulticed after cleaning. Wounds of the feet caused by stepping on sharp objects need treatment to promote drainage, and it is even more important than with wounds inflicted elsewhere to ensure that the horse is protected against tetanus.

Saddle sores are treated on general principles, with especial attention to removing the cause. This is done not by putting padding over the sore but by building it up elsewhere so that the saddle no longer touches the injured part.

Despite its efficient natural protection the eye is injured at times. Common causes are hay seeds (especially if the old-fashioned overhead hay racks are used), and injuries from thorns and whip lashes. Great care must be taken in removing foreign bodies and early removal is desirable, as such things as awns become more firmly embedded as time passes. It is wise to have eye ointment in the stable medicine chest and to apply it several times a day after removing a foreign body or in treatment of other forms of injury to the eye.

Finally, weeping of an eye may be due to blockage of the tear ducts, the passages from the eyelids to the inside of the nostrils down which tears normally flow. If they are stopped up by sandy material or discharges from the eye the tears run down the cheeks, often scalding them. Treatment is given by blowing the ducts clear with a catheter, a simple operation to perform, but not one for the layman to attempt.

3 Lameness: some causes and treatments

Inherent weakness, which makes tissues less able to stand up to work, may lead to lameness. Some forms of lameness can be prevented merely by taking care; it is significant that cases of foot wounds caused by treading on nails by Army horses dropped abruptly when the soldiers concerned were 'put on a charge'. Sore shins are likely to be found if horses are worked when they are very young; strain leads to curbs; movements which impose great demands on the hocks should not be demanded from horses with weakness in these joints.

Horses are kept for working, not for molly-coddling, but work puts on the limbs stresses that did not have to be borne in the wild. Horses in work jar their feet on hard metalled roads; their legs must bear the added weight of a rider and the strain in stopping, turning and landing from jumps; the natural shock-absorbing mechanism of the foot is partly nullified by iron shoes which increase jar, raise the frog from the ground and interfere with the expansion of the foot, while the nails weaken the wall.

Most lameness in the forelimb occurs in the foot; and in the hind limb the hock is the weak spot. Concussion is the great offender in front and strain behind.

Pus in the foot results from infected material reaching the soft structures in the hoof. This may be grit working its way up, but usually follows a penetrating wound caused by treading on a spike or from a shoe nail being driven into the sensitive structures. A loose shoe which turns on the foot, so that the horse pricks its sole with one of the nails, is a common cause of this type of injury. Penetrating wounds which go through the frog are especially serious, as the injury may involve the coffin joint. Even in those cases where this does not happen it is much more difficult to make an effective drainage hole through the rubbery frog than through the hard horn of the sole.

Sometimes the offending nail can be seen sticking in the foot. With other injuries the site must be found by nipping the foot with pincers to find the sensitive area, or by paring away the sole to reveal the entry hole.

Treatment comprises removing the cause, cutting a hole in the sole to permit escape of pus, tubbing and poulticing. Subsequently a plate of metal wedged under the shoe branches to protect the injured part until it has healed will help to keep out dirt. In some cases antibiotics are needed, especially if the coffin joint has been damaged. There should always be cover against tetanus, as the site and nature of these wounds invite infection with this disease.

Thrush, which can often be avoided, may lead to lameness. It is characterised by an offensive discharge from the cleft of the frog; the cleft sometimes splits up between the bulbs of the heel. The disease is favoured by constant moisture; hence it is brought about by wet and dirty bedding and by neglecting to pick out the feet regularly. Cleanliness and packing the cleft with thick string soaked in tincture of iodine, Stockholm tar or a soluble sulphonamide usually effects a cure.

Navicular disease comes on when a horse is in its prime and almost invariably affects the fore-feet only. It is an inflammation of the navicular bone and surrounding tissues. The bone forms part of the coffin joint and is attached to the deep flexor tendon, by which it is firmly held against the other bones, the firmness increasing as more weight is put on the limb. Changes which occur in the bone include ulceration, rarefaction and bony outgrowths.

Hereditary predisposition, mineral imbalance or improper feeding in youth, bad shoeing and lack of frog pressure, faulty conformation and concussion have all been blamed for the appearance of this disease. Factors increasing pressure on the navicular bone, such as long toes or long sloping pasterns, aggravate the condition, as do short upright pasterns, by increasing concussion.

Pain can be relieved with drugs. The horse's gait may be improved by shoeing with rolled toes, while leathers will reduce concussion. But these measures are only palliative. At present there is no known cure for the disease and the operation of neurectomy (which is not entirely satisfactory) may be the only way to keep the horse in work.

Laminitis, or fever of the feet, is a disease with many causes. It is an inflammation of the sensitive leaves which unite the horny hoof to the foot. In the acute stage it is exceedingly painful and may turn into the chronic form, resulting in permanent disability. Predisposing causes are heavy-topped animals such as fat ponies, unfitness, hot weather and badly-shaped feet. Exciting causes include overeating (as when a horse gains access to the feed bin, is put in a lush pasture or is given a big feed of strange food), prolonged concussion, and blood poisoning from infectious disease or colic.

Modern antihistaminic drugs and anti-inflammatory agents are used to reduce the reaction to foods, and these, together with forced exercise to drive the blood out of the feet, will often effect a cure if administered promptly; anaesthetising the nerves of the hoofs will enable a very lame horse to take exercise. Cold applications and standing the horse in water help to reduce the inflammation, and a soft laxative diet is indicated.

The chronic form of laminitis may either follow an acute attack or appear spontaneously. Lameness varies but is not always marked. The outlook is always bad but drastic operations on the foot with exaggerated lowering of the heels have sometimes resulted in improvement.

Neglecting to have horses regularly shod leads to several forms of lameness, including corns and strain of the tendons. A corn is a bruise of the sole in the angle between the wall and the bars. A mild corn is dry, but more serious cases become moist or suppurating and may even become complicated by infection spreading to adjacent structures. They are most common in the forefeet, especially at the inner angle of large flat feet. The usual cause is an injury from the heel of the shoe pressing on the

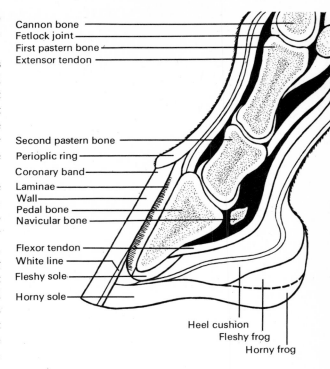

Cannon bone
Fetlock joint
First pastern bone
Extensor tendon

Second pastern bone
Perioplic ring
Coronary band
Laminae
Wall
Pedal bone
Navicular bone

Flexor tendon
White line
Fleshy sole

Horny sole

Heel cushion
Fleshy frog
Horny frog

seat of corn; when a shoe is left on too long the shoe is carried forward as the horn grows until it is embedded in the seat of corn. Treatment comprises removing the offending shoe and paring away the horn over the corn. If there is infection, drainage must be provided and the horn cut away deeply. Tubbing or poulticing will then control infection. Afterwards a shoe must be fitted that does not press on the affected area.

Ringbone is a serious form of lameness associated with concussion, and may also follow strain from twisting or a blow. Ringbones are bony outgrowths on the pastern bones. They are classified in several ways, popular terms being 'true' and 'false' ringbone. True ringbone affects the pastern joint or the coffin joint, while false ringbone is clear of the joints. If a horse with false ringbone is rested in the early stages of the disease and inflammation reduced with cold applications, recovery is the rule; stubborn cases are sometimes needle-point fired. True ringbone is incurable and the prognosis always grave, although unnerving may enable the horse to continue work.

Although there is a hereditary tendency for splints and they sometimes form spontaneously,

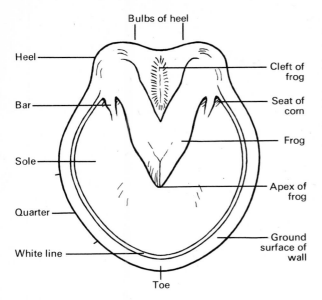

Bulbs of heel

Heel

Cleft of frog

Bar

Seat of corn

Sole

Frog

Quarter

Apex of frog

White line

Ground surface of wall

Toe

UNDERSIDE OF THE FOOT

strain is the usual cause. In the young horse the splint bones are attached to the cannon bone by fibrous tissue, which changes into bone as the animal grows older. The heads of the splint bones form part of the knee joint and if extra strain is thrown on the inner splint bone head the fibrous tissue joining it to the main bone will be torn; bone laid down during the healing forms a 'splint'. The strain is likely to occur when working a young horse, especially if it is turned sharply or if its conformation is such that the inner side of the knee joint takes a greater share of its weight than normal. Cold applications, rest and pressure bandages are the usual, and satisfactory, methods of treatment. A blemish usually persists, and premature return to work will cause it to be larger than would otherwise be the case.

The treatment of strained tendons still leaves much to be desired. A tendon is said to be strained when some (rarely all) of its fibres are ruptured. This is likely to occur in a young, unfit or tired horse, or when an animal gallops into a sudden change of going. Types of con-

formation which put the tendons at a disadvantage, such as long sloping pasterns, long toes, low heels or 'tying in' below the knees, all predispose to strain.

First aid consists of cold applications and pressure bandages. Massage is helpful. Modern treatment includes surgical interference by splitting the tendon longitudinally and using a technique whereby a piece of tendon from another part of the body is inserted into the middle of the affected tendon. Various treatments, including X-ray and infra-red therapy, galvanisation, faradisation, darsonvalisation, electro-massage, ultrasonic applications and the 'black box' have all been used, and some startling and extravagant claims made for their efficacy. Firing has its advocates.

Spavin is generally associated with chronic arthritis of the hock and some animals have a hereditary predisposition to it. Defective conformation increases the liability to strain. Rest for two months while consolidation takes place generally results in lameness disappearing; the use of pain-relieving drugs while work continues may result in the final spavin being larger than it otherwise would have been. Refractory cases are treated by needle-point firing, by cutting tendons near the lesion or even by neurectomy.

A strong ligament, the calcaneo-cuboid ligament, lies at the back of the hock, uniting the point of the hock with the back of the cannon bone. The powerful muscles which straighten the hock, for example when a horse jumps or rears, transmit their pull through this bone and put strain on the ligament. If it partly gives way a swelling forms. This is a curb, which is most likely to occur in young horses, especially those with poorly-formed hocks. Resting and cold applications generally limit the damage and the horse is able to return to work, although a blemish persists. It has been reported that lungeing the patient over small jumps after the initial inflammation has subsided hastens recovery.

4 Ageing by the teeth

Although an opinion about the age of a horse can be formed from some aspects of its general appearance, such as the frizzy tail of a foal or the drawn face of an old animal, it is by examination of the teeth that age is usually determined. The assessment is made by determining which teeth have erupted and by the wear, shape and angle of growth of the front (incisor) teeth. The principles of ageing are simple, but many variations and difficulties arise in practice and even experts often differ.

Horses have two sets of teeth during their lifetime. The first set (known as milk or deciduous teeth) erupt early in life and are later shed; they are followed by the permanent teeth, which have to last a lifetime. The milk teeth are not simply pushed out by the permanent ones but have their roots absorbed and are then shed to make way for the second set.

A horse has twenty-four milk teeth, made up of six upper and six lower front teeth (incisors, nippers or pincers), and three upper and three lower molars (grinders or cheek teeth) on each side. These are replaced by six permanent incisors in each jaw and six permanent upper and lower molars on each side—a total of thirty-six. In addition, four teeth known as tushes erupt, one upper and one lower on each side of the jaw between the incisors and the molars, but nearer the former than the latter. Tushes are normally found only in males, but small ones not infrequently occur in mares.

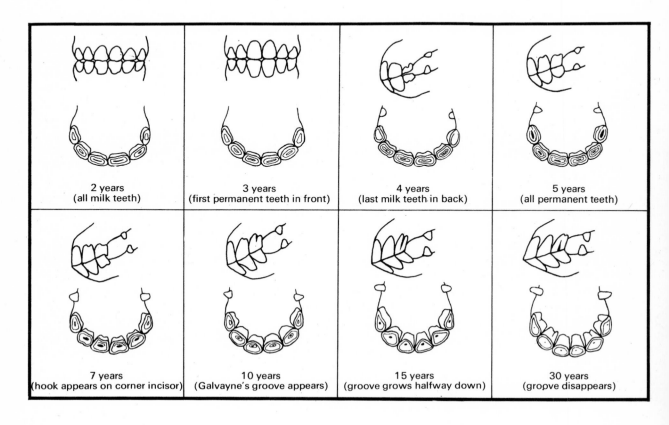

| 2 years (all milk teeth) | 3 years (first permanent teeth in front) | 4 years (last milk teeth in back) | 5 years (all permanent teeth) |
| 7 years (hook appears on corner incisor) | 10 years (Galvayne's groove appears) | 15 years (groove grows halfway down) | 30 years (groove disappears) |

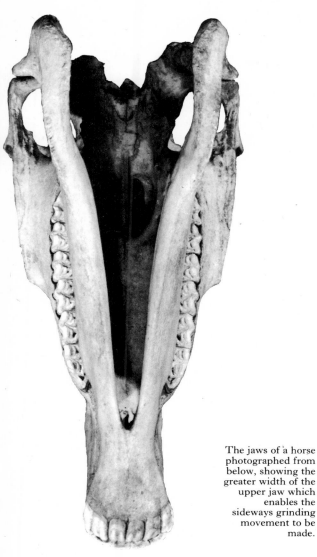

The jaws of a horse photographed from below, showing the greater width of the upper jaw which enables the sideways grinding movement to be made.

Wolf teeth are small vestigial teeth in front of the normal molars.

Up to the age of two years and six months (when the first permanent incisors appear) age is ascertained from the number of teeth in the mouth. By the time it is ten days old a foal has four incisor teeth; these are the two middle pairs, called the centrals. The next pairs (the laterals) appear at four to six weeks, and the corner pairs show at six to ten months. By this time, therefore, there will be a complete incisor set of six teeth in the upper and in the lower jaw.

It is important to distinguish between the temporary and permanent incisors, though this can be difficult. The main differences are that the temporary incisors have a distinct neck, the root being much narrower than the exposed crown, that milk teeth are whiter than permanents, and that there are five vertical ridges and grooves on the outer side of the temporary teeth while in permanents these ridges are more prominent and are two in number on the upper teeth and single on the lower.

The wear of temporary teeth is not such a consistent guide to age as that of the permanent teeth, but signs of wear do appear on the crowns —on the centrals at twelve months, the laterals at eighteen months, and on the corners at two years.

All the temporary cheek teeth have erupted by the time a foal is two weeks old.

The first permanent incisor teeth appear at two and a half years. When permanent and temporary teeth exist side by side differentiation is usually easy because of the difference in size. The laterals appear at three and a half years and the corners a year later at four and a half years, by which time the horse has a 'full mouth', the tushes and permanent molars all having erupted earlier. The tushes of the male come through at four years and dispel doubt about whether the incisors present are of the first or second set.

Although the incisors erupt at approximately the times given, they are not immediately in contact with those in the opposite jaw and it is only about six months after eruption that they start to wear against their complementary teeth.

The eruption of the permanent molar teeth is also a guide to the age of the animal, but the would-be observer may have difficulty in getting even a glimpse of the back teeth of a restless young animal and may well decide that the information to be gleaned from the incisors will suffice his purpose. In any case it is often difficult to differentiate between permanent and temporary cheek teeth, and observation may at best be confined to the number of teeth present.

The small wolf teeth are readily distinguished from the other molars. For practical purposes these may be ignored in ageing, and the remaining cheek teeth numbered 1 to 6 from the front backwards. Numbers, 4, 5 and 6 are not preceded by milk teeth.

The fourth teeth appear at between nine to twelve months, the fifth at two years and the sixth at four years, by which time all the temporary molars will have been succeeded by permanent grinders.

All the permanent teeth are present and in wear by the time a horse is five years old. Thereafter, age is determined by changes in the incisor teeth. It must be understood that these teeth continue to grow throughout the horse's life, pushing out through the gums to compensate for the wearing away of the crowns. Attrition takes place on the biting surfaces (tables) and changes in appearance occur as the tables wear. The rate of wear is fairly uniform, but it can be misleading when animals are reared on sandy soil, which has an abrasive effect, or when, as with Thoroughbreds, they are given hard food early in life.

At five years the corner teeth are just coming into wear, but the enamel which covers the free portion is rolled over and unworn and the teeth have sometimes been likened to seashells in appearance. An unworn permanent incisor has a depression on its surface called the infundibulum or mark, due to an in-folding of the enamel. As the crown is worn down two rings of enamel are seen. It takes about three years' wear to grind the teeth down to the bottom of the in-folding, during which time the mark shows as a dark hollow stained by food.

Thus a five-year-old horse shows the marks on all its incisor teeth but in a six-year-old the marks have gone from the centrals, at seven from the laterals, and at eight from the corners. Although the infundibula have worn away in each case, the sites may still be indicated by irregular rings.

This progress applies only to the lower teeth. Those in the upper jaw have deeper marks which take twice as long to wear away. The upper jaw changes are less consistent, but roughly speaking the marks will have gone from the upper centrals at nine years, the laterals at ten years, and the corners at eleven years.

At seven years it is usual to find that the back corner of the upper corner incisors on each side is not in wear; it forms a projection known as the 'seven year hook'.

The disappearance of the marks is the most accurate indication of the animal's age and it is usual to speak of a horse over eight as 'aged' or 'past mark of mouth', but there are other indications of age after this time and the term aged is also used to mean horses over fifteen years.

At ten years a depression appears in the middle of the tooth on the outer surface of the upper corners. This is 'Galvayne's groove', which by fifteen reaches half way down the tooth, by twenty goes all the way down, by twenty-five has half grown out and by thirty has disappeared. These ages are only approximate, for the groove is not consistent.

The 'dental star' is a yellowish-brown mark which appears on the tables of the incisors at about eight years; it is often not seen on the corners until later. It comes just in front of where the infundibulum was.

The shape of the tables also alters with age. At first they are elliptical, narrow from back to front; by the time the mark has disappeared they are still elliptical but squarer than before. In the aged horse the teeth are triangular with the apices towards the tongue.

When the incisors erupt through the gums they do so more or less at right-angles, and viewed from the side with the head horizontal the incisors form a vertical straight line. As they wear down they project forwards more until, in the very old horse, they are nearly horizontal.

When ageing horses it must be remembered that Thoroughbreds have an arbitrary birthday on 1st January and other horses on 1st May. Teeth erupt earlier in horses bred under intensive systems than in those on free range. The upper teeth usually come through earlier than those in the lower jaw, but being bigger they wear more slowly and look younger.

Part 4
Methods and techniques of training

1 The mentality of the horse

In order to get the best out of any horse, it is necessary first to understand it; genuine communication is possible only through a knowledge of its mental processes.

In spite of a long history of association between the horse and man, many of the primitive instincts the horse developed in the wild have stayed, and still affect its behaviour today. It is important to look back at these early behaviour patterns and the environment that fostered them. The basic physical structure and the mental faculties of the horse have remained virtually the same for 5000 years. The most important characteristics of the horse can be summarised as follows: herd instinct, need for security, the following instinct, love of routine, laziness, excitability, nervousness, sensitivity and courage.

The herd instinct is the strongest of all the horse's basic urges, as its survival in pre-domestication days largely depended on the herd grouping. A horse alone stood little chance of survival. Because of this, horses will naturally want to be with others of their kind. The effects of this urge can be greatly reduced by training, but many horses are reluctant when asked to leave a group, and it is instinct that lies behind most 'nappy' horses' behaviour. The instinct can, however, usefully be exploited during training: a horse will, for example, jump with more enthusiasm if asked to do so at first towards its companions rather than away from them.

Linked with this instinct to be with its fellows is the horse's need for security. In the domestic horse of today security is centred on the stable—or field—in which the horse lives. Horses are generally fairly greedy animals, and there is no doubt that their usually being fed at 'home' also contributes to this. Horses kept on their own are seldom happy, for company also represents security. Horses suddenly isolated will pine not just for companionship but for the security it brings; horses moved to new surroundings will take some time to settle down and regain the temporary loss of confidence occasioned by the move. This is true, though less markedly, even if the horse is in company and is handled by humans it knows and trusts. A horse frequently subjected to strange accommodation—as, for example, a show-jumper travelling to different parts of the country during the summer—will become more adaptable and be less affected by these changes.

When the position of a training area is being considered, the factor of security needs to be borne in mind. If it is placed too close to the stable a horse will find concentration difficult; it should be situated far enough away from the stables—and preferably the proximity of other horses—for distraction to be avoided. It is advisable, however, for a horse, particularly if it is young, to be allowed to become familiar with the area where lessons will take place before they actually begin. Calm is of prime importance in successful training, and only with security will there be calm. A horse in a completely strange field will be looking round, not concentrating on its trainer.

The following instinct of the horse is easy to identify. Like all herd animals, horses were accustomed to looking towards a leader: they are, almost all of them, naturally 'following' animals. This creates, nowadays, a need for a leader that can seldom be satisfied by another horse, though even trained horses will, when out to grass, show tendencies to lead or to follow. In any group of them it is easy to see which horse is 'boss'. It is to man's advantage that most horses have a natural inclination to obey, for it makes them surprisingly co-operative. This becomes less surprising when one realises that in his mastership of the horse—a domination sometimes taken undue advantage of—man is filling a need in the horse which makes his training of it considerably easier.

A solid, inviting cross-country obstacle

A pattern of life which has rhythm, a regular routine, is important to the horse. It encourages security, calm and well-being. It is for this reason that so much emphasis is placed on the importance of regular feeding times and regular exercise. However, an occasional interruption of routine is no bad thing, as the stabled horse without enough activity or any variations in it is likely to become bored. Boredom is a dangerous state of mind which is liable to lead to bad habits and a bad temper.

The love of routine is linked to the horse's natural laziness. In its wild state it spends almost all its time browsing—as, indeed, horses out at grass will do—unless it is disturbed and excited or frightened. Only its willingness to co-operate makes it possible for man to persuade the horse to perform with the amount of energy he requires.

In spite of these characteristics, horses are frequently both excitable and nervous. The horse's ability to run away when danger threatened enabled it in the past to survive predators more crafty or more aggressive than itself. In order to become instantly alert to possibilities of danger, its nervous system had to be highly tuned, and when startled and alarmed now its natural reaction is still to flee. A horse with a rider it trusts can be prevailed upon not to; but it is no good shouting at or abusing a frightened horse, for this will only make matters worse.

Fear is also likely to make a horse excitable, as are conditions that remind it of its wild state— such as galloping—or which it finds unnatural or strange—like being asked to jump. Part of the excitement of hunting and racing comes from the simulation of running with the herd. Obedience produced by training will get over much of the excitability, as the horse will learn to behave calmly in situations that are naturally exciting to it.

It is perhaps strange that in spite of the— already somewhat conflicting—traits of laziness, excitability and nervousness, most horses are also possessed of great courage. Without this courage it is unlikely that they would ever be able to trust humans to the extent that they do.

One important characteristic which is fundamental to our ability to train the horse is its sensitivity. Because it is a non-aggressive animal originally equipped to run away rather than to stay and fight, it has a relatively low pain threshold. In other words, it is very sensitive to touch. Without this sensitivity the subtle leg aids used so unobtrusively on a highly-trained horse would be impossible to achieve. In the early stages of its training the horse responds to aids because it wants to get away from the touch of the leg. This is even more true of the discomfort caused by a bit. The mouth is much more sensitive than most other parts of the body, and a mild bit should always be used until horse and rider have reached a stage of training where the correct use of, say, a double bridle will improve performance. It is less ridiculous than might be supposed to suggest that a horse which pulls badly in a severe bit should be ridden in a bit as mild as a rubber snaffle. With the pain—from which the horse is trying to escape by running away—removed, many horses stop pulling and fighting and will calm down.

As far as training is concerned, perhaps the most useful attribute the horse has is its memory, which is extraordinarily retentive, though some horses are undoubtedly more intelligent than others. As with other animals capable of being highly-trained, there are several points to remember. The first is the importance of making sure that what is being asked of the animal is completely understood and within its capabilities at that time. An imperfectly understood lesson will be wrongly remembered; an animal either mentally or physically unprepared may not be able to carry out a particular exercise. Cause and result must be closely related in time if the result—reward or punishment—is to have any meaning. Thus a horse that has just performed well should be rewarded immediately; one that is being wilful or obstinate must be punished at the time of its bad behaviour. Horses should, incidentally, be sparingly punished. Unsatisfactory behaviour most often results either from imperfect communication or from some outside factor affecting the horse's concentration, calm or confidence. Occasionally, though, it must be admitted, they are just badly behaved, and then they must be treated firmly. A horse always allowed to have its own way will eventually become totally undisciplined and difficult to handle.

2 First steps in training

The early training of a young horse is made much easier if the horse has been accustomed from the start to being handled. Anybody breeding a foal and hoping to train it would be well advised to spend a good deal of time with the foal during the first three years of its life. A prospective trainer buying a three-year-old will also need to devote time to its general handling before any formal training is undertaken.

On these early days the whole future of a horse can depend. It is important to establish from the outset a basis of trust on the part of the horse for the person who is handling it. If the horse learns that it is not going to be hurt or frightened by anything the trainer does, the later lessons will proceed much more smoothly. It should be taught to accept without fear or fuss the presence of the trainer, learn to have its feet picked up, to be groomed, to be led in hand. At this stage it should ideally also become accustomed to the presence and the absence of other horses, and be encouraged to begin to learn concentration and obedience.

All these lessons should be taught gradually and calmly. Unless the horse is deliberately wilful—and horses occasionally can be, at any age—discipline and obedience should be established without any use of force or demonstration of anger on the part of the trainer. A gradual progression of obedience and respect will help the horse in all its later stages of training. If the horse is handled in this way, it should, when the time comes, learn to accept the bit and eventually the saddle and a rider, without undue difficulty.

LUNGEING

The practice of lungeing is in general use in most of the horse countries of the world as a part of the basic training of the horse. The degree of emphasis placed on this exercise and the manner of its execution naturally vary according to the trainer. Some will use the lunge line only for gymnastic exercises designed to supple and strengthen the young horse prior to his being backed; others will rely on lunge work to a far greater extent, regarding it as the foundation for ridden schooling both on the flat and over fences.

Lungeing is not, of course, entirely confined to the training of the young, unbroken horse. It has considerable value in the retraining of the older, spoilt animal and is also used to supple and relax the schooled horse before he is worked under saddle. The essentials of lungeing can be simply described. It is an exercise where the horse circles the trainer, contact between the two being maintained by the line connecting the trainer's hand to the ring fitted on the nosepiece of the horse's cavesson, while the horse's pace is controlled by the trainer's voice and the movements of a long whip held in his other hand.

The principal objects of working on the lunge are:
1. To promote the gradual formation of muscles in the young horse without these being developed in opposition to the weight of the rider. By working the horse in both left- and right-hand circles, equal muscle development on either side of the horse can be ensured.
2. To supple the horse laterally by the equal stretching and contracting of the dorsal, neck and abdominal muscles on each side by the horse's body being bent on the circle.
3. To encourage a tensioning of the spine, induced by the horse stretching his head and neck forwards and downwards. This causes the back to round and the hind legs to be further engaged under the body. The proper engagement of each hind leg is made easier on the circle, as the inside hind must be brought further under the body if the horse is to maintain his balance.

4. To increase the flexion of the joints as a result of greater and more supple muscular development.

5. As far as is possible to flex the spine of the horse and to correct his natural asymmetry.

6. To improve the horse's balance as a result of the increased engagement of the hocks.

These are the physical benefits of lungeing; the mental discipline is equally important, particularly the development of the horse's powers of concentration. Properly carried out, lunge work helps to produce a calm horse accustomed to the *habit* of obedience. It is in this exercise that the horse learns to obey the first of the aids, the voice.

The other vitally important lesson that lungeing teaches is the essential requirement of the riding horse: free forward movement. The urge to go forward is as much the result of a trained mental attitude as it is a disciplined physical movement.

At a later stage of his training the horse may be given his early jumping lessons on the lunge, unhampered by the weight of a rider. Lungeing is also a useful way of exercising a horse who for one reason or another cannot be ridden, or for settling an over-fresh horse before the rider mounts him. Fifteen minutes on the lunge is frequently enough to take the edge off an unruly horse and so avoid the ignominy of being bucked off.

The equipment required for lungeing consists of a cavesson, a lunge line of tubular web material fitted with a swivel hook to fasten on the cavesson rings, and a long whip with a thong. In due course a pair of side-reins will be needed. These are attached first from the cavesson and then from a snaffle fitted both to it and to rings placed at varying heights on a body roller. In some cases trainers dispense with the roller and prefer to attach the side-reins to a saddle. The disadvantage of a saddle is that the height adjustment of the side-reins cannot be made as precisely as it can when a roller is used.

An essential part of lungeing is the availability of an enclosed space in which the horse can work without distraction.

The methods used to teach the horse to work on the lunge will vary according to the particular preferences of the trainer, but whatever methods are employed it is first essential to teach the horse to move freely forward when being led in hand. To make sure that the horse understands what is required of him an assistant frequently leads him round on a circle until he has learnt the words of command. The horse can then be asked to perform work on the circle.

The side-reins are brought into use as a method of encouraging a steady and correct head carriage. Whether they are fitted to the cavesson or to the bit, however, they should always be adjusted at full length until the horse takes up the slack and begins to seek out the bit and to 'accept' it. Only when he does this is it safe to work—for periods of only a few minutes—on shortened reins.

When a horse is being lunged the side-reins take the place of the rider's hands, and the whip acts as a substitute for the legs in pushing the horse into contact with the bit. Only a few trainers lunge a young horse directly from the bit, though the French method is used to place the horse 'on the bit'. It is, however, a method which really belongs to the more advanced stages of the horse's training, and it should be practised only by experienced horsemen.

Specialised aspects of lungeing apart, in general the exercise should be regarded as an essential and valuable part of every horse's training programme.

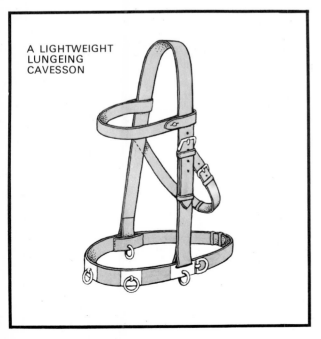

A LIGHTWEIGHT LUNGEING CAVESSON

This sequence of photographs demonstrates progressive stages in work on the lunge. (1) The young horse is first led round the trainer by an assistant, who then (2) moves to a position inside and slightly behind the circling horse. (3) A good, free trot with the horse moving well forward. (4) Crossing a low grid of logs or cavalletti is a valuable balancing exercise as well as a useful introduction to jumping: the horse is led before being sent down the grid at the full length of the lunge rein. (5) A jump in excellent style over an improvised obstance. Note the sympathetic contact maintained by the lunge rein. (6) The horse stands square at halt on the circle.

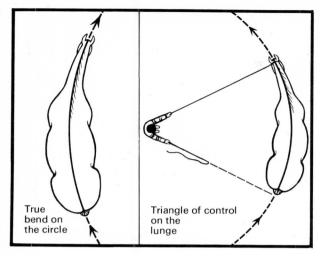

True bend on the circle

Triangle of control on the lunge

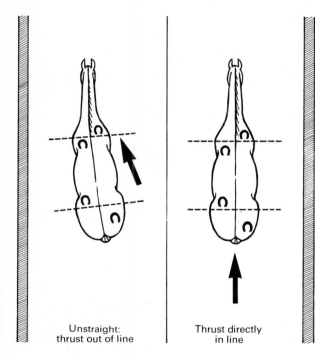

Unstraight: thrust out of line

Thrust directly in line

LESSONS UNDER SADDLE

Once the horse has been backed it should continue its lungeing lessons, both with and without the addition of the rider. By this time the lungeing process will have become familiar and the horse will know what is expected of it. It will be helped to get used to carrying a rider if it first has to do so during lessons that it already understands. Only when the horse has fully accepted the presence of the rider should he begin to take any active part, gradually increasing his participation until the horse is responding to the rider as well as to the trainer on the ground.

The objects of working the horse on the lunge apply equally to the elementary exercises carried out under saddle. In addition, once the horse has learned to accept the rider's weight it must learn to carry it properly as well. It must also, of course, be taught the elementary language of the aids so that it can understand what it is being asked to do. All horses, not necessarily just young ones, greatly benefit from proper schooling. A well-schooled hunter, for example, will not only be a much more pleasant ride, but a much safer one than an unschooled horse; it will be more obedient, more comfortable. will both get less tired and tire its rider less. A well-schooled horse will perform whatever is required of it to maximum effect with minimum effort; the reverse is true of an unschooled animal.

Impulsion is the most important factor of all in schooling—without it, none of the schooling exercises can be properly performed. The horse should first be introduced to the school at the walk, the rider concentrating on riding into each corner rather than allowing the horse to cut across the corners. From the outset the horse should be encouraged to respond to the lightest possible aids; if it does not respond to a light use of the legs the aids should be reinforced by light taps with a schooling whip (which is long enough to be used without the rider altering the position of his hand on the rein) rather than by letting the aid degenerate into a kick.

The horse should be taught to move forward at walk, trot and canter and within each gait to vary the pace. The variations are the ordinary walk (or trot or canter), and the collected and extended walk. At ordinary walk the horse moves freely forward with long strides, a light contact with the bit being maintained. For collection, the stride is shortened by a strengthening of the pushing force of seat and legs on the part of the rider encouraging a greater engagement of the hind legs under the horse's body, and by a slight closing of the hands on the reins to contain the increase in impulsion. In the extended walk the driving aids are maintained but the horse moves forward on a released rein.

The trot is the most valuable pace for schooling. The ordinary trot should be energetic, with plenty of drive from the quarters, the horse covering with its hind feet the tracks of the forefeet. In collected trot the forehand is lightened with the increase in impulsion, the stride is shortened and becomes more vigorous. When the extension at trot is asked for, the horse will lengthen its stride and increase speed in response to the increased driving force of the rider's legs while a light contact with the bit is maintained. Both collected and extended trot should be requested only for short periods.

The rider can either rise with the trot or keep to the sitting trot. The latter should only be introduced when the horse's back muscles are sufficiently developed and it has become reasonably well balanced.

Cantering in the school should only take place when the horse's action is controlled, even and active at walk and trot, and when it has learned the necessary adjustment to balance, necessitated by the presence of the rider's weight, by being asked to canter while out hacking. It is easiest to teach the horse to lead on the correct leg on a circle—that is, with the inside leg—by asking for the transition to canter with the horse bent very slightly in the direction of the movement. It is important to ask the horse to canter from a controlled trot with good impulsion, not to allow it to trot faster and faster until it eventually falls into canter. If the horse strikes off on the wrong lead, it should be brought back to trot and then asked to canter again when balance and impulsion have been re-established.

At all paces, the fullest possible use should be made of the school, the direction being changed by riding diagonally across it and

A young horse being schooled under saddle.

Half-circle
to the right at walk.

Circle right
at sitting trot.

Transition
from trot to canter.

circles of varying sizes being made.

The horse will benefit at a fairly early stage by the introduction of poles laid on the ground, over which it should be asked to walk and trot, and later on by the use of cavalletti. There should be no interruption in the rhythm of the horse's stride, and it is important that the poles, which should be placed down the long side of the school, should be correctly spaced and adjusted to the stride of each horse. At this stage the poles should not be considered as an introduction to jumping, though one of their objects is to lay the foundations for it. They are introduced to help the horse develop suppleness, maintain an even length of stride, improve its balance and pick up its feet. When the horse has become thoroughly accustomed to negotiating the poles when they are laid in a straight line, they can be placed on the circumference of a circle, thus combining their own functions with those of work on the circle.

During all its early training, the horse will be learning to move freely forward, to move straight, to develop evenly and to become supple and balanced. Work on the circle is the best way by far of achieving all these ends.

There are several general points to be borne in mind during the early stages of training. All horses—and young horses in particular—will feel exuberant and have natural outbursts of high spirits at times. Obviously, it is preferable if these do not take place during a lesson, and it is therefore advisable to allow the horse a period at liberty every day. If the horse is being kept out at grass it will have this opportunity in the normal course of events; stabled horses should also be allowed an hour or two in the paddock when they can work off their high spirits and relax. Secondly, concentration is an acquired art; only a little concentration should be asked of the horse at first, and as its training advances work in the school should be broken up by a relaxed ride. Lessons should always be kept short, and be brought to an end before the horse shows any signs of becoming bored— boredom prevents concentration and encourages disobedience. An intelligent trainer will in fact use the hacking periods to advantage as well: riding the horse up and down hills and trotting it over uneven ground are just two examples of ways in which the lessons of the school can be extended to help the horse develop its muscles, balance and wind.

ELEMENTS OF RIDING

In considering any stage of training of the horse it is necessary also to consider the possible effects of the rider on the horse's movement. A horse at liberty will at an early age learn how to balance itself effectively; it will be able to vary pace and speed, to change direction and to turn, without losing balance. The addition of the weight of a rider on its back, however, will necessitate considerable adaptation on the part of the horse, which will need understanding and assistance from its rider.

In order for horse and rider to become a successful combination, the rider must work as closely as possible *with* the horse. One important aspect of this is for the rider to develop a well-balanced, supple seat. The correct position of the rider resembles that of a man standing, with bent knees, rather than one sitting in a chair. The head should be held up, looking out over the horse's ears rather than down at its withers or at the ground. The back and shoulders should be held straight, but not stiffly. The seat should be positioned deep in the saddle, with the legs hanging down naturally so that the heel falls in a straight line with hip and shoulder, and the toe of the foot faces to the front at a slight upward angle. The rider should push down and forwards into the centre of the saddle, gripping with a relaxed, not a tense, grip with the thighs. Gripping with the knees and lower leg will tend to push the rider up out of the saddle rather than down into it.

It is important for the rider to develop a seat that is secure, supple and completely independent of the reins. Flexibility is obtained by relaxing the muscles, balance by the rider adapting his own distribution of weight to the shifting centre of balance of the horse.

There are various exercises which help the rider to achieve a correct seat. Riding without reins (while the horse is exercised on the lunge, for example, or in the school) will ensure that no dependence is placed on the reins in order to maintain balance; riding without stirrups encourages the rider to develop a strong seat and to move with the horse as it moves. As the rider's balance improves and his own muscles develop, he should ride without stirrups not only at the slow paces but for school movements and jumping as well.

Because of the importance of a harmony in balance between horse and rider, the rider should understand how the horse's weight is naturally distributed and how its centre of balance alters as it changes pace. Only rarely is the horse's weight evenly distributed over all four limbs. When the horse moves at speed or is extended, its weight shifts to the forehand as it covers the ground with longer, lower strides, and the centre of balance therefore moves forward. With increased collection the stride is shortened, the forehand lightened, the quarters and hind legs engaged further under the body, and the weight and centre of balance thus move to the rear. The rider should at all times be positioned as closely as possible over the horse's own centre of balance, and it is for this reason that the different seats have been developed for different riding activities. A jockey will ride so that his weight falls as far forward as possible, while a dressage rider will use a seat with much longer stirrups—which also helps the subtle, accurate application of the aids—and his weight falling further to the rear.

A full understanding of the aids and how they should be applied is also of prime importance. The aids are the language which the rider uses to communicate to the horse what he wishes it to do; imperfectly understood and incorrectly applied, they limit rather than improve this system of communication. An inexperienced rider should be given instruction in the use of the aids on a trained horse which will respond when the aids are correctly applied, for he will then be able to feel the result of his application of them. An untrained horse will quickly become confused by unsure use of the aids and will find it increasingly difficult to learn the language.

The natural aids are the legs, hands, body and voice. The legs encourage impulsion and the development of free forward movement, which come from active engagement of the quarters and hind legs, and also control the movement and position of the rear part of the horse. The hands guide the forehand and the positioning of the horse's head and neck. Used in combination, they encourage an increase in collection or extension. The combined use of leg and hand should, however, be restricted to a horse reasonably advanced in its training and understanding of the aids; a young horse should at first be given clear and simple instructions of either leg or hand, used separately.

Equal action of both the rider's legs will increase impulsion and direct the horse straight forward. A pressure applied unequally will encourage the horse to bend round the inside leg, used on the girth, while the outside leg is applied behind the girth and controls the quarters.

The use of the hands is divided into the 'simple' reins, the direct or open rein and the indirect or contrary rein, and the more advanced 'reins of opposition'. The use of the direct rein should first be taught to the horse, and the indirect rein (neck rein) introduced at a later stage.

The weight of the rider's body, as has been explained, has a considerable effect on the balance of the horse, and can therefore be used as an additional aid. The voice, used either soothingly on an excitable horse or more sharply on a lazy animal, is generally also

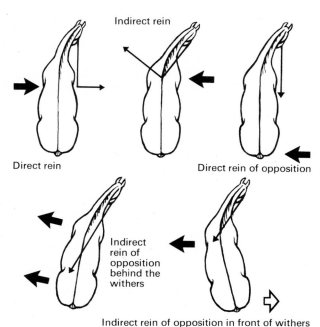

Indirect rein

Direct rein

Direct rein of opposition

Indirect rein of opposition behind the withers

Indirect rein of opposition in front of withers

effective, particularly as it is one aid to which the horse will have become accustomed even before its formal training begins.

An unfit rider will be less able to apply the aids correctly and to use the advantages of a correct, secure and supple seat than will a rider who is fit. Similarly, the horse must be allowed gradually to develop its muscles and to learn to balance itself properly. Most horses, left to themselves, develop unevenly. As a rule, because of the way they lie in the womb, they are likely to develop stronger muscles down the right side of the back, a tendency which is encouraged by their usually being led in hand from the near side when young. They should learn to lead equally well from both the near and off sides in order to avoid this muscular block being further built up. At a later stage in training, work on the circle will help to reduce this natural stiffness. It is perhaps advisable initially to teach the horse by working in the direction it finds easiest (i.e. on the left circle), but as soon as it has understood what is required, work should proceed on the right circle in order to encourage evenness. In the same way, most horses will at first be more comfortable to ride on one diagonal than the other at the trot, but the diagonal should be changed both during school work and while hacking. All these factors will help contribute towards making a horse that is evenly developed, well balanced and responsive.

3 Advanced training

DRESSAGE

Advanced dressage, often called *haute école*, defines not so much a particular set of movements as the refined execution of them. It is their expression rather than their nature which classifies them, and the most essential ingredient of this expression is lightness.

What is lightness in this context? A painter, Max Liebermann, has said that 'art is doing without'; and the lightness that turns equitation into an art is the result of eliminating from movements executed by the horse any force or effort that does not directly contribute to them. Whatever additional effort the horse makes is a resistance which detracts from lightness. Thus lightness is contingent upon the rider's knowledge and tact as well as on the horse's skill and training, which will successfully have straightened it and developed in it a permanent urge to go freely forward. It is only possible to achieve lightness once these important preliminaries have been firmly established.

The urge to advance is called impulsion, and

has been achieved when, rider's hands permitting, the horse will advance on its own, regardless of the nature of a prior movement, and when the slightest pressure of a rider's leg will shift its haunches. Straightness comes with the disappearance of all the horse's undesirable natural asymmetry; once this has been achieved the hind legs will follow in the exact track of the forelegs and the haunches function uniformly, causing the horse's weight to be correctly distributed. Thus a picture of harmony is produced: harmony between haunches and shoulders, haunch and haunch, shoulder and shoulder.

There is no precise distinction between 'ordinary' training and dressage, or between 'ordinary' dressage and *haute école*, though there are some stages of advanced training in dressage which only those specialising in this branch of equitation will need to study. It may, however, be interesting to others—both as non-specialist horsemen and as spectators—to know something of what is involved.

Before any attempt is made at collection, the

A dressage horse during a test moving forward on a circle into the centre of the arena.

horse's paces must have attained regularity and maximum development. There is no real relation between trot and canter, and work to to improve both paces may therefore go forward along parallel, largely independent lines. Work out of doors is preferable to work in the school for this, as the natural impulsion will be greater outside, the horse can be kept on a straight line for longer, and the going offers a variety not available in the school. For instance, it should be possible to trot the horse up a slope, with the consequent flow of weight to the forehand and relief to the quarters; the neck will stretch and the hind legs be engaged much more than on the flat. It is also better to work out of doors towards achieving even strides of the trot by sitting more often to the less frequently used diagonal.

The remedies for crookedness in a horse are work on the circle, shoulder-in and counter-canter. A horse that is naturally bent to the left, for example, requires work particularly on a right-hand circle, when he will bend round the acting right leg, on the right shoulder-in, the true canter on a right-hand circle and the counter-canter track to the left. The spine is straightened by exercises such as these both on the circle and on elements of curves, and is suppled longitudinally by others.

Before going any further let us define the much misused term 'collection'. Collection is a combination of *ramener* and *mise en main* accompanied by lowered haunches and engaged hind legs. *Ramener* signifies a narrowing of the angle between head and neck, the poll remaining at the apex; the *mise en main* is a relaxation at the jaw accompanying the *ramener*. In this way the horse is collected 'above' as well as 'below', along a topline compressed by tightening the natural undulations of the spine.

Ramener and elevation of the neck are obtained progressively and simultaneously by the advance of the entire body towards the head. With a low neck the *ramener* is easily—all too easily—attained, for there is a tendency to overbend; while raising the neck excessively results in a hollowing of the back and misplacement of the hocks. It is essential to work towards *ramener* without haste; do not try to raise the head more than is necessary in order to avoid overbending. Once the quarters are supple and the hind legs increasingly engaged, the haunches

will place the forehand in a higher position. This 'relative' elevation is important.

Collection itself is characterised by the flexibility of both the front and the back of the horse, making it work on 'short bases' to give a flexible equilibrium with great multilateral mobility. This improves both the horse's paces and his changes of direction and speed.

As soon as exercises have made the horse generally reasonably flexible the *ramener* may be introduced. It may now be necessary to deal with a 'contracted mouth'. Any resistance— whether or not it originates in the mouth—will cause contraction there, and thus a relaxed mouth usually indicates the absence of resistance. In the same way that the mouth conveys the general state of the horse, a rider able to finger the mouth into relaxing well will himself help to do away with any incipient resistance more successfully than attempting to do so by using other aids. Of course this is only possible where the resistance neither borders on revolt nor comes from any permanent rigidity of the horse.

The half-turn on the forehand may be helpful at this stage in a horse's training, as are local encouragements by hand, known as flexions. While the mouth prepared by them will doubtless yield more easily, abuse of this method nullifies the effect by limiting it to the mouth itself, without the rest of the body being affected by the benefits of the flexing actions.

The relaxation is shown by a tongue movement similar to that produced by swallowing, and makes the bit ride up and fall back into place with a soft but unmistakeable noise. A slightly opening mouth is enough for this gesture which, quite slow, ought to be devoid of nervousness. The well-trained horse's mouth is mobilised in this way at the rider's very first prompting and ceases as soon as the prompting hand ceases to act.

Before trying the direct flexions leading to the *ramener*, one practises the lateral flexions, which with most horses are indispensable. Their purpose is a gradual suppling of the sides of the head at the point where it joins the neck. By increased tension of the direct rein and yielding of the opposite one, the horse's head is drawn sideways, the trainer being careful to ask for only a little at a time and to keep the head straight on its vertical plane so as to avoid a twist at the poll.

The work on two tracks supples and develops muscles which play a minor part in travel on only one track, increasing the engagement of the hind legs, loosening the shoulders and improving the horse's balance through swift changes between straight and oblique travel and movement from right to left at the half-pass through counter-changes of hand on two tracks. If this sentence covers many lines, the exercises cover a lot of ground in training!

This is particularly true of shoulder-in, which may be performed in various ways. We shall deal here only with that used in training, not for test or show, because it is the most easily stopped and restarted. The horse, uniformly bent in its entire length, moves forward in the direction of its convex side. The size of the circle determines the degree of the bend, and must be dictated by the stage of training the horse has reached. Detaching the horse from this circle by use of the inside rein, which takes on an intermediate rein effect, a few steps of shoulder-in are performed. To stop the movement, all that is required is to ride the horse forward on

the circle, where it travels again on one track but still holds the bend for an instant return to the shoulder-in.

In the half-pass the horse is kept straight, except for a slight *placer* (lateral flexion of the head) causing it to look where it is going. The main difficulty here is to maintain the impulsion and to obtain the engagement of the inside hind—that is, the near hind in half-passing from right to left. If the horse has been trained to engage its hind leg at the prompting of the rider's leg on the same side, this engagement of the inside hind can be controlled. Almost the entire value of the half-pass lies in this, for without proper engagement of the inside hind the outside one will cross so little as to rob the exercise of its purpose, which is to improve engagement by bending hip, stifle and hock joints.

The half-pass may be performed either on straight lines, with the head to the wall, the tail to the wall, or on the diagonal. It is particularly interesting when practised on the circle, where the horse may be placed in one of two positions: the forelegs travelling on a circle either inside

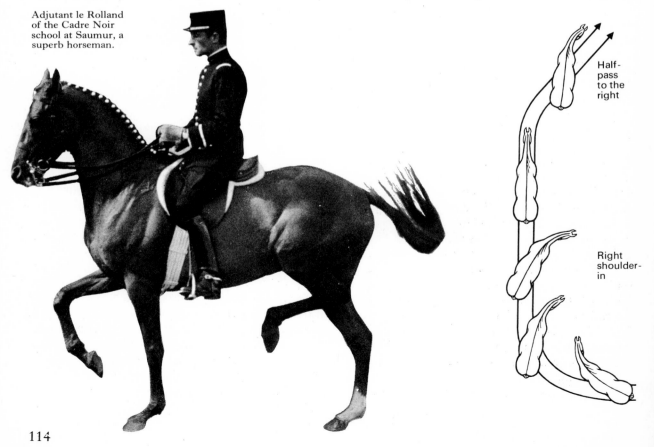

Adjutant le Rolland of the Cadre Noir school at Saumur, a superb horseman.

Half-pass to the right

Right shoulder-in

114

that travelled by the hind legs, or outside it. In the first case the exercise is called haunches out, and in the second, haunches in. Using both these methods, the trainer increases at will the crossing effort of the hind legs over that of the forelegs—haunches out—or of the forelegs over the hind legs—haunches in.

Work at the canter is at first performed at the horse's natural speed, where it can hold a satisfactory balance. The pace is slowed only gradually after the gait itself has been straightened in work on the circle, chiefly at the counter-canter.

When tackling flying changes of leg one must beware of two common faults: an exaggerated slowing down of the pace, and too imperative an intervention of the aids. The flying change can be simply taught: counter-canter in a circle, keeping the horse at a steady pace but tightening the circle to the limit of the horse's ability, then neatly but smoothly reverse the aids, thus demanding a strike-off on the other lead. Repeat the same exercise with increasingly clear demands for a definite change of direction towards the centre of the circle. After a few days of tuition the changes will come easily. Do not, however, ask the horse for changes of lead at every fourth, third or second stride until he has completely mastered single changes.

Single changes are first asked of the horse from the outside to the inside lead on the circle, then on straight lines, and eventually on the circle again but now from the inside to the outside lead. At this stage of training one also goes back to working on transitions, for if the horse is able to strike off correctly and calmly from a walk, canter three strides and return to a walk, he is ready for flying changes at every fourth stride. When the inserted strides at the canter come down smoothly to two, then to one, the horse is ready for flying changes at every third, then every second stride. For changes at every stride, return to the circle and canter on the inside lead: circle once or twice and then ask for a change of leg followed immediately by a second change. Achieve just one change at every stride (track to the left, track to the right), and the horse may be considered as good as trained to them.

The pirouette at the canter is a combination of two movements—that of the pace proper and that of the pirouette itself—and should be worked out in two parts. The prerequisites are a correct and ready performance of a pirouette at the walk and the ability to obtain a single calm stride of canter from walk. In pirouette, the horse's hind legs mark time in the required pace while the forelegs circle round them.

After one full pirouette at the walk, request a second in the same place but this time inserting a single stride of canter during it. Very gradually three or four strides at canter are inserted. This achieved, a half-pirouette at the canter is requested in a corner, at first using the walls of the school as a frame and to encourage the horse to position itself to execute on the spot the pirouette, a movement it already knows, remaining throughout at the slowed canter. The rider should intervene only to maintain the pace and indicate the direction of the half-pirouette. Improvement comes with half-pirouettes being achieved ever further away from the wall, to begin with entering the movement from a half-pass. Only when the half-pirouette is performed easily, away from the walls, from a straight line on a single track, unimpaired in pace or lightness and without any rush, is the horse ready for the complete pirouette.

Passage and *piaffe* are both derived from the trot. Like it, they consist of alternate contact of the diagonals with the ground. Only the times of suspension (both of the total and of each diagonal) are longer. *Passage* is a slow, shortened, very collected, elevated and cadenced trot, while *piaffe* is a collected trot on the spot.

Passage may be induced by slowing the trot and, by burdening the resting diagonal, lengthening the time of the other's suspension, the hands doing the burdening by a neck-reining action, the legs reinforcing the trotting action of the horse. Similarly, the *piaffe* may be reached by slowing down the *passage*.

It is in fact preferable to teach these two movements together. Working into *passage* by slowing the trot, and then into *piaffe* by taking off from the trot, facilitates the transitions between the two airs, which are more difficult than either of the airs themselves. There are several ways of doing this, but the usual method of training is to work the horse along the wall, with the trainer on foot using a longish whip. Without keeping the horse from advancing, the length of stride is gradually reduced by the hand holding the reins, while the other maintains the limbs in activity by light touches of the whip to the top of the croup, the chest or the legs. When, still advancing a little, the horse begins to give a few regular strides of *piaffe*, the lessons are continued under saddle. Initially a second rider may be used, the aids coming first from the trainer on foot only, then from rider and trainer together, and eventually with the rider alone determining the movement. Only two or three strides should be taken strictly on the spot, and the horse should always be ridden forwards on completion of the exercise.

Some of the movements discussed here are difficult ones which only a specialist dressage partnership need know. Others, however, are quite simple to achieve if the necessary groundwork in the horse's training has been thoroughly understood and carefully carried out. It is worth remembering that successful advanced dressage is as much a matter of executing simple movements superlatively well—with maximum lightness, straightness, balance and suppleness—as it is of performing the airs of *haute école*.

JUMPING AND EVENTING

It is no paradox to say that the training of a jumper or eventer takes place primarily on the flat, not over fences. The best of training cannot give a horse jumping aptitude where nature has denied it, but by exercising its body, teaching it skills and making it manageable, training can develop whatever capacities the horse does possess. Thus elementary training on the flat is the same for hunters, jumpers, event horses or those specialising in dressage, though the emphasis placed on the various exercises will differ according to the career the horse will eventually be asked to follow.

To begin with, you cannot do much with any horse that does not obey readily; and since submissiveness is a matter of physical and mental interaction you must first gain, then keep, the horse's trust while developing it to make it able, not just willing, to obey. The kindest horse becomes nappy if overtaxed, and the most able jumper stops and runs out if allowed to get the upper hand. Body and mind are thus inter-

related, and you must know your horse in order to know how best to use it.

Although there cannot be an exact system of training uniformly applicable to all future jumpers or eventers, there are some general rules for any successful training programme. Never ask for an effort or movement unless the horse has been prepared for it; never extend any particular lesson beyond an hour—preferably divide the lesson into two or three short sessions instead; never end a lesson with a tired horse; never pursue two aims at once.

Any horse worthy of being considered trained must reach the level of the FEI horse trials dressage test, which includes only those movements fundamental to the general training process. The jumper and eventer require less collection than the dressage horse, though they must be able to engage their hind legs properly, and have a slightly convex crest and a nearly vertical head carriage to allow the bit maximum effect and the hand action to be conveyed along a properly rounded topline all the way to the quarters. Perfect straightness is not required of them provided they do not deviate on a straight line; but instant, unhesitating forward movement at the slightest prompting of the legs is essential.

Transitions in pace must be effected effortlessly, without the horse fighting or evading the hand. Since this obedience is just as important for changes of direction as for transitions, mounted exercises over fences should not be attempted until smooth control of speed and direction has become second nature.

Although one trains concurrently on the flat and over fences, we will deal here with each part separately. A word first about conditioning, an adjunct to training which in preparing a jumper, not to mention an eventer, plays a very important part. It is a complex process, consisting of outdoor work to develop muscle and wind, and a diet in keeping with the work expected and with the horse's particular temperament as well as supervised physical care, from daily grooming to the sophisticated science of 'interval training'.

Whenever we speak of lessons, we mean a session either acquainting the horse with new movements or, with those already familiar to it, improving their performance. Since any lesson exacts a sustained mental and physical strain on the horse, they should be kept short, even if it means repeating them fairly often. What we call work is performed out of doors, without the necessity of clock-watching. Its chief object is to develop muscle, wind and balance, though during the periods of work we can also usefully check up on the progress made during lessons. Initially work consists of long stretches at the walk, and rather short but regular ones at the trot increased progressively to eight miles or so. Eventually the horse should be able to maintain a good, controlled gallop for between three and four miles. Good muscles and sound limbs are second in importance only to perfectly functioning lungs, heart and digestion. The walk develops all the muscles without tiring them; the trot adds sturdiness to both muscles and joints; and the gallop increases lung power.

Let us deal with lessons on the flat first. Once the horse's confidence has been safely gained, forward movement becomes our chief occupation. In taking over a new horse, green or not, the wise horseman returns to basics and works back up through the successive phases. The first rule should always be not to act with legs and hands at once. When the legs act they must do so neatly, and both hands advance to where contact with the mouth is lost. Conversely, the legs must become inert when the reins tighten for a slowing down of pace or for halt. As progress is made, legs and hands will remain in permanent contact, but both will always still yield slightly before the other pair acts. This includes hand yielding to hand and leg to leg, as when a single hand changes direction or a single leg shifts the haunches, the other having previously given way. It makes the lesson so much easier for both rider and horse.

Even a spurred heel may be incapable of obtaining correct forward movement from a horse that leans on the leg, backs or rears. These are great evils, requiring strong remedies that may be beyond the competence of the average rider. For him we recommend the use of 'rigid reins', which is not only an uncomplicated method but also cannot blemish the horse. Two wooden sticks, ideally polo sticks, are strapped on to the upper eye of a curb bit fitted with its chain on a tighter link than usual, the sticks being cut to a length permitting the rider

comfortably to hold their opposite ends when seated normally in the saddle. From the halt his legs alone request the forward movement, and if there is a defence the hands move ahead vigorously, driving the horse's head and neck forward. This advance of the weight will carry the horse along with it. Rearing under these conditions becomes impossible, and after a few days of treatment the legs alone are almost always enough to persuade the horse to move forward. The only skill required is to combine the action of the rigid reins with that of the legs. Feeling powerless to fight this combination, the horse submits morally, which is what matters; it is never enough to parry a defence against his disobedience—it must be destroyed.

Once forward movement is safely assured, we look for lateral mobility of the haunches. Half-turns on the forehand and the single leg having acquired meaning, we proceed to half-turns on the haunches, and when the legs are sufficiently in control both to prompt forward movement and to shift the haunches, the hands in their turn may begin to exercise control over the effects of the legs.

A puller will act in one of two ways. He either lets himself be carried by the hand, a matter of balance, or he will fight, trying to evade the hand by stretching out his neck and increasing his speed. In both cases the horse must be refused the contact he requires. Intermittent hand action—half-halts in the first case, closing and opening the fingers firmly but gently with steady hands for the second—will do the trick.

We also teach the horse to yield to the opening rein, to neck rein and respond to the direct rein of opposition, and both during lessons and, most particularly, out of doors, exercise it in neck stretching. First at the walk, at the halt if need be, but eventually at a rising trot the neck is stretched when prompted by the hands sliding gently along the reins from the horse's withers to the rider's chest. This exercise is particularly useful because it helps the horse to find and improve his new balance under the rider: the hands not only permit but encourage the forward movement prompted by the legs; the confidence the horse gains in a smoothly-acting hand causes it to seek contact with the hand. It supples and muscles the back as well as the neck—particularly at the base—and

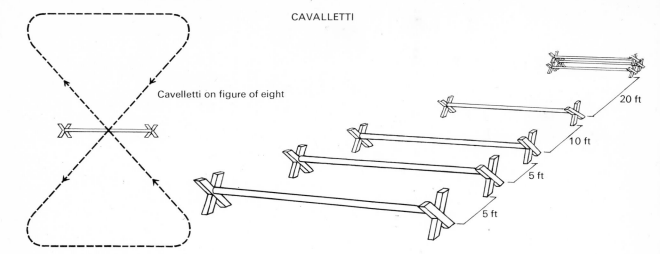

CAVALLETTI

Cavelletti on figure of eight

20 ft

10 ft

5 ft

5 ft

in the right direction; rounding the entire top-line in a convex line it promotes the engagement of the hind legs; and the overall streamlining produced leads to paces covering more ground, without which one cannot even begin to think of collection.

There are three further useful exercises the horse should learn. Shoulder-in leads to the desired degree of collection, supples the horse in all its length, sets it increasingly on the haunches and also gives it assurance in lateral travel. Bent on a circle, the horse describes it once or twice under good impulsion, then leaves it to execute a few steps to the side. The inside rein (left on a left circle for the left shoulder-in) acts as a counter-rein of opposition behind the withers, the legs maintain the forward movement while the horse always remains bent. Just a few steps should be executed, then return the horse to the circle, do another few side steps and back to the circle, and so on.

Rein back is an excellent way to improve engagement of the hind legs, though it must be put off until the rider's legs are sure to obtain instant free forward movement. If not, since its entire value depends on the transitions from walk to rein back to walk, the exercise might do more harm than good.

Counter-canter is best first taught out of doors, where no walls impede us from accustoming the horse to cantering without a change of lead on widely-looped serpentines and without any constraint by the aids. As ease in doing this increases the loops can be tightened, and the

only real difficulty is for the rider not to disturb the balance of his horse.

These exercises, carefully and correctly taught, will enormously improve the balance, suppleness and obedience of the horse.

Now one may start work on the lunge line over cavalletti. The cavalletti (round, not square-cut poles) are set to about eight inches for work at the trot and separated, at least at first, by one of the horse's normal strides. This distance is gradually increased to lengthen the stride. Before approaching the cavalletti the horse should be sufficiently warmed up for the trainer to be able to maintain an active trot. From a single pole and then just two, he will graduate to five or six. While only two poles are in use more than one stride should separate them, so the horse does not mistake them for a single 'fence'. By doubling the distance between them we oblige the horse to take another stride.

Work over cavalletti under saddle should be done at a rising trot to relieve the horse's back. It is an exercise that improves balance, works the back muscles in the proper way, stretches the neck and develops the horse's shoulder movement.

The worst faults in a horse—whether these arise out of ignorance or vice—are cured on the flat; but it is over fences that the worst fault of the rider is generally apparent: his tendency to make his horse jump too often and too high. Wherever possible, the horse should not be expected to perform under saddle anything it has not already done at liberty before, and most

Captain Raimondo
d'Inzeo and the
Irish-bred Bellevue.
The wall stands at
7 ft. 2 in.

itself properly round uprights, work more at the trot and practise neck stretching over the fences. A horse not stretching properly over spreads should be encouraged to do so by having a pole positioned on the ground at a suitable distance on the landing side.

To help the horse get going, one might let three or four cavalletti precede the fence. They should be set up at maximum height (about one and a half feet), and the distance between them adjusted accordingly. They will also encourage the horse to take off at the right distance from the fence itself.

The next stage is to combine the two kinds of fences, first by setting up an upright followed by a spread. First these should be separated by three normal strides, this distance gradually being reduced down to one stride and then to just one very short one, to teach the horse to make maximum use of its abilities without relying on speed. Once this exercise is being successfully performed reverse the positions of the fences and repeat it.

Once the horse is going happily, quietly and freely at liberty, lessons under saddle can begin. The first fences, at a height far below the horse's scope, should be approached slowly. Return to walk between each jump, trotting or cantering only for the last few strides before each obstacle, for by doing so you will oblige the horse fully to use itself, and will have increased control over him at the same time.

When none of this work poses problems work on training courses can begin. The speeds required in competition can be practised, for the horse must be able to approach a fence with

exercises should be performed at the trot. Such are the general rules. I personally do not recommend the use of a ground-line or guard-rail before a fence except perhaps with an exceedingly awkward horse or one at the very outset of its training, for it will teach the horse to judge its fences by the foot rather than by the top, a bad habit later in competitive jumping. The fences used for training should be wide along their length and have thick, brightly-coloured poles.

We want the horse to use its neck correctly, to raise its shoulders and to stretch properly over a spread. Depending on its natural form over uprights and spreads respectively, em-phasise work over one sort of fence or the other. All poles on uprights should be in the same plane and in sufficient numbers to keep the fence from looking hollow. Low, wide oxers make the best novice spread fences; once these are raised, watch out again for hollowness, and make them more inviting by building them in an ascending line. If the horse fails to wrap

An inviting indoor
jumping course.

long or short strides to order, depending on the nature of the fence itself and its relationship with the rest of the course. So variations of speed at the canter are now requested, both on the flat and over fences. Begin by counting the normal strides taken between two points, and then either rein in and push with the legs after each stride, to shorten it, or with legs pushing and hands rhythmically accompanying the movements of the neck, lengthen it.

The horse should be taught to jump both upright and spread fences at an angle. Construct jumps that can be approached from either side, and ride the horse through a figure of eight with the fence at its centre. The loops should at first be narrow enough for the horse to reach the fence almost straight; as the loops widen, the angle of approach widens too. This exercise works wonders with horses that have a tendency to run out always to the same side. If you have a horse that runs out to the left, approach the fence from the left so that it is almost impossible for the horse to turn away to that side. To make doubly sure, stay on the near lead for your right leg to keep the haunches left and oppose a change in that direction.

If your horse is skilled in turning in the air it will land over a fence facing a new direction, which will save precious seconds in a speed competition. This turn is made during suspension. If the rider wishes to turn left on landing, he should turn the horse's head squarely to the left during the jump, tightening the left rein while the right hand yields and the left leg acts well behind the girth.

Introduce your horse gradually to different kinds of obstacles. The first banks, open water, lake and drop jumps he is asked to negotiate should cause no trouble if they are small and easy and an experienced horse gives the novice a lead. If hunting can be looked upon as a means rather than an end in itself, a little hunting can be useful at this stage.

Wherever jumping lessons take place—in an enclosed space or across country—they should at first be kept to a very moderate speed. For every obstacle there is a preferred speed—preferred because it allows the horse to jump with the minimum of effort. The question of speed is very important in both show-jumping and eventing, and merits careful attention. In competition the correct speed for any particular fence cannot always be maintained as there are generally other speed achievements to be considered, but in training the horse must be brought up to confident, easy jumping by being taught at ideal speeds. Only when these have been so successful that the horse is really happy and relaxed should the speeds be varied.

To summarise, therefore, the basic training of a horse on the flat develops his physical capacities and the self-confidence he needs both in himself and in his rider, for it establishes a mutually comprehensible language which enables the rider to convey his meaning to the horse clearly and precisely for instant obedience. Training over fences improves the horse's form, teaches it to make better use of its natural abilities and gives it practice in coping with increasingly complex obstacles. Stable care and feeding must allow the horse to sustain his efforts without coming to any harm and, very importantly, the horse's breeding, aptitudes and conformation must give it enough natural qualities to enable it, with training, to perform satisfactorily.

Part 5
The world of sport

1 Racing

FLAT RACING

The first record of a race in England dates from 1174, in the reign of Henry II, and took place at Smithfield. Until the time of Charles II, horses used for racing in Britain were home-bred horses known as the racing 'galloway', sometimes the 'hobby horse' or 'running horse'. It was not until the seventeenth century gave way to the eighteenth that the importation of the three famous Arabian horses from the east took place; three horses which were to have a profound effect on racing all over the world, for they led to the establishment of the Thoroughbred.

In the early days of racing the most usual distance for a race was four miles, and races were frequently run in heats. It was un-remarkable for contestants to carry as much as twelve stone in weight. Under these conditions close, exciting finishes must have been the exception rather than the rule, and it may well have been lack of spectacle as much as any humanitarian feelings about exhausted horses that led to a gradual reduction in distance and the abandonment of heats, though this method of racing did persist well into the nineteenth century.

The English Derby, still regarded as the world's greatest test for a three-year-old over a mile and a half, was in fact first run at Epsom in 1780 over only a mile. It is the three-year-old races that have become most popular on an international scale. In Britain, apart from the Derby, there are four other Classic races: the St Leger (first run in 1778), the Oaks (1779), the 2,000 Guineas (1809) and the 1,000 Guineas (1814). In France, which now holds a position of considerable eminence in the racing world, there are the Poules d'Essai and the Prix Royal Oak, equivalents of the Guineas and the St Leger respectively; the Prix Diane (equivalent of the English Oaks) and the Prix du Jockey Club (like the English Derby), both run at Chantilly; and an additional Classic, the Grand Prix du Paris, which is run at Longchamp in June.

The British model for three-year-old racing has been closely followed in Europe, unlike the two-year-old tests, of which there are fewer on the Continent than in Britain. In the United States, on the other hand, the emphasis is placed on precocity, with some two-year-old races being held in January. Racing was first introduced to the United States in 1664 by the commander of the English forces invading what is now New York. Commander Nicolls laid out a two-mile course very near to the present-day Belmont Park course, still the best known internationally of the North American courses.

The pattern of meetings is similar on the Continent and in Britain, meetings being held for perhaps four consecutive days. In France, most major meetings are held at weekends, with big races being run almost exclusively on Sundays. In the United States, on the other hand, they may continue for anything up to a hundred days, the average being between fifty and sixty. American racing is usually conducted on dirt-track courses, unlike the turf to be found all over Europe, though with the increase in international competition turf courses are now sometimes to be found running inside the dirt tracks. The most famous Classic races in the United States are the Coaching Club Oaks, the Belmont Stakes and Withers Stakes, all held at Belmont Park, ¬the Pimlico (Baltimore) Preakness Stakes and the Kentucky Derby.

Racing is also a popular sport elsewhere in the world. Australia and New Zealand have a particularly high reputation, and breed horses of as great quality as those produced by France, the United States and Britain. The Melbourne Hunt Cup, run at Flemington Course over two miles, is among the world's most famous handicap races. The Randwick course at Sydney is a well-known one, as are the Auckland and Christchurch courses in New Zealand.

The British introduced racing to other parts of the Commonwealth, too; it is popular in Canada, where the oldest fixed event, the Toronto Queen's Plate, was first endowed by William IV in 1836 and continues to be sponsored by the reigning monarch, and in spite of breeding difficulties caused by the climate, racing thrives in India. Most of the countries in Latin America both breed and race Thoroughbreds. The courses at Buenos Aires, Santiago and Saõ Paulo are particularly well known, and the Grand Premios Brasil and Saõ Paulo is one of the top international races.

Air travel has solved problems of transport to such an extent that the trend is now towards international breeding of racehorses, though because of the difficulties of differences in seasons, climates, tracks, training methods and so on truly international racing seems unlikely to develop. The Washington International, held in the United States in November, for example, can apparently never be considered more than an interesting exercise. The newly-sponsored Eclipse Stakes, the King George VI and Queen Elizabeth Stakes (now, thanks to sponsorship, more valuable than the Derby) and the Champion Stakes, revitalised with Levy Board money, provide in England the principal opportunities for a meeting between Classic horses. For European owners and breeders the world's richest race, the two-mile Prix de l'Arc de Triomphe, which takes place at Longchamp in October, overshadows all other tests for three-year-olds and older horses.

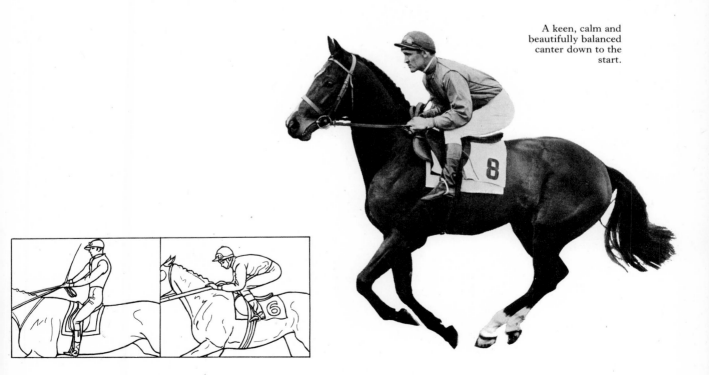

A keen, calm and beautifully balanced canter down to the start.

It is impossible to discuss flat racing without making some mention of the financial aspect. What was once a sport conducted for and by participants, has now grown into a multi-million pound industry, in which the interests of bloodstock and racing for its own sake have become merged with those of spectator-entertainment and gambling. Modern racing derives its principal support from gambling, so it is hardly surprising that it should now be geared very largely to the interests of the betting public, and more particularly, perhaps, to those who rarely visit a racecourse. Enormous sums of money are offered by the big Classic races, and the total turnover of the betting industry is now huge.

Brigadier Gerard has almost become a legend in his own time.

STEEPLECHASING

The sport of steeplechasing, today a highly organised activity, grew almost casually out of races held between private individuals, often to settle disputes about the relative merits of hunters, whose owners would race them from steeple to steeple across country, taking their own line. References to tests of this sort occur with increasing frequency in contemporary newspapers and journals as the eighteenth century drew towards the nineteenth. At about this time, too, it seems that hunting men of the day amused themselves with what are sometimes referred to as 'wild goose chases', in which one rider set a course across country pursued by others. A similar sport was practised by out of season or out of scent sportsmen in the United States during the late eighteenth and early nineteenth centuries, where, particularly in Maryland, the events became known as 'pounding' races, apparently because the aim of the leader was to choose the stiffest obstacles so as to put down—or pound—his pursuers.

Steeplechasing is a minor sport in many countries all over the world, but only in Great Britain and Ireland (its spiritual home) and, to a lesser extent, in France and the United States, has it really become established. In Britain, though the crowded season now extends from late July right through to the following June, steeplechasing has always been linked with the foxhunting season, and the big races are held early in the year. In France, however, the calendar is different, and the Grand Steeplechase de Paris, French equivalent of the Liverpool Grand National, is run in June, as is the big hurdle race, the Grand Course de Haies d'Auteuil.

In the United States, jump racing has moved forward on different lines again. It is now virtually two sports: the hurdle races and steeplechases are held mainly for variety as extra events at some flat meetings; and at the hunt meetings races over timber are held. The most famous, and the most demanding, of these is the Maryland Hunt Cup.

From spontaneous but unruly beginnings, steeplechasing gradually evolved in Great Britain into an organised sport. Today nothing comes outside the rule book. Steeplechase fences, excepting water jumps, must be at least 4 ft. 6 in. high, with twelve obstacles or more in a two-mile 'chase (the minimum distance), and another six for each succeeding mile. A sub-committee of the Jockey Club was the first authority of the sport, and out of it, in 1866, came the Grand National Hunt Steeplechase Committee, which became the National Hunt Committee in 1889.

When the National Hunt Committee was born it controlled a sport still not far removed from the hunting field. The separation was gradual but definite. For example, by 1885 the whole Grand National course had been railed and, more important, it was all grass for the first time. Even before this, the Thoroughbred was gaining ascendancy over his less aristocratic brethren and, as the sport became more 'respectable', so the half-bred hunter faded from the scene. Increasing popularity and opportunity led to the development of breeding for jumping, though with the longer time-lag between conception and reward this does not—and never can—approach the scale of commercial flat race production.

This passage of years between foaling and fruition results in steeplechase breeding being an even less exact science than that for flat racing, since, though certain names and bloodlines appear again and again in pedigrees of leading performers over fences, their immediate sires and dams have frequently reached advanced years—or may even have died—before their progeny can advertise their potential. Because nearly all male steeplechasers are geldings, a sire can only be judged on what he has produced or on his flat racing achievements, and the latter is often not a reliable pointer.

Thanks to Levy Board funds and private sponsors, prize money opportunities for leading steeplechasers have reached levels undreamed of in the first seventy-five years of the NHC's existence. Until several years after the second world war the Grand National still offered the only worthwhile target. The Cheltenham Gold Cup, instituted in 1924, provided a true level weight championship test over $3\frac{1}{4}$ miles, but when the great Golden Miller scored his record five wins in a row from 1932 to 1936 he won only £670 each time for his owner. His Grand National victory of 1934 netted £7,265.

The three leaders coming over Becher's Brook, by far the most formidable obstacle on the gruelling Grand National course at Liverpool, for the second time.

Now, however, steeplechasing has a Pattern of Racing system of its own and the whole calendar is peppered with valuable events. Sponsorship of the Gold Cup led to a prize of £15,255 for the 1972 winner, Glencaraig Lady. Three weeks later Well To Do won £25,765 in the part-sponsored Grand National. Nor have hurdlers been neglected. The Schweppes Gold Trophy, one of the season's hottest handicaps, was worth £9,698 in 1972, while the top weight-for-age test, the Champion Hurdle (started at Cheltenham three years after the Gold Cup) carried a prize of £15,648.

More money in prizes has meant a rising demand for horses and rocketing prices. Though still far from reaching the figures paid for their flat racing brothers (the lack of breeding potential has its natural effect), few eyebrows are raised at bids of £5,000 to £10,000 for horses with any sort of form, the current record of 16,000 guineas having been paid for the hurdler, Major Rose.

But one of the fascinations of the 'chasing game lies in the ever-present prospect of finding a future star, perhaps foaled in some rural Irish backwater, bred for the jumping job but without too much of the look of success about him to push his price up to impossible levels.

2 Show-jumping, eventing and dressage

SHOW-JUMPING

Show-jumping is a newcomer to the world of equestrian activity. It was first mentioned – in a French cavalry manual – towards the end of the eighteenth century, and not until the 1860s are there records of organised show-jumping competitions. In Ireland, which roughly a hundred years before had seen the first steeplechase, the Royal Dublin Society's show of 1865 included a high-and-wide leaping competition; the following year there was a jumping competition in Paris, but this was nearer to cross-country than to show-jumping, for after a preliminary parade indoors the competitors were sent out into the country to jump over mostly natural obstacles. It is probable that in the USSR, where there was strong French influence, there were also jumping competitions at this time.

On the Continent, jumping quickly became widely spread, particularly in Germany and France, where jumping competitions were included in the 1900 Olympic Games, held in Paris. In Turin in 1901 officers from the German army, and possibly also from the Swiss, were invited to take on their counterparts in the Italian army at jumping. The era of international show-jumping had begun, though it is unlikely that any of the pioneers of the sport envisaged its spectacular growth.

A show-jumping competition, at whatever level, is no better than the course over which it is jumped. One can have a field of the best horses in the world, but if they are given a course of too-big fences and impossible distances something like chaos can ensue; if they are given too easy a task, not asked enough to test their ability, the competition will be dull, resulting in a mass of clear rounds and then a 'steeplechase' against the clock to decide the winner. On the other hand, a course of good, solid fences arranged in an inviting way can produce an interesting competition even from inexperienced contestants.

Sophistication of course-building has come about to a considerable extent over the years. At one time the courses at almost all British agricultural shows were very much of a pattern, and that an extremely dull one: six or eight fences along one side of the ring, a similar number along the other, and a water jump or triple bar in the centre.

Gradually the snags were ironed out, especially after the formation of the FEI (Fédération Equestre Internationale) in 1921 which brought some uniformity of regulation, although slates were still in use in Britain after the second world war and 'touches' are still penalised in some national classes in the United States. Generally speaking, however, penalisation is now clear-cut, with four faults given for each fence knocked down, be it with forefeet, hind feet, nose or tail. Only the water still presents problems, for the adjudication still depends upon the human eye, though the use of a plastic tape which is encouraged by the FEI in international competition, indeed is mandatory at CSIO shows (official international jumping shows), at championships and the Olympic Games, at least ensures fairly reliable evidence in the event of a dispute.

The ease with which a show-jumping competition can be judged is, to a considerable extent, a reason for its popularity. Four faults for a fence down, three for the first refusal, six for the second and elimination for the third. Given a digital clock – happily on the increase – to see whether a horse has incurred time faults, any spectator is in a position to see for himself how one horse has done against another.

All that remains is for a course to be built that will produce a competition the spectator wants to sit through. Accusations of lack of imagination are frequently levelled – and with reason – against course-builders everywhere, yet to a large extent the wonder is that they manage to bring in as much variety as many of them do, for basically there are only four different types of fence: the upright, the parallel, the staircase and the pyramid. In spite of this limitation, an imaginative and knowledgeable course-builder can use his basic material, with the many variations of each type, to produce a track capable of getting the best out of a horse at any stage of its development. This of course is, or should be, the aim – to encourage a horse to jump to the best of his ability, not to trap him into making mistakes, which may not only make for an ugly round and unsatisfactory competition but could ruin a horse's confidence for the future.

Having established the class of horse he is building for – novice, Grade B, or top-grade international – the course-builder can then start his plan. Even for a novice the course should not be too easy, for one should assume that the horses have all had reasonable schooling at home. There used to be a tendency to build such easy courses that the most minor of competitions ended in a timed jump-off, but it does a green horse little good to have to scamper round against the clock in competition with others who have gone clear.

For top-class horses the builder uses not only the size of the fences, but also the distances between them, between the various elements of a combination fence, and the position in which they are sited both in relation to each other and to the perimeter of the ring. Although the length of a horse's stride will clearly vary, at a strong canter it will on average be about 10 ft. Fences more than 80 ft. apart are considered as unrelated, which is to say there is sufficient distance between them to make fundamental changes of pace and stride.

If fences are within 39 ft. 4 in. of each other they are considered to be part of a combination fence, which normally consists of two or three parts though it can be more. The distance between fences is what makes them easy or difficult to jump, although this problem has to be considered in conjunction with the shape of each fence. Easy distances between two uprights would be 26 ft. for one stride and 35 ft. for two; between two sets of parallels they would be 23 ft. and 34 ft., with variation for mixed combinations. So given a distance of, say, 29 ft. the rider would have to choose between two short strides or one long one, and his answer would depend upon his horse's ability, length of stride and courage.

How a fence is built will have considerable bearing on how well it is jumped. Thus a flimsy upright with three or four poles will be less inviting, and will be knocked down more often, than one which looks solid from top to bottom. A triple-bar will be cleared more often than an upright of the same height; a fence four feet wide is more difficult than one of twice the width. To some extent the difficulty of a fence is apparent rather than actual – how often has one seen horse after horse making heavy weather of a course and then, as soon as one horse jumps well clear others follow immediately in his wake. The maxim among many event course-builders is to 'frighten the rider but not the horse', and this applies in the show ring as well.

A horse measures the fence to be jumped from where it is in contact with the ground, so if there is no ground-line a fence is more difficult to assess. If there is a false ground-line it is that much more difficult: if, for example, a set of fairly sparse parallel poles has a bush

A perfect take-off at the water jump at the Dublin Horse Show.

Harvey Smith and Summertime,
a highly successful combination.

Both horse and rider
escaped unharmed
from their fall in
Copenhagen.

in the centre a horse may use this as his guide when in fact it is set several inches behind the first set of poles to be jumped. Incidentally, although parallel poles are so-named, usually they are not truly parallel but have the front poles slightly lower than those behind.

An obstacle that has frequently caused a great deal of trouble is the water-jump. This used to be far more true than it is now, mainly because the majority of water jumps were so badly built, with the water either scarcely filling the bottom of the pit or alternatively slopping out beyond the tape. In recent years the standard has improved considerably, and mistakes at this obstacle now tend to happen because a rider, having jumped the upright fences with forethought and precision, reverts to a gallop and a prayer when faced with a stretch of water. When a pole is put over a water jump it usually proves the easiest fence on the course, simply because attainment of the necessary height almost guarantees that the width will be cleared also.

Clearly the size of the fences will depend upon the type of competition: if it is against

The Mexican, Jesus Portugal, on the Derby Bank at Hickstead.

the clock in the first round they will not be too difficult, although at the same time they should not be so insignificant as to give too great an advantage to a horse whose only asset is speed. Jumping is, or should be, the essential element of the sport at all times.

It is significant that when British riders first went abroad after the war they found it almost impossible to keep pace with the continentals, and that the first post-war international victory was by Harry Llewellyn and Kilgeddin in a puissance competition in Rome. Now Britain tends to produce few real puissance horses, which is perhaps why Swank's record, set in 1937, still stands. The puissance is the only type of competition in which jumping alone, irrespective of time, is the deciding factor. Starting with perhaps six fences, a puissance is habitually reduced to two, usually a wall and a triple bar, which are raised for each new round until all save the winner have dropped out. This is sometimes considered an unfair competition, it being thought a poor way to reward a horse jumping clear by making him then jump again over bigger fences until he reaches his limit. True puissances are rarely jumped in Britain, usually being limited to a set number of barrages, probably three, with all those still clear dividing the spoils.

COMBINED TRAINING

Three-day event competitions are perhaps the most demanding and rewarding of any equestrian activity. In order to do well, a horse must combine speed, stamina, obedience and considerable jumping ability; his rider must be knowledgeable and expert in three distinct branches of horsemanship—dressage, cross-country riding and show-jumping. The object of combined training is to test the all-round quality and versatility of the horse.

Combined training is the modern English term for what the French have always known as *concours complet*—the complete test.

It all began—as do so many things of value concerning the horse—with Xenophon in 300 BC.

Over the centuries the great horsemasters evolved systems of training and riding horses which were adopted in whole or in part by cavalrymen, who placed the emphasis upon endurance. Long-distance rides for chargers have been staged for more than three hundred years, the severity of the test being governed by the ratio of distance to speed. Perhaps the classic example was the ride from Vienna to Berlin, held on 2 October 1892. It attracted an entry of ninety-eight officers from the German, Austrian and Hungarian armies. There were rest areas and compulsory checkpoints all along the distance of 370 miles, and the winner— Count Wilhelm Starhemberg, a lieutenant in the Austro-Hungarian Royal Hussars—completed the journey in less than three days. Riding the 15·2 hands horse Athos, a Hungarian half-bred, his time was 71 hours and 26 minutes. The last of the forty-two finishers arrived only fifteen hours later. The distance was mainly covered at the normal military trot interspersed with walking and leading periods.

The French developed the endurance idea with *Raids Militaires*, including one from Biarritz to Paris—a distance of some 450 miles. In Germany the Emperor's prize was awarded to the winner of an overnight journey of some hundred miles, for which ten or eleven hours were allowed. The United States Army followed suit, though it was the French again who developed the first true precursor of the modern three-day event, the *Championnat du Cheval d'Armes*, which was staged by the cavalry around Paris in April 1902. It was concluded by a show-jumping test—as it is today—in order to keep the general public in touch with the proceedings and thus ensure their support.

This event was so successful that it became an annual affair which has continued up to the present day, only being held over during the war years. It was designed to produce an all-round horse and rider, reducing the tendency to over-specialise, and aimed at improving the type of horse being bred and the standard of riding and training. *Haute école* and *reprise libre*, included in the first test, were abolished. Horses were also examined after each phase and awarded points according to their condition, and finally—in 1922—the roads and tracks phase was shortened and a cross-country course introduced. In the same year, too, the event for the first time occupied three full days.

In Sweden a military three-day event was

H.R.H. the Princess Anne on Columbus performing an excellent dressage test.

held at the cavalry school at Stronsholm in 1907; Belgium followed suit in 1910; and Switzerland held their first event at St Gall in 1921. Then the United States joined in, and the Indian Army School at Saugor also ran tests for officers' horses on similar lines. The growing international interest was partly responsible for the introduction, at the 1912 Olympic Games, of equestrian events. They were organised, and—deservedly—won by Sweden, all the competitors at this time still being drawn from military sources.

It was not until after the second world war that civilian participation in three-day events began. The 1948 Olympics were held in England, with the three-day event being based at Aldershot in Hampshire. Up to this time the British had on the whole held aloof from the sport—the officers were busy hunting and playing polo, and were suspicious of everything connected with dressage, which was quite unfamiliar to them. But the post-war era produced a worldwide outburst of enthusiasm for horses and everything to do with riding for pleasure, at a time when the horse's working contribution was beginning to dwindle in importance. A diminution of the military monopoly quickly followed.

The new interest in horses was particularly

strong in England, and it was fostered by the Duke of Beaufort. He had been present at the Olympic Games in 1948 and subsequently gave Badminton Park, his home in Gloucestershire, to be used for what is now perhaps the most famous three-day event in the world. The first event was held in 1949 and was open to civilian riders and, what is more, to women too. Nobody took much interest in this at the time, and certainly none seemed to expect the enormously high quality of performance that has put lady riders in the front rank as three-day event competitors.

Combined training competitions are usually held over three days, though the various phases of the competition have been modified to produce one-day events and Pony Club trials as well. The one-day events were started in the early 1950s as a nursery for the three-day event, and they have grown enormously in response to an increasing demand during the twenty years since they were established. The cross-country phase has had to be reduced in length, and the steeplechase and roads and tracks phases also curtailed, but the principles remain the same and the aim is still that of a complete test for horse and rider.

In any combined training competition there are three phases: dressage, speed and endurance, and show-jumping. The dressage test is designed to show that the horse is educated, balanced, supple and obedient to ride, and though many of the movements included in the test form part of the schooling programme of any horse, others set out to demand from horse and rider a greater degree of schooling and a more polished performance than the average hunter, for example, would acquire.

The second part of the competition, the speed and endurance test, consists—in three-day events—of several phases. There are two on roads and tracks, these being separated by a steeplechase course. Finally comes the greatest test of all: the cross-country phase, a gruelling course of some thirty obstacles spread over between four and five miles of open country. The whole speed and endurance section of the competition will cover some twenty miles, the roads and tracks being taken at a brisk trot or easy canter, the steeplechase course at a good gallop and the cross-country also needing to be ridden at speed, allowing too for the individual horse's ability over solid, and sometimes tricky, obstacles. Only bold, clever horses with confidence in their riders and obedience to them, and being at the peak of fitness, can hope to complete the second day with bonus points in hand and no undue exhaustion.

The third day involves a show-jumping course designed as a final test of fitness of both horse and rider. In spite of the previous day's exertions, horses are expected to be able to complete a relatively modest course; an exhausted or unduly stiff horse will find even show-jumps of this kind difficult to negotiate.

It was the Duke of Beaufort who first realised that the tests involved in three-day events should ideally suit British-bred and trained horses and their riders. Any good hunter who is temperate enough to perform a dressage test and jump a course of artificial fences in addition to galloping across country tackling big fences at speed can succeed in combined training, provided he has sufficient quality. Most natural horsemen who have been following hounds since childhood can master sufficient dressage, in the hands of a good instructor, to satisfy the judges. Strangely enough, the show-jumping phase seems to be the bugbear of many riders, perhaps because the necessity to 'see a stride' and to know whether a horse is right or wrong in his approach is more important in the ring, where the fences come thick and fast and there is little time or space to correct balance and adjust stride, than it is across country, when there is often the width of a field between each jump, and related fences are the exception rather than the rule.

Miss J. Wofford and Kilkerry of the USA on the steeplechase course at Munich.

A French competitor, M. Bentjac, enters the fearsome leaf-pit at Burghley.

In all countries where horses and riding are a natural feature—for driving and riding in the past and for pleasure riding now—the demands of versatility in achievement of combined training are a particularly popular challenge; every year the sport makes phenomenal advances in popularity all over the world.

COMPETITION DRESSAGE

As with almost every other form of physical activity, the art-sport of dressage has long since taken its place in the competitive sphere. Essentially, dressage riding continues to exist, as it began, as a pleasurable activity with two useful functions: to train a horse to be a pleasant ride and in so doing to give satisfaction to the creative urges of the trainer. True creative art can never be competitive in the normal sense of the word, since it cannot be restricted by rigid rules. But dressage, which has certain purely functional aspects, is another matter and those aspects are sufficiently strong to render competition useful in providing a stimulus and a meeting-ground on which progress and technique can be tested and discussed.

The descriptive word 'art-sport' has been carefully chosen because the overriding consideration of good dressage—as of such activities as gymnastics, skating, diving, etc.—is that the form of what is done is at least as important as its content. Every action or movement of both horse and rider must have beauty of style as its aim, to be given final expression in the full development of the horse's power. It is never enough to struggle through a series of set movements without regard to their form. This does not apply, for example, to athletics, in which no account whatever is taken of the style—or lack of it—with which a high-jumper clears the bar. In dressage, style is always of prime concern.

It follows that a dressage competition becomes, in effect, a competition in style. Its object is not to discover which combination of horse and rider can perform the longest sequence of flying changes, the smallest circle, even the highest leap in a *capriole*. The prize will go to the combination that performs a series of clearly defined movements in the purest style. A competition also provides a convenient frame for the display of equine talent that will give pleasure to interested spectators without particular regard to the allocation of marks by judges. It also provides a stimulus for bringing horses and riders together to test their comparative progress throughout the long years of their training.

Standards in competitive dressage vary enormously from country to country, and even more from continent to continent. So, too, do the numbers of those taking part. Europe, itself the womb of dressage, remains to this day the only continent able to produce more than a mere trickle of talent. Even there, some countries have virtually no competition riders of international status, and in many, including such great countries as France, there may be only one or two able to perform creditably at the top level. In others, such as Germany, Switzerland, Sweden and the USSR, where for many generations there has been very active interest, there is today strong support from both spectators and riders. In Germany in particular, dressage can be said to have the status of a national sport. German riders capable of showing horses in Grand Prix dressage competitions, which are, after all, synonymous with the Olympic standard, can be numbered in their hundreds, and they will be watched with intense and informed interest by thousands.

The strength of any country's output in dressage probably rests on the three cornerstones of public interest, financial backing and professional trainers. And although the trainers would not exist in any numbers alone, they are probably the most important and fundamental of the three factors. Wealth in some form cannot be overlooked because it alone can ensure a really adequate supply of horses of high quality and potential. Just as a human athlete of true international calibre is a rare thing, so a true international dressage horse is equally rare and hard to come by, and those riders who always appear to have one or two at their disposal have almost certainly tried and discarded a great many more. Only people with substantial, though not necessarily great, wealth behind them will be able to do this, although such backing may come in various guises. It may represent a long-established cavalry or national school of equitation, or it may be the private fortune of the rider or his sponsor. In all cases it is an inestimable advantage.

As for the professional trainers, their accumulated knowledge and practised eye is virtually essential, even to the most experienced amateur rider, in avoiding or in overcoming problems and in perfecting the style of both partners in the enterprise. In training horses to this standard there is always the danger that a mistake will creep in, and a bad habit become fixed, before a rider working alone becomes aware of it. Thus a horse can be spoilt for life, or at best his educational and competitive progress will receive a serious setback.

The first impression made on any newcomer to the main competitive arenas in Europe may well be a startled awareness of the very high standards of accuracy and of attack that are necessary to make any real impression. He will find the Germans there in force, with all the power of a nation in arms. The Russians usually appear once a year, usually at the annual championship meeting, on the whole showing individual style in which the horses work accurately but move rather as if on rollers, missing something of the fire that stirs the

blood. They will not be in great numbers, but their best will be heading for the top prizes. They provide a shining example of what can be achieved by relatively few individuals operating under conditions that many wealthier nations would consider difficult.

What is the aim of dressage, and therefore of dressage competitions? Even the specialised dressage tests, as well as those forming part of combined training events, are basically designed to demonstrate the extent of obedience, suppleness and lightness of the horse. The Prix St Georges test includes the half-pass, half-pirouette, counter-canter and flying change of leg. None of these movements is really specialised in itself, but they are all difficult to perform outstandingly well. The more advanced tests, the Grand Prix and Olympic tests, do include movements of *haute école* standard, such as *passage, piaffe,* changes of leg at canter at every stride, and so on. Nevertheless, even at this advanced level the primary object is the performance of comparatively simple movements superbly well, and success will depend very largely on achieving this.

It is the precision, the aim at perfection, that makes dressage possibly the most fascinating of all specialist branches of equitation.

Mrs Jennie Loriston-Clarke competing at Stoneleigh.

3 Foxhunting

HUNTING IN BRITAIN

It is not easy accurately to state just when and where foxhunting started in Britain. Although hunting was carried on all over the British Isles certainly since the Norman Conquest, it was almost certainly not until the eighteenth century that packs were used to hunt only the fox.

By the end of the seventeenth century, however, those who hunted—and they were for the most part the great landlords—were beginning to realise that the hunting of the fox provided better sport than that of any other animal. This was because the fox had greater stamina than the hare, had not so strong a scent as the deer, and was more crafty than either, thus presenting in every way a greater challenge to a huntsman and his hounds.

Just three hundred years ago the great Duke of Buckingham, who hunted his vast territories in the north of England, is alleged to have exclaimed that he would willingly exchange a flock of his fattest sheep for a similar number of foxes. By the middle of the eighteenth century, thanks largely to the enthusiasm of such great aristocrats as the Duke of Buckingham and other members of the royal family, hunting the fox was the most flourishing sport in England.

A hundred years later it had become far and away the most popular. Just when even the great landlords were finding it impossible to maintain the magnificent establishments set up to hunt the fox over large areas—the Dukes of Berkeley hunted from Bristol to London, the Dukes of Beaufort from Bath to Oxford—so, thanks to the Industrial Revolution, there were many more of the new gentry who could afford to hunt. As a result, subscription packs were started, hunting smaller areas but much more efficiently organised—the subscribers felt that their subscriptions entitled them to demand good sport.

There was, obviously, a certain anomaly here. The duke, or other noble landlord, owned the hounds and probably most of the country, but other people paid the hunting bills—a fact which the landlord almost certainly resented, as he did the interference of a committee which the subscribers felt entitled to appoint. The nineteenth century is full of stories of rows and arguments and clashes between landlord and followers. A situation so fraught with incendiary problems was bound to take a little time to settle down. It could be said that in some parts of the country it has never entirely settled down.

So often called the heyday of hunting, the nineteenth century was in fact the most discreditable period in its history. The fields were huge and paid little attention to the farmer; foxes, in short supply because of poaching, were invariably bagged; with no traffic-ridden roads, no barbed wire, no artificial manures to steady the chase, hounds were forced on at a tremendous pace, the field riding as if in a race, on unclipped horses many of which, their owners boasted, died of exhaustion every season.

The march of progress and the first world war brought foxhunters to their senses, and when hunting was resumed after the war it was much more like what those who, two hundred years earlier, had first discovered the joys of the chase intended it to be. Between the wars there were still plenty of people who maintained large establishments and foxhunting in those two decades was of a very high order: well organised, producing excellent sport, the country still rideable.

It was a miracle—the result, in fact, of a few dedicated and tireless enthusiasts—that hunting survived the second world war. But it did, and during the last twenty-five years it has evolved as the sport that we know today. Lacking perhaps the style and bravura and colour of previous centuries, it is now far more democratic and far more broadly based; and, indeed, giving pleasure to far more people than ever before.

This is due, firstly, to the fact that far more people today can actually afford to hunt mounted than were able to even in the days before the war. Secondly, there is far less evidence of great wealth among the country landlords and so, with few exceptions—exceptions incidentally which are of great benefit to foxhunting—hunting is far less exclusive: far less a sport for the privileged few. Thirdly, more and more farmers come out hunting themselves, whereas before, so impoverished was their industry, not only could they not afford to hunt but they were dependent upon the local hunt for their livelihood, which made it virtually impossible for them to complain to the hunt or even seek their co-operation. Were it not for the hunt they would be bankrupt. Now many hunts are run by farmers.

A last important factor is that there has been, during the last twenty-five years, the formation of hunt supporters' clubs, which has meant that each year more and more people feel involved with their local hunt. These supporters clubs play a vital part in foxhunting. In some countries there is a danger of their playing almost too vital a part because they tend to dictate to the hunt. There have been cases where continuity is much more in evidence in the supporters' club, where wealth is of no account whatever, than in the mastership or hunt committee, where money is still a major feature. In such cases the supporters' clubs become very powerful.

Fortunately, however, this potentially awkward situation is remarkably rare, and the supporters' clubs do a splendid job for hunting.

Many hunts would be quite unable to exist without them, for they fill the role of ambassadors for foxhunting, popularising the sport among a section of the community that has never before been interested and, even more important, providing a most useful antidote to those opposed to hunting.

Would such a situation ever have been envisaged two hundred or even one hundred years ago? It is, of course, unthinkable: but it may well be that hunting is much better for it. It could even be said that were it not for this development hunting would not have survived.

The fact of the matter is that the foxhunter today has far greater responsibilities than in the past. He has responsibilities to the farmer, to the general public and to the sport itself. In the last century he could enjoy his sport wherever he liked. The whole countryside was his playground. Now even in the most fortunate country there are inevitably a few farmers who do not appreciate the hunt. Unless a proper responsibility towards agriculture is accepted there could well be many more farmers who are opposed to hunting and refuse to allow the hunt over their land.

The hunt has always been a colourful part of the countryside, respected, even loved, by local people. For generations hunting people have made it their business to see that the hunt is very much an integrated part of the countryside. The development of supporters' clubs should safeguard this tradition.

It takes a bold partnership
to stay with hounds over
this sort of country.

HUNTING IN THE UNITED STATES

Hunting in the United States and in Canada is extremely popular. There are nearly a hundred packs of hounds recognised by the American Masters of Foxhounds Association, a body which was affiliated to the English MFHA in 1914. There is also a Masters of Beagles Association, a sport which also has its enthusiasts.

The origins of hunting for sport are to be found in the richly historical states of Virginia, Maryland and Pennsylvania. Thomas, sixth Lord Fairfax, who went to live in Virginia in 1747, is believed to have been the first person to own hounds for hunting—as a sport—in the United States. In those days, when gentlemen lived on their estates in considerable splendour in an era when the importation of slaves was considered quite normal, it was natural that the vast woodlands of the Eastern Seaboard, which abounded in deer and grey foxes, should be exploited for sport.

George Washington, who loved to hunt, kept a diary on hunting between 1768 and 1789. It shows that before he was called upon to serve his country and became its first President he had a lot of fun with his hounds, and passages in the diary show that he had a considerable understanding of them. The Marquis de la Fayette gave him some hounds from France. His huntsman was Billy Lee, who went to the war with his master and, having survived it, returned with him to Mount Vernon to re-establish the pack and continue to hunt along the banks of the Potomac river.

Lord Fairfax's hounds, and those kept at Mount Vernon, were of course private packs, kept for their owners' sport. The first organised hunt club was the Gloucester Fox Hunting Club, formed by the Philadelphia gentlemen in 1766. They kept their pack on the banks of the Delaware river, and it was said to contain 'the best English blood'.

Those areas where Washington and General Howe fought their bitter battles, often over 'a fair hunting country', are today hunted by such packs as Blue Ridge, London, Middleburg, Piedmont, Old Dominion, Orange County (Virginia), Elkridge/Harford, Green Spring Valley (Maryland), Andrew's Bridge, Brandy-wine, Cheshire, Radnor and Rose Tree (Pennsylvania), to name but a few. The little town of Middleburg, situated some fifty miles from the city of Washington, is synonymous with fox-hunting in America as Melton Mowbray is in England. The Red Fox Inn there was established in 1728, so it will be seen that the roots of foxhunting in the United States are nearly as old as they are in England.

Two of the best bred packs of American hounds are the Middleburg and the Essex, which hunt in New Jersey; both packs often take premier awards at the Bryn-Mawr Hound Show held at Malvern in Pennsylvania. The American-bred hound is a special breed, and differs somewhat from the English foxhound. The head is longer and narrower, with ears set on very low; the legs are longer, and do not always have quite the highly arched toes of the modern English hound. It is thought that the American-bred hounds have developed feet perhaps more suitable for the terrain they have to cross. This is dry and hard in some areas, and in others marsh-like—particularly in the Chesapeake Bay area. Conditions such as this hard dry ground and the large woodland areas have given the American hounds extra good noses and a tremendous cry. One would imagine there is a good deal of French blood here.

Harry Worcester Smith (left), founder of the American MFHA, talking to Paul Mellon during a day's hunting in Virginia.

A private pack with the Master in the foothills of the Blue Ridge Mountains.

In packs such as the Elkridge/Harford, for instance, drafts of the very best Heythrop blood have been imported to make what is called the American cross-bred. These hounds are selectively bred and are very fine, being famed especially for their speed. There is, of course, a very close liaison between many of the best hound breeders on either side of the Atlantic.

There are two packs of pure-bred English foxhounds in the United States: the Cheshire and the Arapahoe. The Cheshire was formed in 1913 by Mr Plunkett Stewart, and hunts in the Unionville area of Pennsylvania, while the Arapahoe hunts over the ranchlands in the upland plains west of Denver, Colorado. Mr Lawrence Phipps, Jr, is their distinguished Master, and he has imported only the best pure English blood, notably from the Old Surrey and Barstow.

There is a third type of hound bred in the United States, called the Pen-marydel, a name derived from the states of Pennsylvania, Maryland and Delaware as the hounds are bred from strains bred in those three states – although one also hears of an Irish hound called Mountain who figures in the old pedigrees!

Like the hounds, the red foxes had to be imported. It is believed that they were brought in by the British, and landed in the Chesapeake Bay area. There are now red foxes in most of the eastern states, a slightly smaller variety than the big red fox associated with English hunting. The grey fox, indigenous to the United States, is not as bold as his red cousin, often running in circles and frequently ending up in the top branches of a tree! The deer, which were abundant in the past, still exist in numbers large enough to be a nuisance.

Looking at photographs of meets in the twenties and thirties it would be difficult to distinguish between one held near Middleburg and one in Leicestershire – both boasted large, well-mounted and well-dressed fields, nearly all the ladies riding side-saddle. Nowadays, in the United States as elsewhere, fashion and custom have changed, and the ladies will mostly be found riding astride; the big, quality hunters, mostly TB, are still to be seen in the fashionable hunting countries of the eastern states.

In the eastern states the red fox, and sometimes the grey, is hunted, but further west both the fox and the coyote are quarry. The coyote, a wild dog, usually runs in pairs, and is to be found in the hills and canyons in Colorado, Arizona and California. They will run a considerable distance, and it takes a clever horse to clamber up and down the hillsides, in and out of the canyons where the coyote like to go. It also takes a hound of exceptional nose to distinguish any scent in these dried-out areas.

The hunting season in the United States begins in the autumn and generally continues through to the spring. In some areas the severe winters make it necessary to begin cubhunting early, possibly in July, and hunting may have to close down at Christmas or in early January, depending on how far north one is, until a final few days' sport in late March or early April. In the Boston, New York and northern Pennsylvania areas the really keen hunting people move their horses south when winter closes in, and join the Moore County Hunt in south Carolina, which provides good sport in gently rolling woodlands with a milder climate.

Fences in the United States vary, as they do in other parts of the world. The solid timber fences of Maryland are as famous as the banks of southern Ireland, tough and often high. These rails take (and make) a good jumper. In Virginia fences vary more: some people liken the country to parts of Ireland, with its stone walls and rolling country. There are also panel fences or 'chicken coops', erected by the hunt to enable people to get across country without being too troubled by wire. There are streams to ford, usually wide but not too deep.

There are other natural hazards, too. The warthog, a rat-like animal found in many areas, digs small, perfectly straight, deep holes which are very difficult to see and very dangerous – a horse putting a foot into one of these holes can be seriously injured. Out west, of course, there are other things such as rattlesnakes to look out for; most people carry the antidote with them, for without it the result of a rattlesnake's strike can be fatal. There are also wild pigs and mountain lions (the lynx) which terrify many horses coming across them.

There are hunting traditions in Canada, too. The Toronto and North York were formed over a hundred years ago, in 1843, together with what is now the Eglinton. The Ottawa Valley pack was started in 1873, and there are two packs in the province of Quebec, the Lake of Two Mountains and the Montreal. The hounds used are, like those of the American packs, crossed with English and Irish imports. Naturally the season in Canada is shortened somewhat by the onset of winter, and usually lasts from July to December, with a few days in the spring if the weather permits.

Much further south, in Mexico, there is also a pack of hounds. They belong to Mr Patrick Tritton, an Irishman who has made his home in Mexico and took out some hounds with him which he hunts himself.

People hunt for different reasons – to see their friends, to jump fences, to watch hounds work (which is the best reason of all to the true hunting person); for whatever reason, and in whatever part of the world, the thrill of hearing hounds in full cry is the same the world over.

4 The show world

BRITAIN

The showing classes, which in years gone by were the sole reason behind the staging of any horse show, at any rate in the British Isles, were originally put on for the benefit of the breeders and for the improvement of the breed. To a very large extent, this is still the case today, although there are people who buy a show horse for the sheer enjoyment of owning an outstandingly good-looking animal and pitting him against the best that other exhibitors can produce.

There is no finer place than the show ring — not even, for the pace there is too fast, the sale ring — to learn about the vital statistics of a horse. The conformation of any working animal is, indeed, more than vital. Good make and shape are essential if an animal is to remain sound in work over the years. For an animal designed to carry weight, and to carry it at speed, this is the most important factor of all. Looks are a luxury, but correct conformation is an insurance against disappointment, or even disaster. Whereas quality is desirable, it is the last consideration when compared to classical limbs and a workmanlike frame. If a horse is well made, he is probably a good and straight mover, able to cover the ground and unlikely to strike into himself, brush or over-reach at his faster paces, not prone to the afflictions which go hand-in-hand with faulty action. But even this does not invariably follow.

Judges vary somewhat in the order of their priorities, but nearly every one starts on the ground and works up. 'No foot, no horse' is too basic to require elaboration. Feet that are long and boxy, like those of a donkey, do not provide that all-important contact between the ground and the cushioning frog, nature's provision for the absorption of concussion. The frog atrophies in disuse and the concussion, no longer taken up by a protective cushion, travels straight into the pedal bone; the result is almost always navicular disease.

Flat feet, on the other hand, with the outward appearance of soup plates, indicate dropped soles which lend themselves to bruising on rough surfaces and also cause lameness.

The legs are every bit as important as the feet, and for equally obvious reasons. Convex knees that put strain on the tendons of the forelegs predispose a horse to breaking down, while sickle hocks give rise to symptoms of strain in the hind legs such as curbs, spavins and thoroughpins. Pasterns that are too short and upright, or too long and sloping, are prone to produce unsoundnesses such as sidebone and ringbone — bony deposits which interfere with the free movement of a working part, causing pain and lameness that is permanent.

A horse with good limbs can usually be expected, unless it receives an external injury, to remain reasonably sound throughout its career. Thus the conformation of a horse's body above the legs is more a question of personal preference and is open to debate, though depth of girth is essential for heart-room, strength and stamina. Slope of shoulder, elegance of outlook and conformation behind the saddle are considered in different orders of priority by different judges, who also show their individual preference in what they look for in the ride. Some like a horse that takes a strong hold, others prefer the type that requires only a light contact. Horses go differently, too, for different judges.

The ridden hunter classes are divided by weight, with lightweights to carry up to 12 st. 7 lb., middleweights up to 14 st. and heavyweights from 14 st. upwards. There are also, at the bigger shows, classes for four-year-olds, for ladies' hunters to be ridden side-saddle (one of the most elegant sights in any show-ring) and for small hunters, not exceeding 15·2 hands. The working hunter classes, in which horses have to jump a small course of fences before being judged for their conformation and ride, have also become extremely popular. An importation from the United States, they not only provide a useful outlet for the horse which is a performer but does not come into the category of the top-class show horse, but also a schooling ground for the likely show jumper or potential three-day event horse.

Breeders have plenty of opportunity to show their stock, not only at the annual show of the Hunters' Improvement Society at Shrewsbury but also at all the county and major agricultural shows, which cater extensively for led hunters – brood mares, with their foals at foot, yearlings, two- and three-year-olds. At the bigger shows the youngstock classes are divided into colts and fillies, and at Shrewsbury there are also classes for young Thoroughbreds in each age group.

One of the most interesting shows in the country, also put on by the Hunters' Improvement Society, is the Thoroughbred Stallion Show at Newmarket which opens the season in March. Here some eighty horses compete for the premiums offered by the Society, and the breeders turn out in force to select a mate for their brood mares. Premium stallions undergo a rigorous veterinary examination and are certified free from hereditary unsoundness, which is not the case with any other stallions in the land. In consideration of their premiums, these horses stand at a very reasonable stud fee to members of the Society, who are thus able to use high-quality sires, often with a very useful racing record.

There are, of course, also classes for ponies in profusion, led by the National Pony Society show, the Ponies of Britain stallion show at Ascot in April and summer show in August at Peterborough. Broadly speaking, they follow the same lines as the hunter classes but in the ridden division far more emphasis is – or should be, and usually is – placed on manners. Children are seldom strong enough, or sufficiently accomplished with the exception of the semi-professional children, to control a badly-mannered pony, and if a pony takes charge of its rider or bucks him off it is not suitable to be ridden by a child at all.

There are many ramifications in the world of pony showing. For example, there are the show pony classes, under saddle, in which the

A winning line-up of working hunter ponies.

champion can command a sum which is just about double, at some £6,000 to £8,000, the value of a champion hunter, for reasons which no one seems able to determine. There are the working pony classes, a recent innovation run on the lines of the working hunters, for the ponies who do not quite come into the top-class showing category but usually have more bone and substance and are far more suitable for their young riders, not only in the show ring but in the hunting field.

Then there are the mountain and moorland pony classes, which are either mixed according to size, both large and small, and may be led or ridden – in the former case they may also be divided by sex; or, at the bigger shows, separate classifications are included for all nine of the native breeds of the British Isles – Welsh, Dartmoor, Connemara, Highland, New Forest, Dale, Fell, Exmoor and Shetland.

Arab classes are also held for both led and ridden animals, and they have their own show at Roehampton in addition to classes at many of the bigger agricultural shows. Pure Arabs, part-bred Arabs and Anglo-Arabs all have opportunities for exhibition against others of their kind, and there is a lively export trade both to the Continent and to the United States.

The popularity of the cob has sadly dwindled in recent years and the blood cob is nowadays seldom found. Cobs are confined to a single class even at the leading shows, and if this does not receive more support from exhibitors it seems likely that it will eventually be dropped altogether.

Hacks, however, continue in popularity, and if the standard of training and presentation may be said to have declined in the last ten years or so the classes continue to fill and to provide an elegant contrast to the more workmanlike and less highly educated show hunter. It is hard to describe a hack other than as an elegant and well-made horse, lighter in type than the hunter, with proportions as near perfect as possible, a great front giving a good length of rein, a sweet head, long sweeping movement which stops short of exaggerated toe-pointing and, above all things, that elusive, indefinable quality of *presence*, an essential for any great show horse.

Attached to every category of show horse and pony is a strong professional band of showmen and women, and although the amateur exhibitor is often heard to decry the 'pros', and to maintain that the non-professional is never able to beat them, this is both unfair and untrue. A really good horse will always get to the top, but there are few really good horses about and some of the less experienced amateurs are inclined to regard their geese as swans. In showing, as in everything else, there are tricks in the trade, and the art of schooling for the ring and keeping the horse interested, of trimming and plaiting him to the best advantage, and of producing and presenting him to the judges is half the battle of success. Indeed, a professional show-man can often make a second-rate horse look like a champion, and get away with faults which an amateur would find impossible to disguise.

An adult show class at Windsor

Showing has made the English and Irish horse what it is today – the envy of the rest of the world. For, given the right temperament, the well-made horse is generally the best performer. Without the yardstick and the shop window of the showing classes the quality of horses would inevitably decline, but with the prototype on view for breeders to aim at the standard can only improve.

THE UNITED STATES

Horse shows in the United States must cater not only for a wealth of different breeds but also for three distinct styles of riding – the hunt seat, saddle seat and stock seat, as well as halter classes for all breeds. Because the US is such a vast country, shows cater for many breeds and all styles, and each breed show also caters for the different seats, with the exception of the gaited breeds such as the Tennesse Walker and Saddlebred.

In the hunting country of Virginia, Maryland, Pennsylvania and the Piedmont of North Carolina, as well as California, hunt seat classes largely fill the schedules. California is also a stronghold of the stock seat. The deep South concentrates mainly on shows attracting the three-and-five-gaited Saddlebreds and Tennessee Walkers, which are ridden saddle seat. Florida favours stock seat but also caters well for hunt seat riders.

The average American judge is called on to cope with a great variety of classes. Large shows to some extent delegate their classes by style and breed, an example being the four-day North Carolina State Championships of 1965, in which I showed the same horse in both jumper and Western divisions. Saddle seat and gaited classes, including fine-harness, hackney, harness ponies, roadsters, Morgan and parade were judged by one person; a well-known Arabian trainer officiated in the Western classes; hunters, jumpers and hunt seat equitation came under three joint judges.

In many one-day shows held throughout the country by riding clubs or as part of town celebrations one judge frequently goes through a whole card, assisted only by a ring steward. American judges do earn the fees paid for their services, but they are not required to ride competitors' horses, their evaluation of merit being visual only, which is more favourable as a horse, particularly a show horse, is highly individual, reacting better to his own rider than to a stranger who may or may not be in rhythm with him.

A typical four-day show offers a kaleidoscope of colour, breeds, talents, elegance and thrills. Each day's programme is split into morning, afternoon and evening sessions, the latter offering the cream of crowd appeal classes with open jumping, walking horse, parade horse, and three-and five-gaited stakes. Some shows mix their schedules so that something of everything is exhibited each day, finishing with the championships; others aim to have hunters and jumpers one day, gaited breeds another, and Western at a different time.

Schedules list classes by breed, riding style and judging criteria. If the schedule states, for example, that a pleasure class is to be judged on manners, performance, quality, suitability to rider and conformation, that is the preference order for awarding points. As a rule in junior, amateur, and ladies' classes manners carry a premium, but in the gaited stake classes, where the horse will probably be ridden by a professional, the criteria are performance, presence, quality and conformation – which does not mean manners are unimportant, as they reflect on performance. Many schedules state: 'The judge may require unruly animals to be removed from the ring'.

The hunter division approximates most closely to events found in the British show ring, but the similarity ends with the designation 'hunter'. The American hunter division offers a tremendous variety, being sub-divided into pony hunter, junior hunter, first- and second-year green working hunter, open working hunter, conformation hunter and handy hunter, each class title indicating the category in which an animal may be shown or the prime factor concerning judging.

All American show hunters jump, and a horse entered in the green working hunter division will compete in three classes before the championship and reserve championship is awarded. These three are the first- or second-year green working hunter over fences, green working hunter stake, green working hunter under saddle. In this last the horse, having already demonstrated his ability, is not required to jump.

In classes for hunters over fences, horses enter the ring alone and jump a set course at an even hunting pace, the judging criteria being evenness of pace, jumping ability, manners and hunting soundness. In working hunter classes conformation does not count other than as an adjunct to ability and ease of movement. A hunter must jump on very light contact, seeming to flow over fences, taking off and landing without perceptible alteration of stride. His head must be carried low, reaching out over his fences.

In classes for hunters under saddle horses must gallop on and from the gallop come to a rapid halt, as they may need to out hunting. Some hunter classes are conducted in the ring, but many are run over an outside course giving a better chance to competitors to move at a true hunting pace. Basically each hunter division follows the same pattern, variations being accounted for by a horse's experience, the rider's age and classes open to amateurs. First-year horses jump 3 ft. 6 in.; second-year horses 3 ft. 9 in. Open classes have fences of 4 ft. to 4 ft. 6 in. The majority of American show hunters are purebreds standing well over 16 hands, but though Thoroughbreds are of a heavier stamp than those usually found in Britain. Of interest is the hunter appointments class, where a percentage of marks is awarded for correct turnout – including the carrying of a filled sandwich case and flask.

Closely allied to hunter events are the green and open jumper classes. Many show-jumpers gain their initial experience over fences in the hunter division, where they learn to go with much more stability than their English counterparts. The American show-jumper has a variety of events to choose from, the emphasis being not so much on speed as the ability to jump a really clear round. There are several 'tables' under which horses jump. In some, touching obstacles with any part of the horse before the stifle is penalised by one fault and behind the stifle by half a fault, so greater accuracy is required.

The novice is termed a 'green jumper'. Once upgraded he is known as an 'open jumper', with classes being correspondingly more demanding. Green jumpers may also jump in open classes.

An event popular with all three 'seats' is the pleasure horse class, which is judged on performance, manners, suitability to rider and conformation in that order, unless otherwise stated. All pleasure horses except the Tennessee Walker show at walk, trot (jog for Westerns) and canter, great emphasis being placed on ease of handling. Hunt seat horses must move in a relaxed manner and on very light contact, any animal requiring a suggestion of strength for control being considered ill-mannered. Correct turnout is the same as it is for hunter classes, with horses' manes and tails being plaited. Saddle seat entrants show considerably more impulsion, particularly at the trot, with the horses more collected and more on the bit. The correct tack is a straight-panelled saddle with big skirts to protect clothing, and a double bridle in narrow leather. Horses are shown with loose manes and tails, though the forelock and section behind the bridle is braided with coloured ribbon. Western pleasure horses shown under the stock saddle must work on a loose rein, their gaits being easy, low to the ground and supremely comfortable. High head carriage is penalised, as is excessive use of spurs. Whips, permitted in hunt and saddle seat, are absent in Western pleasure classes.

The pleasure class is probably the only class which is included in every breed association's list of classes, as it is the least specialised. For many horses it offers an introduction to the show ring.

The Saddlebred and Tennessee Walking Horse show as riding horses, which makes them ideally suited to the many pleasure classes schedules include. However, although only shown on the flat and not now being considered working horses, the gaited breeds show in many other classes than pleasure classes.

Walking Horses have three gaits – running walk, flat-footed walk and canter. The difference between show and pleasure types is obvious even to an inexperienced eye. Pleasure Walkers do not have the tremendous action or the presence of their more showy brothers. In apportioning merit the show walker, with a fast, extravagant, running walk, has the edge on his rivals, a full 40 per cent of points being awarded

The striking show stance of an American Saddlebred.

to this one gait; the balance of points is equally divided between the flat-footed walk, canter and conformation. This division offers classes under saddle for two-year-olds upwards, and the monetary awards in the stake classes are high, but the cost of keeping a show Walker is correspondingly expensive, the average show Walker being professionally trained and shown.

Saddlebreds, shown as both riding and fine-harness horses, have two distinct types: the three-gaited horse, with hogged mane and tail, shown at walk, trot and canter; and the five-gaited horse, with full mane and tail, shown at walk, trot, canter, slow gait and rack. Judging criteria for the three- and five-gaited horses are performance, presence, quality and conformation, the whole evolving in a show of controlled energy and brilliant animation whether under saddle or in harness. As with Walkers, Saddlebreds, other than pleasure mounts, are usually produced by a professional.

Saddle seat equitation riders are mounted on three-gaited horses, such animals best showing riders' horsemanship. In both hunt and saddle seats the mounts used are frequently referred to as equitation horses, as they have the utmost reliability blended with correct paces, and although it is the riders under scrutiny that indefinable something attracts the judge's eye.

Thirdly comes stock seat or Western riding. Under this heading is the greatest variety of competitions. Events open to Western riders include pleasure and equitation, judged on a similar basis but with breed and seat requirements different. In more specialised categories there are cutting contests, where the horse cuts a given animal out of the bunch and prevents its return until the rider signals by a hand laid on the horse's neck. Reining classes show the manoeuvrability of the cow horse working at speed. Stockhorse events call for a mount that is nimble, surefooted, able to work a rope and to remain ground-tied when the rider is dismounted. The trail horse negotiates a number of obstacles likely to be found on the trail. Here the judge looks for the horse that is workmanlike and co-operative as well as showing good and easy paces.

No list of Western classes would be complete without a mention of the 'games' events. These are comparable to gymkhana classes but more specialised. Horses are often kept for just one type of event, as competition is needle-sharp and the rewards worthwhile. All Western games are run against the clock. Number one in popularity is barrel racing, a contest over a cloverleaf course. Although entered almost exclusively by girls in larger shows it is no gentle sport, needing courageous riding and split-second timing, the winning ride being separated from the also-rans by tenths of a second. Next to barrel racing comes pole bending—not the type seen in English gymkhanas, but the electrifying sort that makes you wonder if the horse has run at all. A pole-bender changes leads like lightning, then bends nearly double before starting on the homeward run. A crowd-pleaser is Western pickup, evolved from the old idea of rescuing a stranded man. One rider picks another up between given points without slacking pace, necessitating tremendous agility by the man being rescued.

Apart from the three distinct riding seats there are many other classes appearing in American show schedules. Colour bursts into the arena with the Parade horses. The stock saddle used bears little resemblance to a working saddle, being heavily embellished with silver in varied designs, each owner furnishing his horse with the most elaborate equipment money can buy. Indeed, in many cases the equipment far outvalues the mount. The horses used are predominantly Saddlebreds of the heavier sort, standing at around 16 hands, essential in view of the tremendous weight of the silvered equipment. The breed's presence is used to

full advantage, as Parade horses show marked animation and elevation in the parade gait, a balanced trot not exceeding 5 miles per hour. In judging, 75 per cent is awarded to performance, manners and conformation, and 25 per cent to appointments. Flashy palominos and chestnuts are popular colours with exhibitors, their natural attributes adorned with coloured ribbons in mane and tail, the hooves sparkling with gold and silver paint. Not to be outdone by his horse, the rider wears gleaming jewel-coloured fringed shirt and matching trousers, crowned with a fancy stetson, while his patterned boots jingle with ornate silver spurs.

Harness horses and ponies frequent the show ring but again, as with other phases of American horsemanship, there is a wide variety, from the fine-harness horses shown to a four-wheel vehicle, and performing at an animated walk and trot where the emphasis is on brilliant action rather than speed; through the familiar hackneys; and on to the roadsters. The horses are of Standardbred breeding and show at the jog trot —road gait—which means a fair travelling pace, and at speed where the drivers, dressed in stable colours as if on a racetrack, really turn them loose.

Of all American show horses the roadsters, especially when they turn on that blinding burst of power and speed, are the most fascinating, being run a close second by the agile, clever-thinking cutting horses, who surely contradict the often-propounded theory that horses are none too intelligent.

For sheer wealth of beauty in horseflesh coupled with versatility we must surely look to the Arabian shows, where the desert horse is shown under all three riding styles and, in addition, as a side-saddle mount, the ladies wearing elegant and colourful period costumes. Another event is the Arabian costume class, where horses and riders enter the ring at full gallop fitted out either in Bedouin style or, for the ladies, as a version out of the *Arabian Nights*. One other competition popular with Arab exhibitors is the versatility class, where horses show under Western and English tack, the riders making an unofficial race of the change-over. Horses must show true Western and English gaits to be among the prizewinners.

In a country which possesses more breeds

than any other, many of which either originated in Britain or drew on British blood for foundation stock, it is hardly surprising to find all these breeds catered for in such variety. Shows do reflect the regional breeds and styles of riding, but the overall American show scene presents a scope unparallelled in any other competitive horse-loving nation.

AUSTRALIA

Australia has a great variety of activities involving the horse; many of them are adaptations or imitations of spectacles, sports and show events from Britain and the United States, but there are also a number of uniquely Australian sports and competitions.

One of the most colourful and exciting spectacles is provided by rodeo, an important part of the Australian horse scene and a great crowd-pleaser. Rodeos in the various states are arranged in circuits, each fixture lasting for one or more days, with top professional performers travelling from town to town in their big, heavy-laden, dust-covered cars to try to take the attractive prize money away from the local 'ringers' or cowboys.

A uniquely Australian competition, campdrafting, often precedes these rodeo contests. Here, a rider separates a large bullock from a group of cattle, then drives it at the gallop around a large course marked out with upright poles, often using his mount to shoulder the beast over in the direction in which he wants it to travel. The rider, on his speedy, long-striding Waler, must stay right on top of the hefty bullock all the time in order to keep it on course, and if the steer should suddenly decide to change direction and cut under the horse's neck, both man and horse can be in for a nasty spill.

During the last few years American-style cutting contests have been introduced, following the rising popularity of the Quarter Horse in Australia, and this sport is catching on quickly.

Polo is played in many of the country districts, where enthusiasts often use the infield of the local racecourse as a polo field. In certain areas, where the game has been played for

generations, the standard is very high indeed, and a number of Australian polo teams have won fame abroad, the best known on the international scene today probably being the Skenes.

Much more popular, though, is 'poor man's polo', polocrosse, which is played by women as well as men. This Australian invention supplies all the fun, action and thrills of polo for the players at only a fraction of its cost, since each player only needs one mount throughout the game. Polocrosse is rather like a horseback version of lacrosse: the ball is scooped up in a small net at the end of a long stick and is then carried or thrown. This game is played in a much more restricted area than is polo, and the ponies do not have to gallop either so far or so hard – hence the fact that a player can manage with only one mount.

There are a number of one- and three-day events held in various parts of Australia, with the greatest interest being shown in the southern states. The standard here is very high, and Australian three-day event teams have done extremely well in international competitions, winning the gold medal at the Rome Olympics in 1960 and the bronze in Mexico City in 1968.

Dressage in its own right – as opposed to its forming just one part of eventing – is increasing in popularity, and the skill of the accomplished dressage rider and the high degree of training of his mount are much admired. However, since Australians are generally geared more towards active sports on horseback, the higher echelons of dressage activity will probably continue to remain the province of only a few riders.

A bending race at a gymkhana near Canberra.

The start of a race at a 'picnic' meeting.

Endurance riding has recently gained a high place in the Australian equestrian calendar. The big event is the Quilty Cup, held in September each year over a rugged up-hill-and-down-dale course of a hundred miles in the Blue Mountains near Sydney. This demanding sport has been catching on fast, and there are now a number of one-hundred-mile and fifty-mile competitive rides held in various parts of the continent.

Surprisingly enough, foxhunting is a traditional equestrian sport in Victoria, South Australia and Tasmania, where the first settlers introduced foxes from England in order to provide sport for themselves. Near Sydney, the capital of New South Wales, draghunting is also enjoyed, the hounds being followed across the rolling countryside by inhabitants of the big city out for some weekend sport.

Racing is a major Australian passion, and carries on all the year round. The biggest event of the racing year is the two-mile Melbourne Cup. Australian racecourses are noted for their excellent facilities for the public, as the sport is considered top-class general entertainment. The city racetracks are situated among lawns and flower gardens, with large modern stands giving patrons of all enclosures the best possible view of everything that is taking place, from the parade of the glistening Thoroughbreds in the paddock before the start of each race to their final furious battle down the straight.

Most training of racehorses takes place at the racetracks in the early morning, with the horses working out on concentric tracks inside the racecourse proper. Most of the time his horses are working, the trainer will have his eye on the stopwatch. As a result Australian jockeys, who ride almost every morning, develop a very keen sense of timing, which is probably an important factor in their very considerable success abroad, notably in Britain and France.

A very colourful facet of racing in Australia is provided by the 'picnic' race meetings, held in the outback of this vast country, where amateur riders and their grass-fed mounts compete against each other for small prizes on primitive, dusty bushland racetracks. The sport is everything at these unique meetings. Women jockeys have been taking part in special 'ladies' bracelet' races at these fixtures for some years, and in the more remote areas special races are arranged for the dusky-skinned Aboriginal stockmen – who form a large part of the labour force on the cattle stations, and who come yelling down the straight as if their lives depended on it! Picnic race meetings often last two, three or more days, and as well as the fierce amateur competition there is much eating, dancing and drinking for the bush-dwellers during this important annual social event.

Trotting and pacing are both very popular activities, and in the big cities the trotting tracks are lavish installations where meetings are usually held at night under floodlighting. Racegoers can watch the action through the plate-glass windows of restaurants at the track, and going 'to the trots' is a popular family outing.

Hard-fought trotting and pacing races also take place at many agricultural shows, and the close-run contests round the quarter-mile showground tracks provide many thrilling spectacles.

The Australian show ring provides a wealth of other events. Two of the most spectacular are high-jumping and the water jump. In the high jump, riders come racing at a six-barred obstacle with huge wings on either side, and send their mounts soaring into the air to clear it and to land in a variety of startling attitudes in the deep sand on the other side. The world record for the high jump, although unofficial because the contest did not strictly conform to FEI regulations, is held by the Australian horse Gold Meade. Ridden by the intrepid Jack Martin, Gold Meade cleared 8 ft. 6 in. at Cairns, in the far north-east of Australia, in 1946. However, high-jumping has been excluded from the programmes of a number of shows in recent years in response to the much-voiced complaint that it often involves cruelty during training.

The water jump is another exciting event. One at a time the horses come at full gallop the length of the arena in an attempt to clear a wide but very shallow water jump. And it is indeed an impressive sight to see a tall, deep-chested, long-striding water-jumper come hurtling down the showground, suddenly to lift into the air above the glinting surface of the water and land without raising a splash on the far side.

Show-jumping is featured at all Australian shows and, as in other countries, is the biggest crowd-puller. Courses are built to international standards and competition is very keen.

Many types of hack event are featured at Australian shows. There are events for 10 st., 12 st. and 14 st. hacks, ladies' and gentlemen's hacks, educated hacks, open classes and those for pairs and teams. However, the Australian show ring hack is very different from its classic English counterpart. The Australian variety is usually a tall Thoroughbred, perhaps 16 to 16·2 hands, and often a retired racehorse. The contestants are first seen by the judge walking, trotting and cantering in a large circle, then they are called in, lined up and give their individual shows. These generally involve a figure eight at the canter, with great importance being placed on a smooth change of lead.

The Galloway hack events are a special feature. The Galloway category is uniquely Australian, based only upon an animal's height: in Australia, ponies are under 14 hands, and Galloways those from 14 to 15 hands. Finally, there are a number of pony hack classes; the ponies are not always ridden by children, though, and sometimes a silver-haired old bushman will be seen putting a beautifully-prepared pony through its paces.

Every Australian show features a considerable number of best rider competitions, starting with those for very small children (though they

A competitor in the spectacular Mareeba Rodeo in Queensland.

rarely appear on leading reins), and going up the age scale to include adults. Some shows even have riding classes for parent and child.

Carrying considerable prestige on the Australian show circuit are the turnout classes, in which women riders are judged on their clothing, personal grooming, tack and the presentation of their mounts. There are classes for both formal and informal turnouts, and since it is generally the competitor with the newest and best outfit and tack who wins the class, the contest is strangely 'snob' for a country which generally prides itself on its egalitarianism!

In-hand classes in Australian show rings are rich in variety, as the Australian horse world is now the home of many breeds. There are classes for Thoroughbreds, Arabians, Quarter Horses, Appaloosas, American Saddlebreds, Palominos, various breeds of British native ponies – with the Welsh Section A and the Shetland being particularly popular – and a growing interest in the Connemara, Australian pony and Australian Stockhorse.

All the bigger shows have classes for harness horses and ponies, too. Depending on the locality, these can range from the traditional British hackney to general-purpose driving animals. There are not a lot of harness enthusiasts in Australia, but those who are interested in it take great pride in their turnouts.

One of the most recent innovations has been the introduction of colourful parade and costume classes, modelled upon this event in the United States. They are a great crowd-pleaser, since high-stepping Palominos carrying Spanish caballeros, and fiery Arabians with desert sheikhs astride, add an exotic and entertaining note to the show ring.

Classes for stockhorses are in evidence at most shows. The stockhorse can be of any breed or mixture of breeds, and points are awarded for conformation, temperament and general presentation. The horses must give an individual display, usually making a 'dry run' somewhat akin to an American reining pattern.

At all the 'Royal' shows, which are held annually in the capital cities of the various states, there are classes for police horses. The mounted police detachments of the state

Polocrosse at Sydney Royal Easter Show.

governments are very popular, and often give displays such as musical or pattern rides at the big shows. The troopers and their mounts also compete against each other in various events, ranging from those judged purely on presentation to others which resemble fairly advanced dressage tests.

The novelty events are a big feature of most Australian shows. They consist mainly of pole bending and flag and barrel racing. Bending is like its British gymkhana equivalent, and to win you need a fast-starting, agile and responsive animal who has been carefully trained. In flag racing, small flags are placed on a line of poles. The contestants must race out, snatch a flag – one at a time – wheel around the upright, and come speeding back to the starting line to drop the flag into a receptacle before galloping out to collect the next flag. Barrel racing can either resemble bending, or alternatively the competitors race against the clock in a figure of eight round just two barrels.

Across the Tasman Sea in New Zealand, many of these Australian activities can also be found. The New Zealanders also make a feature of working hunter classes at their shows, and dressage is very popular, too, in these lush green islands.

5 Mounted games

GYMKHANA EVENTS

Mention mounted games to any Pony Club members in Britain and their thoughts will automatically turn to the annual competition organised throughout the United Kingdom culminating in six teams competing in the final of the Prince Philip Cup at the Horse of the Year Show. But the origin of mounted games goes far further back into history than 1957, when this competition was first held.

Equestrian games have formed part of man's riding activities for thousands of years. In the earliest days, games on horseback were used as a form of training for the rigours of war, and cavalry regiments were some of the first to invent mounted games. It was essential, when facing the enemy, that a soldier's mount should be exceptionally quick to turn and manoeuvre in order to avoid the attacks of his opponent. As one watches the agile little gymkhana ponies galloping in and out of a line of bending poles and turning on the proverbial sixpence, it is easy to step back in time and see mediaeval knights jousting for honours in the lists. Indeed, some of the sound effects from today's competitors would have done justice to many an ancient battlefield.

In South America, where ponies are used in everyday work for rounding up vast herds of cattle, some of the oldest mounted games are still played. The agility of the pampas ponies has resulted in a demand for these tough and handy animals by the best polo players all over the world. Although there is a genuine Pony Club polo tournament organised each year, there are other forms of this game which definitely come under the heading of mounted games. Cushion polo, which should only be attempted by fairly competent riders, is one variation, and involves the passing of a cushion-type object from one rider to another while the

Tskhenburti, a national game in Georgia in the USSR.

Points are lost if water is spilt from the buckets carried by these Australian pony club competitors.

opposing team tries to wrest away the 'cushion'. As in polo, riding-off is permitted, but a firm umpire is absolutely essential to check any dangerous or rough play. Paddock polo can also be played and this requires a larger, softer ball than that normally used in adult polo. Ex-polo ponies make excellent gymkhana mounts.

Mounted games today consist of the well-loved gymkhana events which have always formed part of the smaller show's schedule. They provide an opportunity for the everyday pony and rider to compete in events expressly designed for the maximum of fun and enjoyment without requiring a top-class or particularly well-bred pony. No matter the shape or appearance, with a little practice at home even the hairiest pony can become proficient at bending and potato races. Gymkhana events are judged purely on performance and although a pony with a little more breeding will probably have an advantage on pure speed over its less aristocratic brothers and sisters, this is not the whole secret of success in such events. The pony must be extraordinarily handy and obedient to hand and leg, willing to stop and go instantly it receives the aids and, in many cases, the less well-bred pony will be calmer and quieter when confronted with the strange objects that appear as part and parcel of some of the events. Approaching a stuffed sack lying on the ground can strike a pony rigid with terror, and it is only by endless hours of practice behind the scenes that one's pony can

be persuaded to approach this hideous object. It is in cases like this that the less highly-strung pony will score.

Training at home to improve the pony's response to the aids can be a great help in competitions. A fast start, for example, is a tremendous advantage over one's rivals. Equally, a pony that is trained to stop dead at a given signal will save precious seconds in certain events. It is only with practice that a pony will become used to such things as balloons flapping round, and it is also as well to get the pony used to the sound of a balloon exploding, as this is quite likely to happen during the course of a race. The sound of a potato dropping into a bucket can conjure up unbelievable terrors if the pony is not used to it. As in all branches of equestrian sport, practice makes perfect, and for mounted games there is the added advantage that no expensive equipment is required; just with a few bending poles, the odd bucket and a sack anyone can school their pony to their heart's content.

It was with the ordinary Pony Club pony in mind that Prince Philip presented his trophy for a national mounted games championship. This gives Pony Club members the chance to compete at one of the major shows. The thought of riding at the Horse of the Year Show in the autumn encourages prospective members of branch teams to practise for months in advance and work their way through the preliminary rounds before achieving a place in the coveted last six teams who go through to

153

Wembley. More important are the aims and objects behind a competition of this type – to encourage team spirit and good sportsmanship. As the races are run mainly on a relay basis the team co-ordination has to be first class. Both riders and ponies must be capable of anticipating their team mates' next move and, judging by the support given to teams in the finals, there is no lack of team spirit among the supporters either. From the beginnings of the Prince Philip Cup in 1957, the championship has proved an extremely popular event; nearly 200 branches now take part. Each team consists of five members under sixteen years of age, who ride ponies not exceeding 14·2 hands. They must be ridden in snaffle bridles and no whips or spurs can be used. Each team has a non-riding captain who is probably the team trainer as well.

Most Pony Club branches have always used mounted games of one sort or another as a form of exercise and entertainment after the more serious riding which takes place during a working rally. Ponies and riders alike enjoy and need the relaxation after an hour and a half or two hours of concentrated instruction. A quick game of musical sacks, a bending race or a flag relay race helps to provide variety at the end of the rally and will ensure that ponies and riders finish the day on a high note. Similarly, an informal team competition among the different 'rides' can act in much the same way. An impromptu musical ride can also be organised, which never fails to appeal as all the members try their utmost to maintain the continuity of the ride.

Once it has been decided to enter a team in the championship the team trainer will organise the prospective members for practices. Cold winter weekends seem a far cry from the electrifying atmosphere of the indoor arena at Wembley, but it is during the winter and early spring months that the prospective team must be drilled until the five members are finally chosen for the regional round in the Easter holidays.

The different races are devised by a committee and the games for the year are circulated to all branches well in advance of the competition. The events are expressly designed to test the skill and timing of the competitors as well as

Agility and obedience are important when every second counts.

including favourites such as team bending, which perhaps more than any other event tests the degree of schooling and obedience of the pony and the skill of the rider, and the potato-picking scramble where vaulting on and off a moving pony is essential if success is to be achieved. A pile of potatoes is placed in the centre of the arena, a bucket is set out for each team and for a given time two members of each team gallop back and forth depositing as many potatoes in their own bucket as they can. The secret of this event is continuous motion. The pony must be trained to describe an oblong using the bucket as a pivot while the rider must be capable of leaping on and off at the right moment.

Several races require a particular skill and athletic ability on the part of the rider. For example, no matter how fast the pony, it will not win a sack race unless the rider is capable of hopping at high speed like a demented kangaroo. But again the pony can help. A well-trained mount will assist greatly if the rider clasps tightly round the pony's neck and is half dragged to the line by a willing partner, though an over-keen pony may well leave its rider trailing behind in an untidy and uncomfortable heap. In the stepping-stone dash, to take another example, the balance of the rider as he hops from one obstacle to the next will be to no avail if the pony refuses to trot alongside. Simple variations of relay races are always included in the schedule, and these test the co-ordination of the team; other races may require the pony to carry two riders at once for short distances. A most popular race involving two riders on one pony also requires a good eye and a true aim. This is the sharpshooters race, which involves two members racing on one pony to an 'aunt sally'. On reaching a marked point in front of the aunt sally, one rider dismounts and attempts to demolish the aunt sally with the supply of balls provided. On completion of this task, he remounts behind the other rider and gallops back to the finish. The simplest form of two on one pony races is the Gretna Green race, when one pony and rider gallop to pick up a second rider and simply gallop back to the finish. A simple race to organise, requiring no equipment except a marked finish.

One entertaining event originated in Russia: pushball. Two teams attempt to push a huge soft ball over their opponents' goal line. This requires a bold pony, one who is quite prepared to lend its weight and is trained to do most of the pushing. Pushball is also played in the Netherlands and is always an amusing spectator event.

The emphasis in the Pony Club is mainly on skill at particular events which are easily adapted as team races, but at local shows there is still a wide variety of events to be found. Pace races such as trotting and three-pace races are popular, as is the bucket elimination. Here the competitors jump in single file over an ever-decreasing line of buckets or cans. The slightest touch to a can, refusal or run-out results in elimination and the event continues until either all are eliminated or there is only one can left. In the latter case the long-suffering steward has the unenviable task of finding a winner by sending the remaining competitors over and over the single can until the numbers are reduced to a winner. As it is essential for the judge to stand directly in the path of the oncoming horse, in order to see if there is any deviation from the central path, it is a stewarding job that is not entirely popular as there is a distinct risk of being mown down as the competitors advance!

Apple bobbing or ducking does not seem to feature in gymkhana schedules quite as fre-

quently as in the past. This was often the last event of the day and, provided the weather had been kind, it was often a welcome end as one plunged one's head into the water trough of bobbing apples, hoping to emerge with the apple safely clasped in one's teeth. Obstacle races too, used to be popular, but they require a lot of equipment to be successful. Crawling under tarpaulins, diving through swinging motor tyres, threading needles, devouring currant buns and perhaps jumping an unusual obstacle – all are part of this most comical of races, for the spectators if not for the competitors. Inevitably one competitor would become almost irrevocably wedged in a tyre or the tarpaulin would claim a victim as some poor unfortunate thrashed about in a vain attempt to find a way out into the open. But they were fun, these complicated events, and if not wholly a test of horsemanship, they tested one's ability to remain calm under a variety of trying circumstances.

Varieties of polo have already been mentioned; a chapter on mounted games would not be complete without describing briefly some of the slightly less hectic but equally enjoyable organised games. Mock pig sticking can provide a fast and exciting game as riders attempt to 'stick' a stuffed sack which is dragged along on a long cord by one rider at a fast canter. Mock hunts can help to introduce younger and inexperienced members to the mysteries and thrills of the hunting field and are to be recommended, especially in areas where members are likely to get little or no real hunting. Again this takes a vast amount of organisation but such an event can provide much-needed instruction to any members who are not likely to be able to hunt regularly, who are nevertheless able to learn about the sport.

Criticism is often levelled at gymkhana events in that they may produce rough and careless riding, but a well-trained, well-ridden pony is a joy to watch and will always score over the inadequately trained combination. It goes without saying that such events can improve a rider's balance and agility in the saddle, and there can be little doubt, too, that the majority of ponies thoroughly enjoy the excitement and fun which is to be found in this branch of horsemanship.

6 Polo

Polo is the fastest team game in the world. And when you consider that it involves hitting a ball of a mere 3 inches in diameter with a long and strangely-balanced bamboo mallet from a galloping pony, with an opponent always trying to thwart that procedure so that the play is constantly twisting and turning, it is also, perhaps, the most difficult game of all to master. It is certainly one of the finest spectator sports.

Where did it originate, this tough and complex game, which is played between two teams of four on a grass ground, 300 yd. by 200 yd. in area, with goalposts set 24 ft. apart? Probably in ancient Persia where it was known as *changar* – a mallet. The word polo is derived from the Tibetan *pulu*, meaning a ball, and developed its present character in India where the British Raj learned it from the native princes. Indeed it was introduced into the western world by the English, a match staged between cavalry officers at Hounslow in 1868 being the first sign of the game in Europe. The strokes, tactics and style of play were further developed by John Watson, who became known as the father of English polo. Up to the first world war the grounds were all in the London area – Hurlingham, Ranelagh and Roehampton – and it soon became a highly fashionable game, an integral part of the London season.

Polo was first played in the United States in 1883, Meadow Brook being the American headquarters, and the initial match for the Anglo-American Westchester trophy was contested in 1886. Owing to the war, and thereafter to the overwhelming superiority of teams fielded by the United States, this famous competition was discontinued in 1939. But with the contemporary upsurge of British polo, it has been revived in the form of the Coronation cup, which has since 1971 been competed for annually at Windsor Park or Cowdray Park.

Perhaps because of the continentals' preoccupation with pure equitation, polo was never played across the Channel on as large a scale as in England or the United States; but in South America the Argentines, with their wealth, their natural facility for ball games and their handy little ranch ponies (*criollos*), soon came through as undisputed leaders of the polo world. By 1970 there were 3,000 players in Argentina, 1,000 in the United States and 400 in Britain.

In 1899, the English imposed a pony height limit of 14·2 hands, and owing to their indigenous breeds and particularly strong supply of ponies of the small type, they provided the chief market for mounts in the polo world. But in 1916, when polo had fallen into abeyance in Europe, the Americans abolished this rule, other countries conformed, and the average height went up to from 15 hands to 15·3 hands. In 1909, the American handicapping system was also adopted internationally. It rates players from −2 to +10 goals, but is no indication of goal-scoring capacity: it is simply a yardstick to indicate a player's grading in the polo world. The term 'high-goal polo' means that the aggregate handicap of each team entered in a particular championship is around nineteen and upwards. In the case of medium-goal this would be in the region of fifteen to eighteen.

The winning team in polo is that which scores most goals, that is to say the one that contrives, according to the rules, to strike the ball most often between their opponents' goalposts. The duration of a match is generally a little under one hour. And, because polo is played at a more or less continuous gallop, it is necessary to change and rest ponies; the game is therefore split into periods, or 'chukkas', of seven-and-a-half minutes' duration. The big tournaments are now divided into five or six chukkas and the smaller contests into four.

The players are numbered one and two (forwards), three, and Back. The duties of number one are: in defence, to ride off the opposing Back and prevent him from having an uninterrupted hit at the ball; and, in attack, to give him the slip and await a pass, or to ride him away from his goal mouth and so leave it open for the number two to score. The number two is usually the stronger of the two forwards and should be the driving force of an attack and the principal goal-scorer. Number three, the pivot of the team, is usually their best player, so this is the most suitable place for the team captain to play. He will often initiate attacks, and his first objects will be to send the ball up to the forwards and to intercept attacks. As principal defender, the Back must be thoroughly reliable. He must be a safe hitter, especially with backhanders. His aim will be to pass the ball to his number two; he will mark the opposing number one. The opposing number two and three also mark each other. But the positions are not rigid and the essence of good polo is in flexibility of teamwork, in changing positions as the game dictates.

A tiresome feature of polo from the spectator's point of view, even in matches of the highest class, can be the frequent temporary cessation of play by the umpires owing to fouls. There is no offside rule, players may impede their opponents by knocking and hooking their sticks, lean into them and 'ride them off'. In fact they will endeavour to do so at every opportunity. But owing to the inevitable hazards of a fast-moving stick-and-ball mounted duel, certain rules have to be stringently enforced: the penalties for riding across another player's 'right of way', misusing one's stick, bumping and zigzagging, are given instantly and severely, in the form of 60-yd. and 40-yd. free hits at one's goal, or free shots from the place of the foul. The 'right of way' exists during every moment of the game and is possessed, by and large, by that player who is riding most closely in the direction in which the ball was last hit. It is an offence for another player to cross this line.

A bell is sounded at the start and end of each chukka, though play is continued until the ball is hit behind or over the side lines or, in the opinion of the umpires, lies in a neutral position. If a match ends in a draw, additional chukkas are played until one more goal is scored.

It is much harder to teach a non-ball-game player to hit a ball from horseback than it is to teach any ball-game player to ride well enough to play polo. The beginner need not be a

A fine back-handed stroke during the final of the Smith's Lawn Cup.

high-class horseman, but he must be able to concentrate on hitting without having to think about his riding, must also be a sufficiently competent horseman to get the best out of his ponies. The same principles apply as in most other spheres of equitation. A good seat is the top requirement. This is particularly important in polo, since many shots have to be taken leaning right out of the saddle, at the gallop. The best way to achieve both firmness and balance is to ride regularly without stirrups, and also to do plenty of schooling exercises to keep supple at the waist and shoulder: the polo player must be capable of moving the upper and lower parts of his body more or less independently.

The polo pony must be able to move off sharply from the walk to the gallop, to stop abruptly, rein back, turn very tightly and suddenly on either the hocks or the forehand, pirouette and swerve in a manner that is probably quite unnatural to him. So the polo horseman must fully understand the aids, and develop good hands as soon as possible; on the one hand he must have very good control and, on the other, generally avoid spoiling the mouth, temperament and performance of nicely-made ponies.

The beginner will probably learn the strokes from a dummy horse in a polo pit, a small wire-enclosed court with a sloping perimeter floor that returns the balls, and a flat centre on which is placed a wooden horse with a saddle. There are four basic polo strokes: the offside forehand, which is the equivalent of the racquets game's forehand and is the most generally used, the offside backhander, the nearside forehander and the nearside backhander. The first aim in hitting should be to develop a stylish swing, so that the stick head may properly gather momentum and the shaft guide it to the ball. The head will then expend most of its energy in driving the ball, and the remainder of it in the course of the follow-through. But the pit is inclined to give a feeling of false accomplishment, so as much practice as possible should be done from a quiet pony — as soon as possible at the canter and gallop.

The polo pony must possess speed, stamina, great agility and good response. He will need a similar quality of conformation as that expected of the hunter and event horse; he should have a nice straight humerus, a deep stifle and plenty of depth through the heart and lungs; he ought to be well ribbed-up to afford a rounded loin; he should have a round well-shaped foot set on a long flexible pastern; and he will show an alert, kindly eye. He must have enough weight and stature to carry his rider well and to be affective in riding off, so he should not be much under 15 hands; at the same time he should remain a pony, with a pony's smooth and low-galloping action, so that the base from which the stick-stroke is made stays reasonably constant. He should, therefore, be well under 16 hands.

Where are the pony paragons to be found? Among the British owners, Lord Cowdray breeds his own English Thoroughbreds, of which he possesses a string of thirty, and some of the Americans breed mainly from American blood. But the great majority of ponies in play today come from Argentina where, with a vast amount of space available and limitless cheap labour, the *criollo*-English Thoroughbred cross is easily mass-produced and shaped. These ponies, made and polo-schooled, can be bought for £600 to £1,000.

There are four chukkas to a practice match and no pony is up to more than two chukkas a day. So the beginner will ride at least two ponies in each game. But he may not have to buy them. Some clubs hire ponies for £3 to £4 a chukka, which is quite a reasonable price when you reflect that, anyway in England, each costs £300 to £400 a year to keep in forage, farriery, wages, transport and equipment. But it is surprising how the keen and promising beginner is encouraged and actively helped, and how little he may pay for his polo. Many who have advanced on the handicap list have been sponsored for teams to the extent that their sport has come more or less free.

The most useful influence in offsetting the cost of club ponies and other expenses is spectator attendance. Considering what an eminently exciting game this is to watch, it is surprising how small a following it has, though the audiences are growing every year.

7 Driving

Driving a horse appears to have been a sport as well as a means of conveyance from the early centuries, the Greeks and Roman charioteers being perhaps the earliest known exponents of driving more than one horse as fast as possible. In England, the setting up of wagers of every description was a major sideline among sportsmen during the seventeenth and eighteenth centuries, and it was not long before horses, both ridden as well as driven, were being exploited by their owners into earning considerable sums of money by this means.

Newmarket, which has always been the centre of horse-racing, was often the venue of these activities, and in the latter part of the seventeenth century a Captain John Gibbs won £500 by driving a four-in-hand to a light chaise up and down the steepest part of the formidable Devil's Ditch on the Heath. For this feat it is reported that he had the chaise built on to a jointed 'perch' (the main connecting rod between the front and back axles) so that the vehicle moved more easily over the undulating ground, the horses being very loosely harnessed, and without a pole between the two wheel horses.

Almost a hundred years later, in 1750, another chaise match, which was of sufficient interest to warrant its being illustrated by the artist James Seymour, also took place on Newmarket Heath. This was for the much higher stake of 1,000 guineas, and was between the Earls of March and Eglintowne against Messrs Theobald Taafe and Andrew Sproule. Four horses postillion driven should draw a four-wheeled carriage containing one passenger for a distance of nineteen miles in under an hour. In fact this journey was performed in 53 minutes and 27 seconds, and since the horses were Thoroughbreds who virtually ran away for the first four miles, it was not perhaps so surprising that they achieved this record. This match was the first of many triumphs for the two noblemen: Lord March, who became Marquess of Queensberry, and was later known as 'Old Q,' had a strange spindly-looking vehicle specially built as lightly as possible to his own specifications, and it was his idea also to use well-known racehorses ridden by professional jockeys.

By the late eighteenth century driving had become a very fashionable pastime which was sponsored by the then Prince of Wales—later George IV—and many young men about town started to bribe the professional coachmen into teaching them to drive a team by allowing them to 'have a handful'. This was of course strictly forbidden for safety reasons, but it took place nevertheless, and so a great many first hand, and at times hair-raising, stories of the coaching days have thus been handed down. This fashion for driving also led to the formation of several driving clubs, the last of which was the Coaching Club, which recently celebrated its centenary year. The British Driving Society is another

A perfectly turned-out pony and gig drive out into the country.

modern club, formed in 1955 and now with some fourteen hundred members. It was inaugurated in response to the recent renewal of interest in driving, and provides for members who drive singles, pairs and tandems.

Despite the fact that the appearance of the railways virtually put an end to coaching as a means of travel, the urge to drive four horses remained, and a revival of the sport took place with many old stage coaches being run on their original routes. The eighth Duke of Beaufort was one of the instigators—in 1866, in partnership with a Captain Haworth, he devised a scheme of putting a coach on the road to Brighton, with subscribers paying for the privilege of driving it on different days. This system was soon copied by other sportsmen, and more and more subscription coaches took to the road, although for limited seasons and in summer only, until in 1908 one of many events to be recorded in road history took place. This was the arrival from America of Mr Alfred Vanderbilt with two road coaches, the Viking and the Venture, and teams of horses. Mr Vanderbilt ran his coaches between London and Brighton during the summer until 1914, when, with the outbreak of war, it was ended abruptly by finding that at one of the stages his horses had suddenly been commandeered by the Army!

With the arrival of peace, enthusiasts became busy again, and coaches were soon running to Brighton, Hampton Court, Oxford and Tewkesbury. This in turn ended in 1939, and although with petrol rationing during the war a few people took to driving horses, no one visualised that it could, or would, ever become popular again under modern road conditions. But old traditions die hard, and it was not long before one or two teams of horses were being put together, and yet another era of driving had begun.

Horses had, however, by now become treasured possessions, so while it was unlikely that old-time achievements of driving excessive distances and speeds would be attempted, yet it was felt that something more than sedate trotting was needed in order to maintain driving as a sport. At some shows, therefore, driving competitions, both competitive as well as against the clock, have been staged. These involve the negotiating of small obstacles such as driving through narrow markers; stepping over raised poles; and backing into and out of gateways, etc.

On the Continent, in the meantime, all types of harness, including teams of up to twelve stallions in hand, had been displayed, and eventing—involving negotiating rough ground and steep hills as well as driving through water—have been achieved. This activity is now officially recognised as a sport by the FEI, and rules for both pairs and four-in-hands have

Emerging from the water during a marathon drive in Poland.

been drawn up. These competitions are similar to those held for riding horses, and involve presentation, dressage and cross country work at varying speeds, as well as an obstacle course, and are held over several days.

Apart from these competitions held on the Continent, in which the Hungarians, Germans and Austrians are the principal participants, driving as a sport is actively pursued in a number of other countries as well. In the United States a lavishly-produced quarterly journal containing illustrated articles of driving interest is published by the Carriage Association. This society also arranges courses of lectures and meets of carriages in historic settings, and despite the fact that distances are so great its many members manage to attend horse shows and organised functions, as well as driving entirely for pleasure in their own areas.

In Scandinavia, too, there are many enthusiastic driving sportsmen, and the Danish Driving Society is a thriving concern. Similarly, in Belgium, Holland and Switzerland, Spain, Portugal and Italy, keen drivers are also to be found, although France, which produces so many elegant and attractive items on harness and carriage themes, appears to be sadly lacking in drivers, although harness racing is, as in the other countries, an active pastime.

Although it is true to say that most horses can be driven as well as ridden, certain breeds show a greater aptitude for harness, and a number of these have become popular all over the world. In Holland, both Friesian and Gelderland horses are extensively used in harness, and the latter, with their outstanding looks and showy action, have become very popular in England as coach horses. Similarly, the German breeds of Oldenburg and of Holsteins, which are broken to harness on their stud farms, are also exported to other countries, and a team of Oldenburgs is at present in the Royal Mews in London. In Austria, Lippizaners and Haflinger ponies are the main harness breeds, and these too are finding their way into England. Elsewhere, Arabian horses, as well as both Anglo-Arabs and part-bred Arabs, are bred and used extensively for sporting driving in many parts of the world. Another universal harness breed is the hackney, which, though primarily intended as a roadster, is now largely used as a show animal.

In almost every part of the world driving enthusiasts are now to be found, and these range from the elderly to the very young. Competitions such as those staged abroad are now also held in Britain, and with H.R.H. the Duke of Edinburgh as an active participant, they may well prove that while racing has always been considered the sport of kings, driving is, perhaps, the sport of princes.

8 Harness racing

Harness racing is one of the oldest horse sports. Chariot racing certainly existed in Roman times, and probably in the days of the Greeks, Egyptians and Assyrians. It now takes place all over the world, particularly in Europe, North America and Canada, Australasia and New Zealand.

Modern harness racing is divided into trotting and pacing. In both forms, a single horse pulls a very light sulky and is guided by one driver. Trotters move diagonally, as horses generally do, while a pacer's legs move laterally –i.e. the two nearside legs move forward together, followed by the two offside legs. Some people mistakenly regard pacing as an unnatural gait. It has been accepted for many centuries: Chaucer wrote about 'a proper amblynge little nag', meaning a pacer, and royal courts frequently mounted their ladies on pacers, for the movement is more comfortable than that of the normal trot.

The United States is undoubtedly the leading country in harness racing, and nearly all international records are held by American-bred horses. The world pacing record is held by Steady Star, an American horse, with a time of 1 minute 52 seconds for the mile. This gives an average speed of just over 32 m.p.h., which

compares favourably with the Derby record, held by Mahmoud, of an average speed of just over 35 m.p.h. The world trotting record currently stands at 1 minute 55·2 seconds over a mile.

The predominance of American-bred harness racehorses is now being challenged by pacers from Australia and New Zealand and by trotters in France. (Harness racing, though popular on the Continent, is mostly limited to trotters; though in Britain pacing races are held.) The first dollar millionaire stakes winner in pacing history was the horse Cardigan Bay, bred in New Zealand, while a French trotter, Une de Mai, is now well past the $1½ million mark. $2 million in prize money looks within her compass, which would make her not only the biggest money winner in harness racing history but in world equine history, for no Thoroughbred racehorse has as yet reached this figure.

The breeding of harness racehorses divides itself naturally into trotting and pacing strains. It is evident from watching even the youngest foals that pacing is a natural gait, and it is in fact very difficult to persuade a natural pacer to trot conventionally. The hobbles generally worn by pacers are not a restrictive device, but merely act to accentuate an already natural action. Trotters wear no form of hobble; they are much more likely to break their trot. In a race this does not involve disqualification, but the driver must pull back in order to re-establish the trot, and in doing so will lose valuable ground.

The conformation of a good harness racehorse is different from that of a Thoroughbred. The criteria, however, are also different, perhaps the most important being that the horse does not have to carry the weight of a rider on its back. The set of the head and neck, the absence of a good riding shoulder and the sloping rump are all factors which perhaps contribute to the performance of the Standardbred at its particular sport, though they would be regarded with

A fine pacer on the racetrack during training.

The finishing post: trotters on the Vincennes track in France.

disfavour in other spheres. In spite of the iron-hard going of limestone racing tracks, neither trotters nor pacers seem to suffer unduly from leg trouble, though great attention must always be paid to their action, so that they do not damage themselves, and to the way they are shod. Free and level action, which can be assisted or marred by shoeing, is the most essential attribute of a successful harness racehorse.

Harness racing is today one of the growth sports. Any competent horseman can, with a little familiarisation, drive a racehorse, for whether the reins are two or ten feet long many of the same principles apply. To sit behind a good-quality, well-behaved horse and be pulled along the track at nearly 30 m.p.h. is exciting in itself; in a race it is that much more so, and this excitement communicates itself to the spectators.

Pacers closely bunched at the Australian Horsham Show.

Index